# FROM COLTS TO RAVENS

# FROM COLTS TO RAVENS:

## A Behind-the-Scenes Look at Baltimore Professional Football

by John F. Steadman

TIDEWATER PUBLISHERS
CENTREVILLE, MARYLAND

Library of Congress Cataloging-in-Publication Data

Steadman, John.
From Colts to Ravens : a behind-the-scenes look at Baltimore professional football / by John F. Steadman. — 1st ed.
p. cm.
Includes index.
ISBN 0-87033-497-2
1. Baltimore Colts (Football team)—History. 2. Baltimore Ravens (Football team)—History. I. Title.
GV956.B3S68 1996
796.357'64'097526—dc21 96-49754
CIP

Manufactured in the United States of America
First edition, 1997; second printing, 1997

To Mary Lee

The best cheerleader, copy reader, and wife
any sportswriter ever had. I got lucky.

# CONTENTS

# PREFACE

No, it will never be the same. It's too much to ask, an unrealistic expectation. Baltimore's football past has been momentous . . . turbulent, too. The good times and the bad. Cheers and tears, which is kind of what the game of life is all about. Now it's a new beginning.

The Baltimore Colts struggled valiantly to make the grade, and their public never failed them—ownership failed the public, not once but twice. In 1950, the owner sold the entire franchise for $50,000, including two future Hall of Fame players, Art Donovan and Y.A. Tittle, plus a governor-to-be, the only one the National Football League ever produced. For the record, his name was Edward J. King of Massachusetts, a middle guard in a five-man line.

Then, after a two-year wait, a football team came back, the ill-fated Dallas Texans, bankrupt and with no place to call home. Adopted and nurtured by Baltimore, inheriting the Colts' name, they ultimately became the best team in all of football.

But once again, in 1984, they were stripped from their place of long residence and literally driven away to another city where they and their uniforms with the horseshoes on the helmets never seemed to fit the surroundings. Indianapolis.

Hopefully, the designated replacements, the Baltimore Ravens, will realize their responsibility and provide a more permanent type of pleasure. That's what sports were intended to be, going back to when cavemen without headgear scrimmaged with a rock.

Baltimore has been subjected to more woe and discomfort, brought on by its team owners, than any municipality on the face of the football universe. Now a new team, the Ravens of Baltimore, once the Browns of Cleveland, are here, seeking acceptance where the Colts once played.

Since the start of pro football in Baltimore, I've been privileged to be there—first as a fan for the inaugural game on September 7, 1947, when they were dressed in green-and-silver uniforms, subsequently as a reporter covering the team, as the Colts' assistant general manager for three years, as a sports editor of the *Baltimore News-Post* and *Sunday American* (later the *Baltimore News American*), and finally as a columnist for the Baltimore *Evening Sun* and the Baltimore *Sunday Sun*.

I was never too far away from the sidelines and the front office. I was afforded an up-front view of the proceedings, both glad and sad, and all the while a cornucopia of characters was tumbling around within this bizarre mix of personalities.

I had professional opportunities to do numerous other things, but there are no regrets. A look back reminds me of invitations to join Commissioner Pete Rozelle in his NFL office, to assume general managerships of the Los Angeles Rams and Baltimore Orioles, to become executive director of the Pro Football Hall of Fame, to accept the job as sports director of a major Baltimore television station. But the desire to remain a newspaperman won out every time—in a walk, no contest. Working on a newspaper. How could life be any better? The excitement that came with each edition was something no other business could begin to offer.

Family, friends, and readers will notice something different about the text that follows. It has always been my preference in writing to utilize the editorial "we," thinking it put the writer in the properly expressed role of reporter and not some know-it-all who keeps reminding the world how much he knows or is trying to reinforce a falsified sense of importance.

The "I," to me, sounded pretentious, overbearing, and self-indulgent. The editor of this book convinced "us," or rather me, that using "I" was the more appropriate way to tell this story, that it would make easier reading. "You" will just have to page on to see how this all comes out.

What follows is the definitive story of pro football in Baltimore, as I viewed and reported on it for much of my lifetime. It's not intended as a tribute, a rouser, or an exposé, but merely a chronicle of the history, the enjoyment, and, yes, the heartbreak, associated with some of the more eventful moments in the life of a team and its followers. Through it all, a personal fund of recollections and reflections are drawn upon, which are based on an insight few others were in a position to have or probably didn't even care about.

If any city deserves the best of all good things that can happen in a football way, it's Baltimore. It paid a stiff price fighting the emotional wars. The fans, that's you, deserve a monument for what you've endured. Or, better still, maybe a wing in the Pro Football Hall of Fame.

I wish to acknowledge the following: Tim Haughton, a computer wizard, who spent many hours helping me get to the line of scrimmage (The computer is a game I didn't understand. I still don't!); The Hearst Corporation; *The* [Baltimore] *Sun*, *Sports Illustrated*, Associated Press, and United Press International; the Pro Football Hall of Fame; the All-American Football Conference (long gone); the National Football League (alive and well); all the players and coaches, some famous and others less well known, who made the Baltimore Colts a civic treasure. They contributed to a lifetime of happiness for many, which is how they'll be remembered—with an epitaph of joy.

# FROM COLTS TO RAVENS

CHAPTER 1

# FOR THE GOOD TIMES (ONCE AGAIN)

It was akin to hearing that Niagara Falls had somehow been rerouted to the Mojave desert. Or that space exploration had revealed the moon was indeed made out of blue cheese. Or the Pope himself had renounced his faith.

Well . . . almost.

So it was with the Cleveland Browns coming to Baltimore. Seemingly more fiction than fact, except it was all so true. Las Vegas, which will put a price on anything, would not have dared advance odds on such an unbelievable development.

That the Browns, one of the most successful of all National Football League teams, looked upon by their devoted followers as a civic landmark, were defecting from their happy home of forty-nine profitable years, was looked on as preposterous. Not that Baltimore was any bad place to be, far from it, but rather that Cleveland football had been a bellwether of stability, the future of its franchise never in doubt. The team was a tower of respectability, and its attendance, far and away among the best in the league, was a constant.

And down on the field a team performing amidst a wash of fanatical enthusiasm was lifted by the spirited crowds that identified with the Browns and the subtleties of the game they knew so well. This was a city, Cleveland, trapped in all the emotional entanglements that develop after you give heart and soul to a cause. All of the same could be applied to Baltimore because it, too, once had its team, the Colts, pulled away in an earlier case of grand larceny.

But the Cleveland Browns moving to Baltimore? Even in a world of constant change, where nothing is a surprise anymore, it taxed the limits of believability. There was skeptical reaction, then astonishment. Finally, when the confirmation came, a bitter backlash of resentment erupted, touching off the National Football League's most troublesome controversy in its up-to-then seventy-six-year history.

It was judged too bizarre to be real when whispers were heard that this "oak tree" of a franchise—founded, nurtured, and revered in Cleveland—was being uprooted and transplanted to Baltimore, a city that had suffered unrelenting heartache itself over what had happened similarly to its team twelve years before—the infamous midnight heist to Indianapolis. The man doing the moving this time, who approved of it all, was Arthur B. Modell, who had owned the Browns for thirty-five years and was regarded as a force for conservative reasoning, always advocating stability and upholding the bylaws and constitution within the National Football League. He was handsome, smart, charming, articulate, approachable, and obviously a deal-maker. He had, in the sternest of terms, spoken out against the previous indiscriminate transfer of NFL franchises, such as the Raiders going from Oakland to Los Angeles and the Colts to Indianapolis.

It was believed universally that Modell certainly wouldn't be a part of any such crass maneuver. Putting an entire team in motion wasn't his style. But the Browns were skipping out of town without offering a word of advance notice, and this didn't correlate to Modell's reputation. He originally came from Brooklyn, gained control of the Browns in 1961 and, even though a run of championship seasons had eluded him, was regarded in Cleveland as a first-class citizen, a forceful leader, a patriot of the city, and a philanthropist who was considerate of his fellowman. Modell was besieged with honors over the years, both in and out of football. His son, David, kept telling him he belonged in the Pro Football Hall of Fame at Canton, just down the road from Cleveland.

That he had only one title to show for his efforts, the Browns' 1964 shutout of the Colts, wasn't that disturbing, except in Cleveland. When it came to an overall assessment of his ownership there wasn't too much that was lacking, except a Super Bowl. After all, in Pittsburgh, the revered Art Rooney, founder of the Steelers, had waited forty years for his team to win anything. Besides, solid sports organizations are more than just about winning, even if the casual fan doesn't think so. It is important that teams create a sense of being a good neighbor to merit public respect. They had to be more than mere hosts to a game on Sunday afternoons. And Modell fit this mold.

The advance scouting report depicted him as humorous, persuasive, likable, and innovative. Always eloquent at press conferences, he told jokes and offered one-line wisecracks to relax the listeners. Among some owner-colleagues, but not all, he was appreciated as a stand-up comedian.

He was not quite Bob Hope, who was raised in Cleveland, but he was entertaining. Also, among those who watched him closely, he had an almost insatiable desire to be loved and respected. This, of course, is a normal human characteristic. The slightest criticism bothered him, which meant he also was considered sensitive and self-centered, stubborn and emotional. Having the admiration of the masses and those around him seemed especially important. Modell was close to obsessive in his need to be held in the highest esteem. But life doesn't always guarantee such a deal. There aren't that many Art Rooneys among us.

Modell, onetime "boy wonder" of the NFL, self-made, who at age thirty-five put together the $4-million purchase of the Browns in 1961 and had now owned the team for half his life, was moving towards elder statesmanship in 1995 and acquiring an aura that went with it.

Now, in a bolt of lightning that lit up the football heavens, he was preparing to haul the Browns out of Cleveland and bring them to Baltimore, where they would fill the long-lingering void that had been created when the Colts departed so rudely for Indianapolis. Baltimore and Cleveland offered similar case histories. Or did they?

The Colts had been ridden out-of-town by Bob Irsay, an owner who made the unbelievable an everyday happening. Unlike Modell, who pulled the switch without any warning, Irsay procrastinated before he dealt the lethal blow. Threats by Irsay became so commonplace they were almost expected.

Baltimore, despite its annoyance with Irsay, never wanted to believe he'd take the Colts away or that the league would permit it to happen. Irsay might have been a clown, but the public didn't think he was capable of pulling the team away. He even made personal appearances in some of the possible relocation sites, participating, for example, in an absurd pep rally at midfield in the Gator Bowl, while the city of Jacksonville wondered if it actually had a chance to get the Colts from Baltimore. Could he be serious or was this a cruel, thoughtless game he was playing?

It appeared that Irsay, since he had little else to do, enjoyed the tension and the attention his wanderlust occasioned. Besides Jacksonville, his itinerary included Memphis, Phoenix, and Los Angeles, where he promised officials of the Memorial Coliseum he would have "his engineers show up next week" to study plans for installing luxury boxes around the rim of the massive structure that had been home to the Rams before they cut and ran for Anaheim in 1980. His actions, in Los Angeles and elsewhere, were predicated on "fishing" for a better deal. Although so many times his statements about going elsewhere with the Colts were debunked and categorized as mere talk, he was, by design or not, keeping the speculation alive.

Eventually, he landed that "better deal" and in one devastating action, reduced Baltimore to a state of football ashes. Then came trauma—screaming, kicking, and venting anger—as no issue in Baltimore's sports past had ever occasioned. To some loyalists of the Colts it bordered on an act of treason. The Colts of Baltimore, usurped by Irsay, were being carted off to Indianapolis, lock, stock, and barrels of Gatorade. This was a stab in the back, a below-the-belt wallop. It was the painful betrayal of a proud city and its football past. Baltimore had been violated, ravaged, plundered, humiliated, and hurt. Much of the same could be said, eleven years later, about Cleveland and its suffering fanatical fans.

Since that infamous midnight ride of March 28, 1984, when Irsay and the Colts suddenly vanished, Baltimore endured what seemed a bad dream. The move of the team occasioned two reactions: self-sympathy and brutal denunciation of Irsay. The city kept reminding itself of what it had lost; it was a community wronged by a reckless man who knew little about its grand football history and the fans' passionate love for a team. He simply didn't care.

Baltimore kept telling itself this couldn't happen, but the weekly league standings, to the contrary, documented the team's presence in Indianapolis. The Colts were indeed gone from Baltimore after thirty-five years. Some exceptional seasons had been enjoyed; others were not so good—just like any other franchise—but the feeling for the Colts had been personalized, maybe not so much as an extension of one's family but certainly as a close kinship. Now Cleveland was to experience the same abandonment as Baltimore. An anti-Modell mood swept the country, a raging inferno of protest, more intense and far-reaching than what had occurred to Irsay.

The Colts' loss in 1984 cut deeply into the psyche of Baltimore. It was so unprofessional for a team to up and disappear one stormy night in March. A dirty deed had been perpetrated under the cover of darkness, and it brought with it the kind of shame associated with a holdup on the street.

The National Football League, it was thought, was too stable and in charge of its own house for anything so degrading to happen. The city liked to tell itself it had "made" the NFL, but this wasn't entirely true. It was, however, a premise the faithful fans arguably advanced by hypothesizing that if the Colts had not been a part of the so-called "greatest game ever played," highlighted by the epic win over the New York Giants for the title in 1958, that teams in the league would still be wearing faded uniforms and struggling for survival.

As much as this provincial philosophy sounded comforting and lifted civic pride, it was merely that—a soothing boosterism that was pleasing to hear. It certainly wasn't factual because the league was making vast strides in popularity before the Colts took the field against the Giants to decide that still-much-talked-about 1958 NFL championship. It was a game, though, that was going to forge memorable moments in the annals of Baltimore sports and elsewhere, for that matter, because of its enormous historic impact.

The bragging provided an identity other cities couldn't begin to match, but the outcome of any one game, though steeped in lore, could hardly propel an entire league to national acceptability. No doubt, the unprecedented events of December 28, 1958, unfolding in New York's Yankee Stadium and witnessed by a then-record television audience of forty million, made a powerful impression. But to point to that isolated afternoon and arbitrarily insist it "made the league" isn't objective nor does it hold up under the scrutiny of research.

In a manner of speaking, the league had already turned the corner under the leadership of Commissioner Bert Bell, who was among the first to recognize the immense value of television as a means to enhancing an interest in sports. Certainly, Baltimore's loss from the NFL in 1984 was a crime that went unpunished, but the league went on, just as it had when Oakland left for Los Angeles and St. Louis for Phoenix.

A change of venue, with Irsay putting Baltimore out of business, didn't necessarily alter the size of the schedule, downsize ticket sales, or reduce the number of television watchers. If anything, the reverse was true. The NFL had taken on a life of its own . . . rich and important. It became the quintessential public relations machine, under Commissioner Pete Rozelle. It rarely missed a beat. One city being replaced by another wasn't going to make a difference—unfortunate, but true.

But in mid-season of 1995, with Baltimore a football wasteland for over a decade, except for the Canadian Football League's two-year presence, the Browns were bolting from Cleveland for a new home. What made it decidedly different from the Colts leaving Baltimore is that it happened during the season and touched off a spontaneous national reaction. Modell and the NFL, which couldn't help itself, took a vicious pounding from all sides.

If you were keeping count, the scoreboard probably would have flashed a 99 percent negative backlash across America as reflected in *Sports Illustrated*, *The Sporting News*, *USA Today*, *The New York Times*, and *The Wall Street Journal*. Modell was pierced by the flaming arrows of personal criticism and submerged in boiling oil. He first stated that the reason for ending his association with Cleveland was to protect his family's future financial interests. So fans perceived that he had merely found a more fertile monetary field—the greener pastures of Baltimore.

The first suggestion that anything might possibly be going on between the Browns and Baltimore originated from a source of impeccable credentials, a well-connected businessman with close ties to the Maryland Stadium Authority. He knew its membership and clearly understood the workings of professional sports. To this day he remains unidentified, a "deep throat" type of informer, but he could be called a contractor of sorts. And certainly reliable.

He claimed with the strongest conviction that the deal to move the Browns to Baltimore had already been finalized, even before a single report surfaced that they were even talking. Signed and sealed, he kept insisting, while saying the transfer transaction between the parties involved was now a part of history. "No," he told me, his name couldn't be used. I was baffled. In fact, downright skeptical, because of the prevailing feeling that Modell would be the last man to abandon a city that had been so good to him, plus the realization that the same owner enjoyed a reputation as an NFL loyalist who had vehemently opposed other teams making geographical moves.

I made a call to Modell's office in Cleveland on October 24 and his secretary asked my name.

"It's John Steadman," I answered. There was a slight pause and the next voice, clear as a bell, was Modell's: "Oh, my No. 1 man. How are you?"

"No, Art, far from your No. 1 man, just an old broken-down sportswriter."

He laughed but didn't disagree. I told him there was a story circulating that needed checking, specifically a report that he was thinking of coming to Baltimore . . . and bringing his team with him. Was it true?

"I can't comment on that," he answered politely, "but something good is going to be happening." That's precisely what he said—no amplification.

He obviously wanted to get off the telephone, and he said that when he took the call, he thought at first it was the "other Steadman," meaning Jack, the former general manager of the Kansas City Chiefs. That was the end of the conversation. Modell's reply wasn't an admission he was heading to Baltimore, nor was it a denial, but it definitely was a tantalizing indication that something was possibly developing.

From a desk at the Baltimore *Sun*, I immediately headed for the office of sports editor Jack Gibbons, around the dogleg corner of the sports department, no more than ninety feet away, and told him what had transpired. To both of us, it seemed the longest of long shots that anything so astonishing would occur, considering the Browns' well-patronized support in Cleveland for close to half a century. Added to this was the awareness that Modell's reputation was such he'd never do anything that wasn't in the best interest of the NFL.

Hadn't he earlier fought and vocalized bitterly against Al Davis when he pulled out of Oakland and headed to Los Angeles with the Raiders? Hadn't he also said, in a widely circulated comment only the year before, that the Browns would never be leaving Cleveland? "We can't hopscotch franchises around the country," he declared in 1994. "We have built this business on the trust of fans. If we treat that as if it doesn't count, it isn't going to wash."

Gibbons, asking me to stand by, called in Jon Morgan, a reporter assigned to following Baltimore's pro football story developments, and asked me to repeat what had been said only a minute before. I reconstructed the brief dialogue with Modell, but I couldn't reveal the source of the tip because of a promise reporters uphold when given information. You can't compromise a source if you are to maintain trust. It goes with the business, and Gibbons and Morgan understood that.

Two days later, Morgan, after pursuing the lead, had turned up nothing new, apparently, except that John Moag, chairman of the Maryland Stadium Authority, had altered his game plan for luring a team to Baltimore. Morgan, charged with doing the hard reporting and writing, described how Moag differed from his predecessor, Herb Belgrad, in the way he was going about getting an expansion club or seeking an established franchise. Belgrad had been outgoing, enthusiastic, and businesslike. Moag—for the moment anyhow—was more reticent and didn't believe in going public with what he knew or was planning to do.

Speaking about his "game plan," Morgan quoted Moag as saying, "It's an absolutely different effort than what had gone on before . . . the process now has to be a lot quieter, a lot more one-on-one. A lot more businesslike." Tom Guilfoile, general legal counsel for the Phoenix Cardinals, made no promises but remarked, "I think it's a cinch Baltimore will get a team." And a well-connected Baltimore lumber executive, Louis Grasmick, told Morgan, "I really believe the strategy has the potential to bring a team here . . . I think something is going to happen soon."

Still, so far as could be determined, no decision was imminent in this rumored negotiation. Chris Ely, the weekend sports announcer for WJZ-TV, said when he saw the Modell quote in *The Sun* about something "good" happening he went to his news director and told him that from that one statement he believed the Browns were coming to Baltimore. But the news supervisor decided that "there's no way that's going to happen." Others in Baltimore and Cleveland shared the same opinion.

Meanwhile, sportscaster Mark Viviano of WBAL-TV was gathering his own facts on the impending move of the Browns, checking the reliability of it all and, even though far from officially confirmed, went with the report on-camera on October 25. On November 3, he left no doubt that, in his opinion, the move had been agreed to and completed. Detractors were in abundance.

Viviano, standing alone, stayed with the story, and didn't blink an eye. Nor did he soften the content. Other Baltimore television personalities and some radio talk show hosts ridiculed his report and simply said it wouldn't and couldn't transpire.

"Most of the scorn came from within the media," he remembers. "Some people voiced doubt but the longer I stayed with it the more I knew the deal was over and done with. I got a couple of unsolicited phone calls after the first reports. A few identified themselves, others didn't. They were all telling me they knew about what was developing and that the story I had was 'right on.' A few of the callers added a bit more detail, things they knew or heard about." But Viviano didn't need any more help at that point. He had hit the bull's-eye.

Cleveland's newspaper, *The Plain Dealer*, was aware of what was emanating from Baltimore and began to press Modell for answers. One of its leading football reporters, Anthony Grossi, heard the same conjecture—that the Browns were heading for Baltimore—but, after running a check, felt it could be categorized as nothing more than "cocktail party talk." Cleveland's radio and TV stations turned to Viviano for interviews and he complied, apprising them of what he knew and holding to the conviction it was going to happen. The Browns, indeed, would soon be bound for Baltimore.

When I called the NFL office the day after the first unsubstantiated claim, Commissioner Paul Tagliabue was away on business. With him was his assistant, Joseph Browne, but I talked to Greg Aiello, who handles media relations. When I told him there was a need for confidentiality on what I was about to tell him, he quickly answered, "Absolutely, you have it." After hearing what I told him regarding the Browns, he said it was all news to him, something he insisted he hadn't heard mentioned from either inside or outside league circles. No, not even a hint or a rumor.

One of the league's highest officials insists, in retrospect, that Tagliabue and his staff were not aware of Modell's intentions, except that he had "dropped vague hints" that he might be getting out of Cleveland while attending a meeting relating to television matters. The NFL claimed no advance knowledge of Modell's intentions to head for Baltimore.

The first chance I had to write of the developments came in *The* [Baltimore] *Sun*. With the demise of *The Evening Sun* only weeks before, I got the opportunity to remain with the new and expanded Sunday edition of the paper. Without further insight as to what might be going on, I wrote that if Moag had a signed contract in his back pocket for Modell to bring the Browns to Baltimore, it had to be marked "top secret," because the league didn't know about it.

I was later told that confidentiality agreements had been signed between the parties involved. Heavy financial penalties would be assessed if there was a premature announcement. With each passing day, the Browns-to-Baltimore issue increased in intensity. And for one reason . . . it was true. Furthermore, as the original tipster continued to reiterate, it was a fait accompli.

As conjecture proliferated, there was even a suggestion that the team coming to Baltimore wasn't going to be the Browns. In a late night call sports editor Gibbons asked me if I knew of any other pending moves or further details concerning the Browns. If it didn't work out to be the Browns, wondered Gibbons, could it possibly be the Cincinnati Bengals or Phoenix Cardinals? There were recurring reports that both franchises were looking to transfer. And Moag had talked to both clubs.

Mike Brown, the Bengals' owner, had been in Baltimore for an earlier visit. I told sports editor Gibbons it was impossible to hazard a guess, except to tell him the same source I had talked to earlier was still holding to the belief and insisting it was the Browns, yet he wasn't able to elaborate further, or offer new information about how it was going to be done.

During the previous summer, months before, I had been advised by a Maryland official that the Chicago Bears were interested in exploring Baltimore and that Virginia Halas McCaskey and her husband Ed, the chairman of the board and son-in-law of the late team founder, George Halas, were coming for a visit. This was supposed to mean the Bears' entire team might be following at some later date. I knew this to be wrong and told the well-intentioned informant that the McCaskeys had invited the Steadmans and Jim Frey, the former Chicago Cubs' manager who lived outside of Baltimore, to dinner with them at Obrycki's Crab House. Their Baltimore stop was merely to inspect Camden Yards, the baseball park they had heard so much about, with the hope that something similar in football design might be constructed for the Bears in Chicago. The McCaskeys attended lunch the next day with Moag, who took the visitors on a ride along North Charles Street after providing them with a tour of Oriole Park.

Back to the Browns-to-Baltimore scenario. It was a story that wouldn't go away, as much as Cleveland and the NFL hoped it would.

Instead of being put aside as just another rumor or false report, it was taking on additional credibility. Modell knew it couldn't be kept off the record much longer. Moag agreed. Finally, on November 6, the Monday following the Browns' game with the Houston Oilers, a press conference was announced for 11 A.M. at Camden Yards. It was to be held on the main parking lot, close to the exact location where a new football stadium would be constructed.

The formal announcement was to be made, then and there, that the Browns were leaving Cleveland and coming to Baltimore. It was what Cleveland dreaded to hear but what Baltimore had been waiting to be told for over eleven years—that it had a team and was back in the NFL. The way it was evolving—taking a team from a community that had lavished phenomenal support on the Browns—didn't bring total elation to this frustrated city-in-waiting.

The evening before the announcement, the telephone rang at my home. First came a pleasing introduction: "This is John Moag and I want to make sure you know of the press conference tomorrow." When I said I did, he explained that after the main part of the media briefing he wanted me to be the first one to direct a question to Art Modell.

"No, John, thank you, but I don't want to be a part of any press conference that is being orchestrated," I told him. He seemed surprised but corrected the impression by saying, "Oh, that's not the intention at all. We just think out of respect for your long association with pro football that you should have the honor of asking the opening question of Modell." I didn't want to do it, had too much respect for the newspaper business to be a shill, and explained to sports editor Gibbons that I had rejected the idea. Gibbons said, "I agree. That's not the thing to do."

The press gathering, as it unfolded, was what we in the news business facetiously refer to as a "dog and pony show," meaning it was poorly presented, lacked any thread of professionalism, and the roles some of the cast of characters played that day were a sorry embarrassment. It was, at best, an amateur hour without the "hook."

Maryland Governor Parris Glendening bragged about how Modell was first contacted and then induced to come to Baltimore from Cleveland. He held up a Browns' coffee mug and said that on an earlier night, at a meeting in Salisbury, he had wanted a cold drink and it had been served to him in this same cup. Now the dog and pony show, just like that, had turned into "show and tell."

Reporters on hand and those around the country watching on national television, couldn't believe that a public official was bragging to the world about being a part of a clandestine action that resulted in lifting a team from another city. It seemed the essence of bad taste.

Glendening also boasted about the part he played in the scripting, leaving no doubt how he helped manipulate what was described as a secret transaction, with everything but a cloak, dagger, and hidden microphones. He described what a huge financial surge this was going to mean to the economy of Maryland—which was a gross exaggeration because only ten games are played in a normal pro football season and few fans come from other parts of the country to register in hotels or spend money in restaurants. Glendening, willing to explain how the deal worked out, revealed that sessions with Modell and his partner, Al Lerner, were conducted covertly inside the privacy of a parked airplane, owned by Lerner, at Baltimore-Washington International Airport.

Meanwhile, some community leaders in Baltimore didn't feel all that pleased with what they were hearing. It was a playback of, or payback for, in many respects, how the Colts had been pulled away from Baltimore and trucked off to Indianapolis. Cleveland was devastated, ripping into Modell and accusing him of a double-cross, underhanded maneuvering, and calculated deception in the months and weeks preceding the action. Much of the country was irate over how any city, drawing in excess of seventy-thousand a game, could lose a team after a highly supported forty-nine-year residency.

Modell, on the speaker's platform with Glendening and Moag, didn't look himself. It was apparent he was uncomfortable and not feeling his best. This was most unusual since he usually carried himself with a self-assured presence. This, though, was a far more difficult circumstance, one he had never been a part of before. As I studied Modell and tried to read his feelings, an unmistakable picture emerged that this was a man who, at that moment, was exceedingly tormented. If Glendening and his advisors didn't know the historical significance of what had taken place, luring the Browns to Baltimore, then certainly Modell did. He seemed so alone, obviously disturbed by the feelings he had to have deep within himself. It wasn't easy. At that moment, he was irrevocably turning his back on Cleveland—home, friends, and business associates—a city where he had been once revered and where he had made contributions to a better way of life through helping myriad charitable causes.

Why then did he discard Cleveland and embrace Baltimore? He insisted it was to assure his heirs-to-be of a solid financial future. He also claimed he was taking a fiscal beating in Cleveland, despite the fact that home attendance was booming and broadcast income from the league and from radio and television accrued close to $40 million. Three days before he headed for Baltimore, Modell, in an interview with *The Plain Dealer*, was reminded he had previously promised there was no chance the team would ever move.

But then he quickly revised his position by saying, "As long as I owned the team and as long as I was given any cooperation at all, but the game has changed considerably. The Cleveland Browns have had some tremendous financial difficulties since the free-agency market opened up. And the picture has changed. As for my proclamation that I would not move the team, that's gone, that's null and void because the game has changed considerably. My ball club right now is not in fiscal, financial shape to sell."

But that certainly wasn't Cleveland's fault. If Modell couldn't turn a profit on the enormous home crowds he was drawing, perennially the first or second best in the league, plus the vast television income, then he was not the able businessman he was reputed to be. He had, in the past, made questionable investments outside of football in a radio station, the production of a movie, and other expensive ventures, along with having one of the league's highest payrolls for players and a front office that was top-weighted in number of employees when compared to most other clubs.

From the outset of the Cleveland-to-Baltimore move, I believed there was a strong personal reason, having to do almost entirely with Modell's ego, that caused him to cast a wandering eye towards Baltimore. For his entire career in Cleveland, going back to 1961, the other team in town, the baseball Indians, had been a doormat. There were a few brief flashes of success but nothing substantial. Usually, the Indians were considered out of the race by Mother's Day or, at the latest, the Fourth of July. Then in 1994 and 1995, the hottest ticket in Cleveland was the chance to see the Indians play in their new facility, Jacobs Field, which was similar in concept to Baltimore's Camden Yards. The Indians, simultaneously with the park opening, and in an act of perfect timing, became the most improved team in all of baseball. Suddenly, after almost four distressing decades, they were successful and exciting. For the first time in what seemed to be eons, Clevelanders were talking Indians. Baseball conversation was everywhere: street corners, saloons, restaurants, offices, and loading platforms. Cleveland had pennant fever.

Under the circumstances, with the Indians drawing so much favorable attention, the belief persists that Modell's vanity caused him to think about taking his football team to Baltimore. Sports have been known to do this to a man. There was his own misguided feeling that he wasn't truly appreciated—a false assumption on his part. The ego aspect, as much as anything, contributed significantly to the transfer of the Browns' franchise to Baltimore. Modell had difficulty, after all those years of standing front and center, being relegated to the role of "second banana." For virtually his entire time in Cleveland, thirty-five years' worth, the Browns, and only the Browns, were the foremost team in town, which made Modell the paramount franchise owner.

Along with the resurgence of the Indians and their making it to their first World Series since 1954 (when Dwight Eisenhower was in the White House), the Browns were no longer dominating the first sports page of *The Plain Dealer* and other northeastern Ohio newspapers. They were relegated to a below-the-fold position or placed on the second or third page of the section. The Indians suddenly were the lead story because public interest warranted every inch of editorial play they were receiving. Father Art and son David took the popularity of the Indians quite personally. There seems little question, then and now, that this was a significant force, maybe even more compelling than any promised financial bonanza in Baltimore, that drew Art Modell towards the crab flats of Chesapeake Bay.

Modell was dismayed, too, by the fact that a new arena had been built for the Cleveland Cavaliers of the National Basketball Association, which they didn't need, and a museum for rock 'n' roll music had been created, along with the attractive park for the Indians. It was, to him, an insult that he hadn't been taken care of first, but at least on one occasion, during an interview, Modell said he realized the time would come when his stadium problems would be properly addressed. When the buildings were being planned, he didn't raise any objection because, after all, he controlled Cleveland Stadium, where he was the landlord. So Cleveland was lulled into a feeling of false security with the Browns. It would move at some later date to assist Modell. There didn't seem to be any urgency because he knew his turn would come.

The city fathers allowed themselves to believe there wasn't any timetable they needed to meet. They figured since Modell was so much a part of Cleveland life he was one of them, a good friend and neighbor, and also that as a businessman he realized not everything could be done at once. The problems inherent in trying to bring about the renaissance of a city were monumental. It was generally understood that eventually the Browns would be housed in a new stadium, even if nothing had been promised or put in writing. Such an optimistic rationale was all wrong, as details of the November 6 events in Baltimore were to prove.

Modell also had an unusual arrangement at Cleveland Stadium, constructed in 1931 by the Osbourne Engineering Company, the same firm that built the original Yankee Stadium. The stadium was erected on a landfill by the Works Progress Administration with the dream that an Olympiad would follow. But that didn't happen. Modell, in helping to bring order and improvements to the huge double-tiered horseshoe, formed a management group to control events that were held there and to pay for its upkeep. He was taking the burden off the city. In 1974, Modell established the Cleveland Stadium Corporation and signed a twenty-five-year contract. This added to the widespread feeling that he was one of them, a Clevelander who would be with the city in the good times and the bad.

It's estimated Modell spent $18 million on improvements, including installation of 108 luxury loges and a new scoreboard and playing field, among other changes. But there's just so much you can do with an old stadium, as Baltimore, Los Angeles, Detroit, and other cities have learned.

The fact that Modell was in charge of Cleveland Stadium meant the Indians were his chief tenant. He set the rental scale and the concession percentages. Baseball and football, meanwhile, coexisted on a reasonably amicable basis. Modell, though, was in total control.

The Indians finally decided they wanted to be in charge of their own destiny, which meant they would no longer be answering to Modell or paying him rent. They went off on their own, moving to an exclusive place to play, newly constructed Jacobs Field, in 1994. Just like that, baseball in Cleveland made an immediate comeback. All the attention given to the Indians, well-earned after a long drought, bothered Modell even if he didn't make his feelings known in a press release. The spotlight was playing on the Indians, as never before, in a city where Modell was always top dog . . . in or out of the end-zone "dawg pound."

Son David, groomed to be the eventual front-office quarterback of the franchise, told a group of Cleveland-area newspaper reporters only weeks before the departure news broke that the Jacobs family didn't compare to the Modells and accompanied it with an all-out blast of personal criticism and the use of vile language. It startled the reporters to hear such an unexpected diatribe, right there on the field at Berea, Ohio, the $15-million training and office showplace that Art built for the exclusive comfort of his team.

Mary Kay Cabot, of *The Plain Dealer* staff, said she couldn't believe the unprovoked explosion and the nature of the comments about the Jacobs family and the Indians' success. "Older members of our sports department, over the previous couple of years, had told me I was too willing to buy into what the Modells were saying but I wasn't alone," explained Cabot. "Other reporters believed them, too. We never guessed, under any circumstances, that Art would betray Cleveland. That's exactly what it was—a betrayal. Total deception. It was entirely that."

Initially, the Browns' move, even among some positive-thinking members of the Baltimore business leadership, wasn't hailed as any celebrated coup. It was perceived as an unethical and dastardly thing to do to Cleveland, almost a carbon copy of what had happened when

Irsay kidnapped the Colts and hauled them off to Indianapolis. If Baltimore's anguish over what had been inflicted on it by Irsay was so troubling, then why was the same game of "stealing a franchise" now being condoned? One important figure in Baltimore business circles, recognized throughout the nation for his momentous achievements, quietly refused to head the club's ticket drive when asked if he would be available to handle such a role. He made it known he wasn't going to be used as a tool, nor was he interested in trying to sell something to friends and associates when he believed the premise was entirely wrong.

Significant, too, and reminiscent of that March night in 1984 when the Colts made their disgraceful exit, was the awareness that Baltimore could no longer be considered the martyr, the Joan of Arc, of football. It had aggressively, under the dictum of the governor, sought to satisfy its frustrations by going after the Browns, a team of renown. Not bothered by any implication of wrong-doing, Baltimore, through the Glendening/Moag maneuver and the interest evidenced by Modell, had ensured that similar pain was being inflicted upon another city.

Instead of demonstrating mutual respect for Cleveland, Baltimore had gone on the offensive to take what it could get. Some Baltimoreans were now dealing with a sense of guilt over how Cleveland had been victimized by a Maryland governor and his appointed Stadium Authority chairman, who had achieved what they wanted, but, in the process, had broken the hearts of Cleveland's loyal followers. Again with Modell's compliance.

Leonard Burrier, more widely known as the "Big Wheel," who roamed the stands and sidelines leading cheers for the Colts, then the Baltimore Stars and the Baltimore Stallions, didn't like the way it happened: "I'm glad for Baltimore that it got a football team," he said, "but I'm unhappy at how it came about. Here's a city, Cleveland, that sold out a seventy-thousand-seat stadium. I can't understand how with all the TV revenue, NFL products revenue, concession revenue, he [Modell] says he's losing money and has to get out of there."

To attract the Browns was an enormously expensive undertaking—tantamount to a giveaway. It was as if the streets of old Baltimore, in a bad way financially since the city was losing businesses and population, had overnight been paved with gold. From a financial standpoint for the city and state, there was little to be gained, but at least Baltimore had realized its objective of having an NFL team, regardless of the cost. Modell, in agreeing to desert Cleveland for Baltimore, would get a rent-free $200-million stadium built to his own specifications with public money. The contract would run for thirty years. He also would receive the profit from parking and concessions, plus half the revenue from all other events, such as concerts, soccer matches, boxing shows, tractor pulls, that might be held in the planned 68,400-seat stadium. In addition, Modell would have the right to charge a permanent seat license (PSL), meaning he could extract a fee from a fan before actually selling him or her the ticket.

It represented a selfish abuse of the public, but Glendening and Moag had agreed to it, with the ceiling placed at somewhere around $74 million on the income that could be raised from PSLs. This was later reduced to $65 million by Modell but some Browns' officials were saying it had cost $125 million in expenses to move the team. Believe that if you want. The club estimated that a sizable number of employees might be moving, but, the final count, according to publicity director Kevin Byrne, was around fifteen—hardly a significant total.

Along with fighting a losing battle for almost twelve years and being deprived of pro football, Baltimore was satisfied it finally had a team in hand, yet some citizens told themselves it was a shame it had to be Cleveland that was victimized. Measured another way, Baltimore, at the time, wasn't displaying the same degree of emotion it had shown when the Colts were pulled out from under them in 1984. Instead, there was more public empathy expressed for Cleveland than Glendening, Moag, and Modell, or anyone, anticipated.

With Modell delivering a franchise to Baltimore, the immediate feeling among fans was more surprise than anything else; they were not doing cartwheels about Harborplace. Denise Koch, a WJZ anchor personality, gave this perspective on what was happening around her: "This is a day when there should be unrestrained joy, but I don't find it. Call it a bittersweet attitude. In truth, as much as I hate to admit it, Cleveland is being hurt at Baltimore's gain."

Among a sizeable element of Baltimore fandom, no doubt the majority, there was pleasure that a team was finally on the way, regardless of what it took in giveaways to bring it about. The mood, however, though generally upbeat, couldn't be described as euphoric. The prevailing attitude with some of the more fanatical followers was that regardless of how a team arrived, even if it was painful for Cleveland, it was justifiable, considering the way Baltimore had been kicked around and treated so rudely by the NFL. This could never be denied. The league, in its incompetence, had abused Baltimore.

It also meant, however, that the city and state were available for exploitation by any owner who was more interested in money than in respecting and upholding tradition. Ethics, unfortunately, have become passé.

CHAPTER 2

# LONG, HARD STRUGGLE

What Baltimore and its love-starved football romantics wanted was a team—any team. It had to do with feeling good and replacing frustration with exhilaration. There was kind of a trapped-in-the-end-zone desperation that surrounded the possibility of getting an NFL franchise. Even Art Modell, of all people, had voted against Baltimore when it had last applied.

Baltimore, like any other city of note, considered itself major league caliber. It wanted parity with all the rest, something it believed had been lost when Irsay took it on the lam after saying he "wasn't going to move the goddamn team."

Baltimore, endeavoring to enhance its standing, had fought a long, hard battle to gain national and international attention. It was no longer a place bracketed between Washington and Philadelphia. Outside of a great hospital (Johns Hopkins), an all-lump crab cake, and the most famous baseball player of all time (Babe Ruth), there wasn't that much to relate to in Baltimore's past. Indeed, Thomas D'Alesandro, Jr., Baltimore mayor from 1947 to1959, had uttered a for-then whimsical observation regarding an enormously successful urban project undertaken by the city of Pittsburgh: "I don't think we can do it because, after all, Pittsburgh has the Mellon family and all we have are watermelons." But the city, with D'Alesandro giving early hope to such an effort, had renovated the Charles Street business hub and later the spectacular inner harbor area. His friend William Donald Schaefer, who later became mayor, helped bring the latter phase to fruition but, of course, previous mayors, such as the two D'Alesandros, father and son, along with Theodore R. McKeldin had provided the early impetus.

The old wooden piers along Pratt and Light streets gave way to what eventually became Harborplace, where an attractive setting of upscale shops and restaurants, combined with the shipping and nautical activities of the port, created an appeal for the home folks as well as a lure for tourists.

Prior to the make-over of this part of Baltimore, the citizens had a feeling of self-doubt. It was an inferiority complex of metropolitan proportions. The condition dated back to the first half of this century, a period when conservative Baltimore, rarely making a splash, was considered nothing more than a whistle-stop.

From a sports perspective, Baltimore had the Orioles, a team synonymous with baseball success, that involved itself in the life of the city. Also Pimlico and the Preakness, referred to as the second jewel in the annual Triple Crown thoroughbred series. The Colts were once included in the same regal realm, even exceeding the Orioles in popularity for a considerable part of their time—but football had been gone since 1984.

Again, what Baltimore coveted, in the fall and winter, was to be restored to the mainstream of so-called upper-crust Sunday afternoon sports-going society. Pro football would give it that much-sought-after appeal. With all respect to those spirited, well-intentioned replacements who tried to fill the void, they just didn't measure up. The Stars of the United States Football League, which Baltimore had in name only in 1985—the team practiced in Philadelphia and played in College Park, Maryland—and later the Canadian Football League's Stallions, who merely tugged at the heartstrings in what was a two-year fling (1994–95), never developed into serious relationships with the fans.

Not that the Stars and Stallions weren't successful in their own separate ways; they were talented, well coached, and winners on the field. But, again, Baltimore wasn't buying the label of anything it considered to be lower in stature than the NFL. Because of the Stars and Stallions, Baltimore is the only city in the world that can lay claim to winning championships in the USFL, which went out of business, the CFL, and the NFL.

So, for mere bragging rights and earning league titles, Baltimore is three-for-three. It never held membership in a league it couldn't win, except in the All-America Conference—which, of course, was dominated by the then-invincible Browns of Cleveland.

Baltimore was too good a city, with a proven football background, to be continually rejected by the NFL. Anything less than a first-rate offering was unacceptable. This could only mean the NFL.

For eleven years, the franchise was among the missing, but in some respects it seemed that they had been gone much longer. The Colts were in decline as a centerpiece from almost the moment Irsay bought the team in 1972, which was twelve years before the exodus to Indianapolis. Some of the Baltimore mourners, choked with emotion and overreacting, were quick to equate the loss to a death in the family. This, of course, was misuse of the language. The move of a sports franchise is an enormous money-making machine for the owners and players; it could never be compared to losing the life of a loved one. It wasn't life or death, but a beloved team that the fans in Baltimore had created. Now it was being stripped away.

Baltimore, with all its enthusiasm, had what could be described as an indigenous weakness. It took the fate of its teams on too personal a basis, as if winning or losing made the surroundings any better or worse for the populace. The drinking water tasted as good as ever and the tax rate didn't decline, regardless of the standings. The unpredictable Irsay was responsible for the loss of the Colts, after tarnishing their good name, and then packing them away in Mayflower moving vans to another business address.

A man I know quite well would later roll down the window of his car and curse loudly at every Mayflower truck he encountered, be it in Homeland, Hampden, Hampton, Highlandtown, or even out on the open highway. In this instance, it was another classic case of wrongfully blaming the messenger. The Mayflower company, based in Indianapolis, with its huge and gleaming eighteen-wheelers, had only enabled Irsay to evacuate under the cover of darkness.

Even National Football League Commissioner Pete Rozelle didn't know the Colts were pulling out of Baltimore until they were gone.

Baltimore attempted in the courts and before the Congress to correct the wrong, but the verdict was irrevocable. Rozelle had earlier wanted the Raiders to remain in Oakland, where they enjoyed astonishing support. In a bitter antitrust trial in 1982, the Raiders and Los Angeles Coliseum Commission won the favor of a jury hearing the case and the team was declared free to go south, from the Bay Area to Southern California.

This became the genesis of some owners' new game plan, even if the commissioner didn't agree. Teams, by way of the precedent established in the Raiders' case, were able to roam as they wished. No restraint could be exercised or tether applied. The league realized, after losing Oakland as a franchised member, in a case costing over $100 million, that it couldn't deter or control teams from picking up and going where they wanted. Podunk, if they desired. Peoria the next day. Anyplace they decided to hang a helmet. Rozelle, accustomed to continuity, as was the rest of America when it came to pro football, fought to protect the rights of cities, but it was a hopeless cause. The NFL continued to lose the legal arguments, which only added to Baltimore's woes. Rozelle attempted to restore order to the league but the owners, in this case, were calling the signals.

Irsay himself had even voted against allowing the Raiders to move out of Oakland for Los Angeles in 1982. The minutes of the league meeting showed he was dead-set against it. Then Bob reversed himself when he wanted to take the ball out of Baltimore and put it in play elsewhere.

When Irsay hit the road only two years after Oakland took off for Los Angeles, there was no legal recourse. Not even Hurst "Loudy" Loudenslager, the most fanatical of all the legendary Colts' fans, had any impact on the decision. This was a man who turned part of his house into a museum for the team and had his wife bake expensive walnut cakes every time a player or coach had a birthday. He customarily showed up at BWI airport to send the team off on a road trip and was waiting there when the players returned, regardless of how late it was Sunday night or how early it might be Monday morning. Meanwhile, he'd be playing the "Colts' Fight Song" on the portable recorder he carried with him.

Baltimore was broken in spirit over the loss of the Colts. The cleated heroes, in blue and white, were gone. Franchises were now on wheels. The court ruling in the Oakland case determined they were transients and could migrate any time they wanted. If the thought occurred to them they might even change residences at half-time, although to this point that hasn't been tried. The Colts' property, including uniforms, game equipment, tackling dummies, office furniture, medical supplies, and pictures off the walls, had been carried away in Mayflower moving vans for Indianapolis.

One thing the Colts failed to take out of Baltimore was the band uniforms. They obviously forgot. At the time, band president John Ziemann had them at the tailor for cleaning and repairs. He later called Harriett Irsay, Bob's wife, who was a friend of the Ziemanns, John and Charlene, and she told him to keep on marching. In other words, the uniforms belonged in Baltimore because that's where the band was. Harriett wanted the band to keep them. Too bad Bob didn't feel the same way about the football uniforms and the players who wore them.

There was so much wrong about the defection that hope lingered that something would certainly be done to quickly amend the situation. A belief existed that the league couldn't do without Baltimore. Suffice it to say the league made out quite well, which again was damaging to the pride of a community that put too much emphasis on the value of a team. The cruel departure of the Colts precipitated, in the souls of fair-thinking men and women, a belief that a franchise replacement would, in short order, somehow wind up on the white marble stoops of old Baltimore. First, after Irsay shanghaied the Colts, it was the New Orleans Saints that might be coming to Baltimore, following a story that a group of Marylanders was attempting to buy them and change their name to the Baltimore Saints, or whatever.

That was a brief hope that went up in smoke. New Orleans, drawing crowds in numbers that Baltimore never approached, had a domed stadium and a constituency that was always going to be there—they had been tested to the depth of their loyalty by prolonged losing streaks. But New Orleans to Baltimore? No chance.

Without a doubt, the most positive action Baltimore took was when Mayor Schaefer asked Henry Butta, a Baltimore business leader, to decide if Memorial Stadium could be improved enough to satisfy the NFL or if a new stadium was necessary. Before embarking on a renovation of the existing stadium, Butta personally solicited contributions from corporations to finance a fact-finding survey.

Results of the study commissioned by Butta showed a new stadium was needed and that its location should be downtown. The preferred spot was several blocks to the south and east of the Camden Railroad Yards, where the Baltimore Gas & Electric Co. had an operation known as Spring Gardens. From twenty-one potential locations, Spring Gardens was rated number one. However, acquisition of the land and the cost of moving huge storage tanks made building there prohibitive. Camden Yards, number two on the list, got the call. Butta was ready to go.

Then came an opportunity in 1988 to attract the St. Louis Cardinals, but owner Bill Bidwill, after making visits to the city, put it to a vote of his family. The final choice was Phoenix over Baltimore in a photo finish. Just like that, the St. Louis Cardinals became the Phoenix Cardinals. Originally in 1920 they had been the Racine Cardinals and later the Chicago Cardinals.

Bidwill, friendly but in a quiet sort of way, kept his own counsel and never tipped his hand. At one point in his discussions with Herb Belgrad, the Maryland Stadium Authority chairman who preceded Moag, he indicated he was prepared to make a decision that would please Baltimore. He seemed receptive to what he had been told. Bidwill knew the area; he played high school football at Washington's Georgetown Prep and had even scored a touchdown against Loyola High School of Baltimore.

Before completing travel plans for his team, he came to Baltimore on frequent inspection visits, attended a party hosted by Mary and Sig Hyman at their residence in Stevenson; he appeared to enjoy himself but was noncommittal. That's just the way he is: secretive, a loner, difficult to read.

Jack Buck, the prominent play-by-play football and baseball announcer from St. Louis, offered poignant insight on Bidwill's character by saying, "He's a fine, fine man. He just does things differently than the rest of us. I'd go so far as to say you could have been camped out under his dining room table for the last six months and never heard a word mentioned or had any idea of what he was intending to do in regard to moving the team."

Bidwill's ultimate choice was Phoenix, where he immediately fumbled the kickoff. He overpriced the seats and got off to a stumbling start. The average ticket for the 1988 inaugural season was $38, plus a premium of $1,650, $900, $600, $250, $150, and $50, depending on seat location. The second season they were reduced considerably and lowered again the next year, 1990, when the average dropped to $30 and more than half the seats, 43,864, were $20 or less.

Phoenix was annoyed with Bidwill before it had even gotten to know him. It was a poor beginning for the new owner in town. Shortly thereafter, Bidwill was hospitalized for a gallbladder operation, and *The Phoenix Gazette* sports editor Joe Gilmartin, gifted with a delightful touch, wrote a classic line saying that during the Bidwill surgery the "doctors took the bladder out and left the gall in."

Bidwill, despite his detractors—and Gilmartin isn't one of them—is a decent, though introverted, man who endeavors to do the right thing, has a love of the NFL and understands its history—which is far more than can be said for most of his contemporaries who are in the business of owning teams. Too many NFL owners stay up late at night trying to invent new ways to clip the public.

After the Bidwill turndown of Baltimore, which had much to do with his family preferring the warmth and scenic vistas of Arizona's Valley of the Sun, there was nothing more for Baltimore to do than anticipate league expansion. It was the only sensible option, a policy established by Governor William Donald Schaefer, who was devastated by the loss of the Colts. He also insisted he wasn't interested in robbing any other city of an existing franchise. However, if any owner had already made up his mind to move, he would at least listen.

Baltimore, meanwhile, was a free agent, trying to make itself look attractive to any suitor who happened along the street but, more importantly, intently pressing onward in hopes of realizing its ambitions for expansion.

At one point, the New England Patriots, owned by Victor Kiam, were supposed to be ready to give up on Foxboro and its modest facilities. The stadium in Foxboro was erected in 1971 at $6.1 million, a comparatively low cost as prices went, then and now, and looked every penny of it. Would it be a team such as the Patriots that might be receptive to transferring to Baltimore, where the promise for guaranteed profits included everything but ownership of the Chesapeake Bay and mineral rights in Western Maryland? In its working man's past, the NFL would have been elated to have something half as good as what it had in Foxboro, but now the league was playing to the swells, and team owners wanted elaborate facilities that it expected cities to pay for so they could become richer and flatter their own importance.

It was first said the reason the NFL couldn't enlarge from twenty-eight to thirty clubs was because it lacked a labor contract with the players' association. This was interpreted as a foot-dragging tactic because a previous expansion had been implemented normally at a time when the league was involved in trying to arrange a collective bargaining agreement with its players. After holding off expansion for as long as it could (why cut in another two teams for a slice of the profits until they were forced to do so?) the league eventually, in March of 1990, named an expansion and realignment committee. It subsequently followed up by announcing it would add two clubs for the 1994 season, a decision that was eventually put back for another year.

Baltimore now was in the race with St. Louis, which had lost the Cardinals to Phoenix; Oakland, whose Raiders had fled to Los Angeles; Memphis, San Antonio, Jacksonville, Nashville, Raleigh-Durham, Honolulu, Sacramento, and Charlotte, and only two would be selected. From a field of eleven prospective cities, only Jacksonville, Charlotte, Baltimore, Memphis, and St. Louis survived the final cut. The hoped-for prospect of expansion also made Baltimore realize, even earlier, that it must project itself by assembling an impressive ownership group.

The city didn't lack for interested applicants. One of the first out of the starting block was Nathan Landau, a Bethesda, Maryland, real estate developer and an important fund-raising figure in the Democratic party. His candidacy didn't last long. He was supposed to be aligned with Bob Tisch, a former U.S. Postmaster General, who had all the money that was ever going to be needed; Herbert Haft, who was chairman of the boards that directed the Dart Group, Track Auto, and Crown Books; and Vernon Jordan, a member of a District of Columbia law firm and past president of the National Urban League. But Tisch, after hearing Landau had made it clear that he would be in control, informed him that under no circumstances was he interested in any such partnership.

Meanwhile, Landau hired a research expert to compile extensive profiles on every owner in the league: their backgrounds in business, hobbies, homes, and the names of their wives and children. But he never got a chance to utilize the information. The Landau effort slowed down and, for reasons known only to himself, expired.

Tisch also said he wanted to go it alone and pulled away from his link to Landau. There was no shortage of other reported applicants, including Al Lerner of Cleveland, a minority partner in the Browns with owner and friend Art Modell; Ed Hale of Baltimore; Bart Starr, the former Green Bay Packers' Hall of Famer; and "Bubba" Smith, the former Colts' defensive end who had "gone Hollywood" and was playing in movies and acting on network television. Some would-be Baltimore owners were underfunded, others simply had no chance. The feeling existed that some were either coming out of the woodwork or tumbling from the sky.

Tisch, though, was afforded a strong inside track in the early part of the franchise race. He was extremely wealthy and had been a neighbor in Scarsdale, New York, of Commissioner Rozelle. Tisch had the money, zillions of it, and also the proper connections, from the top down—starting with Rozelle.

Baltimore, once it had Tisch aligned, felt pleased about itself. And it should have. Rival cities, such as Oakland and Charlotte, virtually conceded that Tisch represented a guaranteed ticket for Baltimore returning to the NFL. He also was the brother of Larry, who controlled CBS, and thus, was in position to know most of the owners. They certainly knew him. He owned the Loews' hotel chain and, just to have a Maryland address, and maybe a place to sleep, bought a hotel in Annapolis, formerly the Radisson. Tisch even went out for a sight-seeing cruise on Chesapeake Bay, established a quick rapport with Governor Schaefer, and conferred with a Baltimore friend of Rozelle, one Sig Hyman, for local knowledge.

It was felt there wouldn't be much competition with Tisch around. Other Baltimore bidders for a franchise knew Tisch would be tough to beat. Memphis and Charlotte knew it, too. His affluence and influence translated to a sterling reputation in the corporate world, which is what the NFL has become. Tisch had what none of the others possessed—imposing stature in all areas of business and a national profile.

Leonard "Boogie" Weinglass, a self-made success story, who had founded the Merry-Go-Round Enterprises, Inc., made his franchise interests known. He was thrilled to be challenging for a team. Football was going to be fun and "Boogie" believed he could convince the NFL that a once-poor kid from Baltimore, homegrown and making it on his nerve, deserved to be in control. Impressed and amused by his personality, the league in some ways allowed him to figure his chances were much better than they actually were. "Boogie," whose unpretentious ways highlighted his beguiling charm, even had a nickname for the team: it would be Bombers, but he was getting way ahead of himself.

Then, for Baltimore, came the toughest break of all, a sudden, out-of-the-blue development. The city quickly went from being the standout front-runner to a nondescript place back in the pack with all the rest of the competing cities. Although deeply involved with Baltimore and its pursuit of a team, Tisch had learned that some members of the Mara family, including Mrs. Helen Mara Nugent and her children, Tim Mara and Maura Mara Concannon, were going to sell 50 percent interest in the New York Giants. Tisch was contacted. Would he be interested as a possible buyer? He responded instantly.

One reason he was influenced to go after an expansion team in Baltimore was because it was only an hour away by plane from his home. He would be able to leave suburban New York on a Sunday morning and be in Baltimore in advance of the kickoff. Earlier, he had considered buying the Dallas Cowboys before Jerry Jones bought them from H. R. "Bum" Bright, when they were on the market in 1989, but backed off from an offer because the round trip on game day, even by private plane, would have been too long for comfort. So, without any prolonged discussion regarding the Giants, he paid $85 million for half-a-team with an option to buy the rest at a later date.

It was a clean and appealing deal for part ownership of a valuable franchise, carrying the name of the nation's leading city, even though it played its games in New Jersey. Hours before the Tisch decision was publicly disclosed, he called Sig Hyman, Rozelle's Baltimore friend, to inform him of his change in plans. It amounted to distressing news for Baltimore. Hyman was disappointed but understood. In the next sentence, he suggested Tisch should notify Govenor Schaefer as soon as he could because it wouldn't be proper for him to learn about it by reading the next morning's newspaper. Next Hyman told Tisch that after he talked with the governor, he might want to call me because I had enthusiastically advocated his ownership, and he did.

Schaefer was stunned—after all, he felt confident he was riding a sure winner—but in his conversation with Tisch, said he realized why a man with a chance to get partial ownership of a team, plus an opportunity to buy total control later, would be more interested in being located in his hometown than waiting for a new club in Baltimore at some undetermined date in the future. George Young, the Giants general manager and a native of Baltimore, said, "That was a major defeat for Baltimore. If Tisch had remained in the expansion chase, there's little doubt he would have gotten a team for Baltimore." In retrospect, that was as close as Baltimore was going to get in the expansion derby.

Tom Clancy, the heavy-hitting author, who had lived near Memorial Stadium before he became famous and was a Colts season ticket holder with his father in the top deck at Memorial Stadium, right above "Orrsville," as he liked to say, announced his intentions to buy a team. So Clancy joined the hunt, later to include Jim Robinson, a Baltimore movie producer who had struck gold in Hollywood and was reeling off a flow of box-office hits. Clancy and Robinson were attention-getting names, and they were from Baltimore, which made it all the better. Additionally, John Mackey, the Hall of Fame tight end, was brought into the group by attorney David Cohan, who was Clancy's friend and also a legal advisor.

Weinglass, who had movie mogul Barry Levinson with him and ex-Colt Joe Washington, plus a cast of thousands if needed, was looked on as a sentimental favorite. He demonstrated vibrant optimism and, after one league meeting, predicted "Baltimore is a lock, a sure-thing," but, unfortunately, it didn't work that way. Modell, for one, laughed it off and publicly minimized Weinglass's chances. "Boogie" believes Modell shot him down because of a secret agenda he had all along—like coming to Baltimore himself. Most all of the competing entrants tried to align themselves with recognizable names from sports and entertainment. Clancy and Robinson engaged John Unitas, the Hall of Fame quarterback, to represent them and, likewise, Ted Venetoulis, a publisher, political analyst, and former chief executive of Baltimore County.

The simple strategy was for Unitas and Venetoulis to make calls on league owners in an effort to garner support so that when it came time to decide on cities they'd favor them with their votes. Unitas was to draw a fee of $25,000 per team visit, paid to him by Clancy and Robinson, and was assured of being included in any ownership alignment that might result. Unitas and Venetoulis must have been doing an effective job because the league office, after hearing about their mission on behalf of Clancy/Robinson, suddenly said it didn't want prospective owners of expansion teams engaging in any such method of lobbying—cease and desist—as if they were doing something illegal or unethical.

They were pulled up right there, rather abruptly, but there was never any assurance that Jerry Richardson and his Charlotte contingent had been asked to stop meeting with the owners of existing teams. Of course, Richardson had a head start and had worked the team owners, making the rounds, long before Clancy/Robinson/Unitas/Venetoulis had formed a foursome. At that point, most all of Richardson's preliminary work had been done. He got there early and cultivated important relationships, doing exactly what Unitas and Robinson were doing—visiting the owners. Raymond Berry, then coaching in the league, opened doors for Richardson and made it possible for him to gain entree to various club officials. But when it came time to pick a coach for Richardson's team, Berry was given little consideration. Too bad. Such treatment offended Berry and also his friends.

The league, early in the expansion effort, had a prescreening process, interviewing those ownership candidates considered creditable from the cities that indicated interest. The meeting was held at one of Tisch's New York hotels, what had been formerly known as the Summit but renamed the Loews.

Herb Belgrad, who directed the formation of the Maryland Stadium Authority after being appointed by Governor Harry Hughes, was in attendance for league meetings representing the state, and continually lobbied in the lobby and other places. He was, unless the governor was present, one of the official leaders of the delegation. So was Matt De Vito, chief executive officer of the Rouse Corporation, a man of prestige and integrity, who impressively outlined Baltimore's position from a business perspective.

De Vito would have made an outstanding owner for Baltimore had he been tempted to go in that direction. But he certainly couldn't have been expected to be interested after witnessing the way the city was eventually treated by Commissioner Tagliabue and the NFL.

Baltimore's other would-be owners, in the final countdown, were the Glazers, father Malcolm and sons Joel and Bryan. They had showed up in the city without a calling card or any kind of an introduction, just a family coming in "cold" and announcing an interest to bid for a football team. In fact, the Glazers arrived at the advertising/marketing office of Image Dynamics, explaining they heard it was an ideal public relations firm to hire for gaining proper attention and access in Baltimore.

Although the visit was flattering, company president Phyllis Brotman said she couldn't represent them as a client because of a previous commitment to assist a group headed by a friend, Bart Starr, the former Green Bay Packers quarterback and a Hall of Fame member, who also was hoping to head up a Baltimore expansion effort. Brotman advised the Glazers to try the Leffler Agency, headed by Bob Leffler, who also worked for the Cleveland Browns and, in the waning seasons of the Colts in Baltimore, had handled their advertising and promotions.

After the preliminaries regarding expansion and questioning by the NFL had concluded, Weinglass, Belgrad, and De Vito returned from New York to Baltimore by train and, as they compared notes, felt good about the way they had been received during the early interviewing phase. Clancy believed he had personally done well, too, saying, quite candidly, that "most of the time my record shows I can be effective."

Clancy had spent a sizable portion of his own money to prepare an impressive video to introduce himself to the league and its owners. He commissioned a first-rate production that ran twelve minutes and showed him playing pool and firing guns with leading military figures in his own shooting gallery on his estate in Southern Maryland. It was an elegant presentation. If they gave Academy Awards for such ventures, then his certainly would have been nominated. The video was packaged and shipped air express to each NFL owner, along with a case of six of Tom's best-selling books, all autographed. On the outside, in bold gold-leaf lettering, was stamped: Another Blockbuster from Tom Clancy. It was by every measure an attention-getter, something way out of the ordinary, a valuable and unique gift. It weighed eighteen pounds. It was as expensive as it looked, probably costing in total as much as $60,000 to produce, package, and deliver.

Already, but slightly prematurely, "Boogie" was proclaiming his own victory. He named himself, this man of upbeat cheer, a solid shot at becoming the knighted one, ahead of Clancy/Robinson and the Glazers. In the aisle of the railroad car, on the trip home from the New York meeting, "Boogie," so typically, was bouncing about with boundless exuberance. He predicted Baltimore to be a sure winner—whether he was picked or not—but was, no doubt, personally high on his own chances. There wasn't any music playing but "Boogie" was dancing, intoxicated with enthusiasm. And, yes, also dreaming of the wonders of owning a pro football team in his own hometown.

CHAPTER 3

# ANOTHER RUDE JOLT

From a field of eleven cities, all with early visions of becoming expansion selections, the league preserved only five for serious down-the-line consideration. Those still included in the hunt were Baltimore, St. Louis, Charlotte, Memphis, and Jacksonville. And you might like to think of them in exactly that order of preference. Unfortunately for Baltimore, as subsequent events were to prove, the National Football League wasn't in accord.

At a meeting in the NFL office, 410 Park Avenue in New York, a short punt from the Waldorf-Astoria, I had the chance to go one-on-one with Commissioner Paul Tagliabue during a congenial and informal meeting. A group of fifteen men, including sportswriters, former team general managers, coaches, scouts, and historians from around the country, had been invited to help select the seventy-fifth anniversary team of the NFL under the masterful organizational hand of Don Weiss, one of the commissioner's first-line assistants.

I told Joseph Browne, the director of communications, that I'd like ten minutes of Tagliabue's time if he had availability on his appointment calendar. Somewhere during the discussion of Chuck Bednarik, one of the best who ever played the game, one of the commissioner's staff said that Tagliabue was free to talk and he would like me to join him in his private office. I excused myself temporarily from the effort of picking the all-time NFL all-stars and joined the commissioner. I told him I was speaking for myself, not the Sunpapers or the city of Baltimore. Strictly Steadman.

Tagliabue was an interested listener. I mentioned that what I was about to tell him wasn't rehearsed, that it was coming from the depth of my soul and the observations were based on background acquired from being around the NFL since 1950, back to a time when I wasn't much more than a small boy. I explained how Baltimore had been given such a bad deal by Irsay and, before that, Carroll Rosenbloom, and ahead of him, Abraham Watner. Baltimore was way overdue for having a decent NFL club owner.

It was a personalized report, complete with anecdotes, a review of history, but I never drifted away from the defined purpose—describing why Baltimore deserved to be chosen for a return to the NFL. The commissioner listened, smiled at some of the recollections, and asked questions. I told him Art Rooney, the late beloved owner of the Steelers and a frequent visitor to Baltimore, had said, "After what that Irsay and Rosenbloom have done to your city it's lucky it's still standing."

I pointed out to Tagliabue that he might be tempted to perceive some of my comments as born of provincialism, but they weren't intended to be that way. I knew better, I told him, probably as well as anyone, about the positives and negatives of Baltimore, but Baltimore didn't need to sell itself. Its record spoke volumes. For thirty-five years the city had helped create a large slice of significant professional football history. Of the cities on the expansion list, Baltimore was far and away the best via any yardstick he wanted to use—size of television market, per capita income, diversity of businesses and industries, plus a long relationship with the NFL. I told the commissioner why not take Baltimore and St. Louis, both of which had been deprived by owners going elsewhere, in the upcoming expansion contest, and deal with the best of the new cities, such as Charlotte and Memphis, at some future date? This would, most emphatically, present the ideal opportunity to clean up the past indebtedness of the NFL to Baltimore and St. Louis.

Tagliabue had earlier emphasized that Baltimore's having three possible expansion groups competing (Clancy/Robinson, Weinglass, and the Glazers) made no difference to the league. Such interest, he said, was to be regarded as an advantage. The other cities each had only one clearly defined ownership in place. Speaking of Charlotte, he asked what I knew about Jerry Richardson. Even though my mission was to carry the ball for Baltimore, as a self-appointed representative, there was no way I could suggest anything negative about Richardson's personal character, background, or business acumen.

Tagliabue, of course, was already well-versed on Richardson. He didn't need for me to tell him anything, except I knew Richardson better and for a longer period of time than any individual in the league; our association went back to 1959 when he was a rookie from Wofford College who joined the Colts as a thirteenth round draft choice. My opinion of Richardson was sky-high. That he represented Charlotte, a Baltimore rival, was something that couldn't be held against him. I mentioned the fact that Jerry, after quitting the Colts, had become a momentous success story and, at last count, had 120,000 employees in his fast-food empire that included Denny's Restaurants, some Hardee's outlets in the south, and various other chains, plus Ogden Catering that serviced stadia and ballparks with concessions.

Richardson had played for the Colts two years, in 1959 and 1960, and left the club because General Manager Don Kellett would not advance his salary to $10,000 a year. Prorated, it would have meant $21 more a game for a twelve-week season but Kellett wouldn't budge. Richardson, just as adamant, soon headed home to Spartanburg, South Carolina, and with one hamburger stand, which he paid for with his money from the Colts win over the Giants in the championship of 1959, began to work his way towards becoming a multimillionaire.

There is strong reason to believe if he hadn't committed to Charlotte, his interest would have been centered on putting a team in Baltimore. When asked, he never denied such a possibility. In fact, Jerry talked about it with friends in what amounted to serious discussions. Max Muhleman, who heads a marketing firm that worked with Richardson, said he wouldn't be surprised to learn that such a possibility had existed. Yes, Richardson thought seriously about actually giving up on Charlotte and casting his lot with Baltimore, but felt that since he had made a commitment he didn't want to break his word. I pointed out to Tagliabue that Jerry was a straight-shooter, had followed the NFL closely, and would be an asset, without any question. I also mentioned if he got a team it would make him the first owner to come from the player ranks since George Halas founded the Chicago Bears in 1920 as player-coach-general manager-owner-ticket taker.

Instead of ten minutes with Tagliabue, my time extended to close to a half-hour. A sportswriter had tried his best to brief Tagliabue on Baltimore, not a hard-sell but hopefully an informative one, maintaining objectivity. There was talk with Tagliabue about the Colts' Corrals, the well-known network of fan clubs that had stayed in existence since 1957. More than half of the thirty-two Corrals were still functioning, although there was no team to cheer for in Baltimore. Similarly, the Colts' Band, which had been together since 1947, continued to march and play at parades and even performed during NFL half-time shows.

As the conversation was about to conclude, I asked Tagliabue directly what he thought might happen regarding Baltimore and the NFL. He said there was no way to foretell the outcome; that all factors had to be weighed but Baltimore was certainly going to get every consideration, which is what any commissioner would be expected to say in an expansion situation. Then he offered a comment that stunned me. "If you take Baltimore and St. Louis," he said, "restoring those franchises first, then what you've done is really not an expansion." I didn't quite follow such a disturbing line of thought but countered by saying it was important for the league to take care of unfinished business, to clean up the errors of the past and correct the mistakes that had eliminated Baltimore and St. Louis.

Ultimately, instead of Baltimore and St. Louis, the combination voted for acceptance was Charlotte and Jacksonville. In all fairness to Tagliabue, I don't believe this was any secret prearranged plan but merely one of the possibilities the league was considering. The proximity of the Washington Redskins to Baltimore was considered a barrier. Yet Tagliabue never brought it up.

With the Redskins holding a backlog of season ticket applications going back over twenty years, another team in the area would certainly do them no harm. After all, hadn't the Redskins and Colts, in the past, coexisted for thirty years? I left the conversation with Tagliabue pleased that some things had been clarified on Baltimore's behalf, but seriously concerned that he had virtually discounted restoring Baltimore and St. Louis as any kind of a priority. More important than anything I might have introduced was a firm belief that Tagliabue, who had a residence in Potomac, Maryland, and was acquainted with the Baltimore situation, couldn't overlook the many assets the city offered—headed, of course, by a new stadium ready to be built, officially approved, with all funding in place and assured by the state legislature. No other competing city could make that claim.

The Baltimore audience also had for decades demonstrated an almost cultlike fanaticism towards the game, and its geographical location made the city a close fit to New York, Philadelphia, Washington, and Pittsburgh. It would be a perfect choice for being placed in the same division with any of those teams or in any revised alignment that might come later.

Relative to division identity, Wellington Mara, president of the New York Giants, had earlier made a special point to encourage Bidwill, when he was between St. Louis and either Baltimore or Phoenix, that he would personally like him to seriously consider Baltimore. It would have turned that section of the Eastern Division into a convenient and inexpensive home-and-home bus trip for the Giants, Eagles, Redskins, and Cardinals, which is what Bidwill said they would have been called had he opted to accept the Baltimore offer. But, like a lot of other things in life that make so much good sense and are supported by sound reasoning, it didn't happen.

After Irsay hauled the Colts away, there was strong feeling about the city that it wasn't going to allow itself to be turned into a convenient money-making place for other NFL clubs to utilize as an exhibition site.

Customarily, the clubs use the good name of charity by sharing a percentage of the proceeds but the two teams, collectively, go home with most of the revenue. "There's nothing tougher to sell than an exhibition game between two teams from someplace else," said Franklin "Pepper" Rodgers, who was representing Memphis in its ongoing quest to be accepted in the NFL. "We've put on seven exhibitions over the years and each one constituted a tremendous amount of hard work. I think we've had enough of that because we in Memphis have nothing more to prove. We've paid that exhibition price more times than we should have."

Memphis was frustrated beyond belief because when the league had last expanded, in 1974, and awarded memberships to Tampa Bay and Seattle, it was promised in writing that it would be given special preference the next time the expansion matter was on the agenda. Well, Memphis, decades later, is still waiting. Since Baltimore didn't have a desire to join in the exhibition scrimmages, it figured, the same as Memphis, that it didn't need to add anything else to its résumé. Still, with St. Louis and Charlotte hosting exhibitions, Baltimore didn't want to give the impression it couldn't fill up Memorial Stadium.

With only that purpose in mind, to take the exhibition challenge and stamp out any lingering doubt, Belgrad and the Maryland Stadium Authority booked the Miami Dolphins and New Orleans Saints for a summertime appearance in 1992. Chip Mason, a leader of the Greater Baltimore Committee, and Matt De Vito, speaking for the business community, emphasized how it was important to "make a statement" by buying the exhibition tickets as quickly as possible. In a matter of six hours, the stadium was virtually sold out. This was another positive sign for Baltimore, of course, but was the league going to be impressed, or was the entire expansion race and its seemingly ever-changing rules a rotten charade? The Baltimore presentation, not the exhibition but what surrounded it, evolved into the most emotional football scene the city ever experienced.

Colts' players from the past were introduced individually to the crowd. Sixty-nine in all were on hand. It was a football homecoming unlike any that Baltimore, despite all its past glories, had ever witnessed. A sentimental journey into the past. "It made an old dog feel young again," remarked Tom Matte, a Colt alumnus. The two visiting teams, preparing to play, stopped what they were doing in their loosening-up drills to view the demonstration of the crowd and the thundering tribute it was paying its old heroes. The Saints and Dolphins teams and their coaches actually turned their attention toward the veteran Baltimore players, some of whom they had heard of but who, for the most part, represented merely a list of names to the younger athletes in uniform.

For the record, a crowd of 60,021 was present. The Saints won 17–3, and no one cared. After all, it was a glorified scrimmage, a mere exhibition. The Colts from out of the past, even some who had played in 1950, such as Sisto Averno, Paul Salata, and Art Donovan had retained the affections of the public. They cheered their names, an almost maniacal eruption of enthusiasm.

Having witnessed every NFL game the Colts had played, plus sporting events of all kinds, I knew there was never a stadium crowd anywhere, in any circumstance, that created so much sustained noise as on that hot summer evening in Memorial Stadium. Did Baltimore want the NFL to come back? The din answered that question in an amplified way. Had there been an applause meter on the premises, the machine would have been pushed to the breaking point. The late Jim Finks, general manager of the Saints, said, "There has never been anything like this anywhere in the country that I've ever seen or heard about. Baltimore deserves to be back, not only for the show it put on tonight but for other important reasons, and you can quote me as extensively as you want."

Roger Goodell, among the representatives present from the league office, said he once lived in Washington and came frequently to see the Colts play but he, too, had never seen a crowd react in such a way. Pete Elliott, executive director of the Pro Football Hall of Fame, present to award John Mackey his Hall of Fame ring, asked, "Tell me, please, how long has anything like this been going on?" Elliott had played at Michigan, been to the Rose Bowl as a player and coach, and said he had never observed a stadium exploding with so much personalized emotion. The rallying call, advanced by the Stadium Authority, was "Give Baltimore the Ball."

Mackey received his Hall of Fame ring in the middle of the field surrounded by other Colts' Hall of Fame players, including Art Donovan, John Unitas, Lenny Moore, Jim Parker, and Gino Marchetti. Again, the crowd went into a frenzy for Mackey, who always added Baltimore Colts under his name whenever he signed an autograph. "I don't in any way want to be confused as an Indianapolis Colt," he said. "I played for the Baltimore Colts and I'm proud of that. The Indianapolis Colts mean nothing to me."

But, fourteen months later, when it finally came time to take the expansion vote, none of the revelry and reaction from the exhibition meant a thing to the NFL.

Finks, a friend of Unitas and also of Baltimore, had been prominently mentioned as a likely successor for the commissionership when Rozelle went into retirement in 1989 after twenty-nine years of extraordinary achievements. Certainly Finks was more than qualified, having been a former player with the Pittsburgh Steelers and general manager of three NFL clubs. He was outgoing, approachable, and had enough of the "old school" knowledge of the game to qualify as a highly attractive candidate.

Finks came close to getting the job but ran into opposition from a clique of new owners who felt they were being circumvented in the process. They took a strong position and refused to yield. Tagliabue, the league's leading attorney since 1969 from the firm of Covington & Burling, got the nod after two of Finks's supporters from the "old guard," Mara and Modell, changed their stance and went the other way. Both agreed, with a logjam on their hands, that Finks couldn't be elected so they backed away from their initial candidate. "The truth of the matter is that Paul Tagliabue is as much old guard as anyone," commented Modell. "Paul Tagliabue and I have worked together for years."

It was a terrible disappointment to Finks but even more so to his family and friends. He became ill shortly thereafter and died in the spring of 1994 from lung cancer. There's little doubt that had he become the commissioner he would have been out in front championing the cause of Baltimore as his number one choice for expansion.

While the league was preparing to decide on a commissioner, Jack Kent Cooke, owner of the Washington Redskins, referred to Tagliabue as a "beltway lawyer," which was hardly intended as a compliment. But Tagliabue rallied in the stretch run for the commissionership, with help from Mara and Modell. This meant he was in full command when the NFL expansion issue was eventually decided in late 1993.

Governor Schaefer was not enamored of Tagliabue. He didn't consider him a friend of his or of Baltimore. In 1993, six months after the Super Bowl was played, Schaefer wrote the commissioner a letter of protest over the rendition of the National Anthem. He addressed his complaint as "Dear Sir," a rather cold salutation, to be sure. Here's what Schaefer told Tagliabue about the way the National Anthem was presented:

> The National Football League never ceases to amaze me and Baltimore seems to be on your personal whipping post. The latest slap took place during this year's Super Bowl. While this may sound trivial to you, I have received a lot of angry letters from people who took great offense at the singing of our National Anthem. Miss Cole [Natalie] presented what I can only call an interpretation of the National Anthem—somehow blending it with America the Beautiful. The result, aside from an incomplete Anthem, was that the historical context of the song, written in and written about Baltimore, was simply lost. I have been urged to do everything from introducing legislation in our state

legislature condemning the league for this slight to boycotting the Super Bowl in the future. I chose not to. However, you show very little interest or concern for the state you live in [or the city where our National Anthem was written].

As the league's expansion effort dragged and just when it seemed that, at last, something positive was going to happen, the Baltimore ownership list was again decreased. It was a blow when Clancy suddenly withdrew, only four months before the matter was to be decided. Not as devastating as Tisch going in another direction, but it hurt. Clancy had wanted Peter Angelos, a Baltimore attorney of prominence and a former candidate for mayor, to join him in the football pursuit with Robinson. But Angelos, invited by Clancy to hear about the football plans, wondered why someone wasn't addressing something more essential—buying ownership of the baseball Orioles from Eli Jacobs. "I thought getting involved with the Orioles was more urgent," Angelos said later. "There was a chance that down the line we might lose the team and I felt baseball in Baltimore was more important than any other sports endeavor. That's why I turned my attentions to seeing what could be done about buying the Orioles and assuring they remain."

As it played out, Angelos bought the Orioles at auction for a record $173 million. And Clancy joined with him as the second largest investor in the baseball club by reportedly writing a check for $20 million. Clancy, in announcing his withdrawal from the pursuit of an expansion team, one that played with an oblong ball and wore shoulder pads, explained, "I don't think football would be economically viable. I've seen the finances of other clubs. An owner with another team called and told me to get out, that it wasn't going to be worth the cost."

Robinson, the movie mogul, didn't want to go it alone and had only gotten involved because Clancy had recruited him. The NFL, although it didn't see it coming, quickly commented that Clancy's resignation would not hurt Baltimore's upcoming chances. League spokesman Greg Aiello put it in reasonable perspective when he said, "Baltimore was in the enviable position of having three viable ownership groups—three times as many as any other city. Now it only has twice as many. They only need one."

When the league, later that year, met to address the expansion issue, two cities were to be picked but, as it turned out, only one got the nod—Charlotte, the prohibitive favorite. The league gathering was held in Rosemont, Illinois, a suburb of Chicago. I arrived early and casually walked into the empty meeting room that was being prepared with tables and chairs. No one was there so I went about examining the surroundings or, as "hoods" say, "casing the joint." It was too early for guards or NFL security personnel to be posted, but microphones were at the ready. And, surprisingly, a large electric map of the United States had been erected at the front end of the long, narrow room.

It turned out the map was a working tool that was going to be utilized to influence the outcome of the voting. It was designed to work against Baltimore. No doubt of that. During the league discussions of where to go with expansion, the map was turned on, and bulbs marking each league city were illuminated. It was a subliminal attempt to strongly tilt the playing field away from Baltimore; it could hardly be anything else. The owners, attending the meeting and looking on, saw the lights of New York, Washington, Pittsburgh, and Philadelphia, as well as all the other cities in the NFL. But then when the expansion lights blinked, Baltimore was sitting there, just as it always has, within 38 miles of Washington, 98 miles from Philadelphia, 210 from Pittsburgh, and 215 from New York. The graphic made an impact, saying: Why give the Middle Atlantic states another team when it already has five (including the Jets and Giants) so closely grouped together? That was the message being transmitted by the NFL—in lights yet!

The close proximity of several clubs was certainly true, but Tagliabue and his prejudiced cohorts failed to point out that the large population along the northeastern seaboard always supported the NFL. Also there was undeniable evidence that the Redskins, Eagles, Steelers, and Giants were established members of the league for well over half a century. The major manufacturing cities—New York, Pittsburgh, and Philadelphia—all working class, were strongholds of the game. Why the bias against Baltimore?

Back to the map. From Washington to Atlanta there was a blank space. So when the light flipped on to show Charlotte, it was a master stroke of promotion. It was far enough away from Washington, to the north, and Atlanta, to the south, to make good sense to the owners that this was one place where the NFL should be represented. Then, too, they were enamored of Richardson and what he represented as an incoming member of their fraternity. The vote for Charlotte became nothing more than a formality.

The other empty area highlighted on the electric map was St. Louis, with Kansas City at the opposite end of Missouri, New Orleans to the South, and Minnesota to the North. That wasn't difficult to figure. Now all they had to do was work to fill the void that existed in St. Louis. However, lease arrangements on the new domed stadium in downtown St. Louis were encumbered. The league was afraid to vote on a second expansion slot because the threat of legal action was being heard from the competing ownership groups within the city of St. Louis.

Tagliabue thought it best to back off, if only temporarily, to see if the problems and the in-fighting could be resolved before making a choice. Confusion reigned. St. Louis, under its then-muddled conditions, desperately needed protection and additional time. The league quickly called "delay of game," and the meeting ended with Tagliabue and the club owners agreeing to sidestep the issue for the time being. This accommodation would work against Baltimore. The city was ready with all the prerequisites in hand but the league had ignored its most attractive applicant.

The commissioner did announce to the waiting world what had been anticipated—that Charlotte was the winner for 1995 expansion and the other site would be chosen at a later date. He promised the verdict would be forthcoming in a matter of a month to six weeks. Baltimore apparently had not been counted out, but the game was virtually over for Memphis and Jacksonville. The battle for the last remaining opening, it was agreed among the majority of seasoned observers, would come down to St. Louis versus Baltimore, two cities of similar social and ethnic characteristics that once had teams and lost them through no fault of their own.

While St. Louis leaders went back home to try to reach a solution, matters got worse. The possibility of legal action was not going to go away and, if the NFL made a move, taking one bidder over the other, there was no doubt it would lead to long and costly litigation. This allowed Baltimore, with the difficulties in St. Louis, to take on the look of being an almost automatic choice. Newspapers around the country seconded the motion. Jacksonville was afforded little hope and actually attempted to *withdraw* its own expansion candidacy. The prospective lead owner for Jacksonville, one Wayne Weaver, who had made his fortune in the shoe manufacturing business, was disgusted over the way the expansion effort was being conducted and decided to pull out. But the league didn't want this to happen. The game it was playing was rife with deceit and duplicity.

In fact, this was the second time Jacksonville had tried to back out and put the entire expansion effort to rest. During the previous July, the Jacksonville City Council failed to approve $112 million for renovation of the Gator Bowl. This perturbed Weaver, a personable, self-made man who didn't have the advantage of a college education, but who had been enormously successful selling shoes and earning money. He announced the campaign for an NFL franchise was over for him and shut down the Jacksonville expansion office. However, the league got him to change his mind a month later. The power of NFL persuasion.

If St. Louis couldn't straighten out its entanglements then Baltimore would almost certainly get the second franchise. The NFL would have no other options, except to name either Memphis or Jacksonville. Baltimore was decidedly in the forefront... except the league didn't want this to happen. What it had was a secret agenda.

Remember all those lights on the map? Jacksonville, which was a mere "safety valve" for the league if it got boxed-in and couldn't go to St. Louis, was advised in the strongest of language not to abandon its expansion fight or, if it had already resigned itself to getting out, then by all means to change its mind and jump back in the race as quickly as possible. It didn't know it at the time but Jacksonville was the newly designated favored son, placed on standby, if St. Louis's ownership act fell apart again.

Where did this put Baltimore? Still on the outside looking in at the biased and unfair game the NFL was playing, where the rules seemed to continually change as the expansion discussions evolved. On the morning of the final vote, a league official received a call from retired commissioner Rozelle, living in Rancho Sante Fe, California, who had been extremely careful not to interfere in any way with league matters after leaving office. Rozelle wasn't about to make Tagliabue's role any more difficult by injecting his own ideas or opinions, but he was available as a sounding board or to give advice, if asked.

As with an ex-president, he wanted to allow Tagliabue, his successor, freedom to make up his own mind without exerting any pressure. But this time it was different. Rozelle felt something should be done for Baltimore. He solicited a favor, but was careful not to ask for it in so many words, or to let himself be quoted in interviews. He just wanted his opinion to be made known to the top echelon of the league. He had great confidence in Baltimore and wanted to see a team returned there, hoping that the owners and commissioner would signal "touchdown Baltimore." He didn't press—that's not his style—but typically, for him, kept his request low keyed.

Rozelle wouldn't impose himself on Tagliabue, or anyone else, because that would be a violation of his own code of business ethics, yet he wanted to do what he could for Baltimore. The message was conveyed but nothing changed. It was the eleventh hour, and the clock was moving. Rozelle's intentions, unfortunately for Baltimore and the league, were ignored. His request regarding Baltimore was blatantly ignored.

While the owners gathered for their meeting, Don Weiss, a veteran of the NFL wars, was relaxing in a mezzanine chair. I had known Weiss when he came into the league, shortly after Rozelle arrived. A smart, respected individual who always dealt the cards straight and was exceedingly fair, Weiss had been a sportswriter with the Associated Press, and was a man who didn't know how to lie or play games with the truth. What are Baltimore's chances today? I asked. "As good as any of them," he answered. "Yes, I mean that. I don't know how it's going to come out but you're definitely still in this thing."

Baltimore figured it had a lot going for it. From the time Charlotte was selected to start-up time for the next meeting, when the second city was to be chosen, Baltimore had downsized its ownership lineup. A new name was now atop the leader board. It was Al Lerner, who had earlier been mentioned as a possible owner but then had pulled away. Lerner was a friend of Modell's, a neighbor in Cleveland, and a 5 percent owner of the Browns who took Modell in his private plane to all the Browns' road games.

Lerner had been president of Baltimore's Equitable Bank before it was acquired by Maryland National, which was later sold to NationsBank. Out of this triple-play, Lerner "spun off" MBNA America, a credit card company that has enjoyed exceptional acceptance. He also is chairman of the Town & Country Trust, a developer of apartment complexes in the Baltimore metropolitan area. His reputation, the country over, is as a strong, perceptive, and astute competitor in business. One of his earlier jobs, after he was discharged from the Marines, was working for a furniture store in Baltimore.

Although it was presumed Lerner was well known by the other NFL owners since he was Modell's game-day traveling companion, such wasn't the case. Most of them had heard his name, knew he was associated with Modell, but knew little else about him. They were aware he was usually seated in Modell's private box at the games, home and away; he was known as Modell's friend and carried the reputation of a financial genius.

Lerner, who at times was described as a silent partner of Modell's, was rarely mentioned on the sports pages. This is the way he liked it. His ample resources would have allowed him to buy a team, without a doubt or a debt, because the $140-million expansion price was something he could have handled—right out of petty cash. The NFL current era is no place for a poor boy, and Lerner had all the necessary resources. Making it even more difficult is the fact that the new expansion clubs would not share in league TV revenues or profits from NFL properties for two years.

Governor Schaefer felt Lerner was the man who could, at last, rally the Baltimore endeavor and get the ball in the end zone. Others agreed. Since it was obvious the previous would-be owners, Weinglass and the Glazers, hadn't gotten much of a reception, Schaefer put forth the name of Lerner, virtually side-tracking the other groups. Important members of the Baltimore business community told him this was the direction he should go. Lerner was recruited, reluctantly or not. He was going to provide Baltimore with its best shot. That was the general reaction in Baltimore and also among league sources.

Lerner, however, refused to outline or discuss his specific interest in Baltimore, or even return reporters' calls, in the days leading up to the NFL's decision. He was there on the morning of the meeting, but he didn't make an appearance in the lobby. Lerner, interested in keeping a low profile, entered the hotel via a little-used entrance, neatly avoiding the media crush that was waiting for him both inside and outside the building.

The Baltimore delegation, headed by Schaefer, De Vito and Belgrad, were confident Lerner was going to be the "game breaker," the man who would be able to push the ball over the goal line. But a strange and surprising development presented itself. Lerner spoke for only a few minutes to the owners. Some of his listeners were to say later he made no attempt to "sell" himself, except to say he was a candidate for a team in Baltimore and wanted them to know of his desires. Then he left the hotel the same way he had come in—by a back door, a secret exit plan. He was driven to the airport and boarded his plane, but those not in the actual meeting room, such as the media and representatives of the competing cities, never knew he left.

They assumed he was continuing to huddle with the owners, pleading the case for Baltimore. Instead, he was long gone. Was there some kind of secret strategy at work that no one completely understood? Sometime later, Modell, carrying a light shoulder bag, left the meeting by way of the lobby and walked outside to hail a taxi. As he got in one side of the cab, I opened the opposite door and, since he didn't object, joined him in the back seat. He told the driver to take him to the airport, where he would join his friend Lerner, who was there waiting for him. Modell explained they were heading to New York for a charitable fund-raiser.

During the cab ride, I asked Art what happened. "Well, the timing wasn't right for Baltimore. I introduced Al in there. Of course, I built him up by telling them how long we had been friends and the kind of guy he is." Do you think Baltimore will get a team? "Yes, of course, you've done everything that's needed. Your governor is a good man and Belgrad is too."

At that moment, it was difficult to envision Modell coming to Baltimore and bringing the Browns with him two years later for virtually the same contract Lerner would have had. The only difference was there was no agreement at that time to charge the fans for permanent seat licenses. That wasn't included in the already bountiful Baltimore offer.

Could Modell at that moment have been thinking of the possibility of coming to Baltimore himself? Or would it be Lerner who would encourage him to make the move? Nevertheless it happened, with Lerner, at Modell's encouragement, providing the link to Baltimore. In a matter of minutes, after departing the NFL confab on expansion, Modell joined Lerner on his plane and was en route to New York. Could they have been contemplating Baltimore for a future football landing?

Meanwhile, the Baltimore contingent was crowded in a hotel room upstairs waiting to hear from either Modell or Lerner. But no word ever came. They had been abandoned, as Modell and Lerner left the meeting without so much as offering even a word of farewell to the Baltimore group. Talk about a final indignity. Was this any way to treat potential partners, or Schaefer, the governor of Maryland, who also was waiting? They didn't know what actually happened until I returned after the cab dropped Modell at the airport so he could join Lerner.

First, I talked in the lobby with sports editor Jack Gibbons and reporters Ken Murray, Vito Stellino, and Jon Morgan to apprise them of what had taken place. Then I went knocking on the door where De Vito, Belgrad, Schaefer, Ernie Accorsi (the former general manager of the Colts and later executive vice president/football operations for the Browns) and others from the Baltimore delegation were assembled. When I told them the story of riding to the airport with Modell so he could join Lerner for a trip to New York, they acted as if I might be hallucinating. They were, in a word, astonished.

The first reaction was that none of this could possibly be true; that some kind of a cruel joke was in the making. De Vito asked, rather incredulously, "You mean to say Al Lerner has left? And Art Modell is gone, too? Well, I have a telephone number for the plane and, if they are still on the ground, maybe I can reach them." He placed calls through various operators, using several numbers that had been made available to him, but it was too late. Lerner and Modell were gone. Belgrad, like De Vito, didn't want to believe they had vanished into the thin November air, bound for New York. They actually ran out on them. And also Baltimore. No courtesy call, no nothing. Totally ignored.

Still, as bad as it seemed, the worst was yet to come. It soon became known that Modell, to whom they were looking for help, didn't even cast his vote for Baltimore. Before leaving to join Lerner, he instructed his son, David, to support Jacksonville over Baltimore. Prior to a voting conclusion being reached, a hurried-up effort had been made to try to get Schaefer to speak before the NFL owners. His presence was requested by Ed McCaskey, of the Bears, always friendly to Baltimore, who agreed if Schaefer came before them again it could help and not hurt the cause.

Schaefer was desperately hoping he'd be able to address them, if only for a minute. But the chance was flatly denied because the league office said Schaefer had spoken at the previous expansion meeting and policy, they insisted, dictated he not be called again. After nearly an all-day wait, listening to the full gamut of speculation about what might be going on inside the meeting, word circulated that Jacksonville was going to be in and Baltimore, Memphis, and St. Louis were out. But it still wasn't official.

The league had a list of rooms where the various ownerships were waiting so, when the time came, they could inform each group of the decision before it was made public at the commissioner's press conference. Unfortunately, Baltimore knew the verdict before an NFL representative ever got to Schaefer, De Vito, and Belgrad. Word traveled fast. Once so hopeful, they were now devastated and disillusioned. Was this any way to treat an applicant for a franchise? How could Jacksonville be ranked ahead of Baltimore as a football city? Had Modell, supposedly a friend, given Baltimore the double-cross? Tagliabue and his advisors had dealt Baltimore a low blow again. Reaction in the lobby, where reporters had gathered, was overwhelmingly pro-Baltimore, anti-Jacksonville.

"I'm as mad as I've ever been," said Rodgers, who was representing the Memphis interests and had a preconceived feeling his city would be bypassed. "We could have accepted Baltimore being picked ahead of us. Baltimore had the best of everything in its proposal. But Jacksonville? Now right there that tests the credibility of this entire process. This makes it all a joke. The two best available cities, Baltimore and Memphis, were passed over." The strongest Baltimore backer was Norman Braman of the Philadelphia Eagles. Another owner, who asked not to be identified, said Braman's speech was powerful and virtually said the city was raped when the Colts were taken away.

In the first vote, Braman, Tisch of the Giants, and Mike McCaskey of the Bears, son of Ed McCaskey and grandson of George Halas, supported Baltimore but the latter two read the tenor of the room and, in the final vote, reluctantly switched to Jacksonville. They knew Baltimore had no chance. Braman was the only one who held the course, even though he was pressured to change his opinion so Tagliabue could announce it as unanimous for the benefit of public reaction. Of course, it would further prove how wide-sweeping his influence had become. This Braman refused to do. He held out, the lone dissenter.

The Jacksonville partisans at the Tagliabue press conference carried on as if it was a victory party, which for them it was. The moment was bitter for Schaefer, who first as mayor and then governor, wanted so much to right the wrong of the Colts leaving Baltimore but had been continually rebuffed. After Tagliabue delivered his remarks relative to Jacksonville, the commissioner was interviewed by Scott Garceau, sports director of WMAR-TV, who asked him, considering all that Baltimore had done, what advice would he now offer to the loser and should the city continue to pursue the goal of seeking a team? That's when Tagliabue told Garceau, on-camera, that every city had to make up its mind and be guided by its own order of priorities, saying it wasn't up to him to dictate such policy to a community because the other options might be to build a "plant or a museum" rather than a football stadium.

Baltimore was crushed at the rejection and the disrespectful way its representatives had been treated. When reports hit the news wires of what Tagliabue had mentioned to Garceau there was more dismay and increased bitterness in Baltimore. When I checked with the league office, some expressed doubt about Tagliabue's having actually said such things. I held the telephone close to a VCR and played the tape for these friends in New York to hear. Without a doubt, he had made the comment, and in so doing piled up more animosity in Baltimore toward the NFL and himself.

The commissioner was vilified but, in truth, three of his advisors were as much to blame for the rejection of Baltimore. Roger Goodell, vice president of operations; Joe Ellis, director of club administration; and Neil Austrian, president, were in charge of advising Tagliabue. They made a recommendation, along with the expansion committee, and Tagliabue was in agreement. Goodell, Ellis, and Austrian simply gave the commissioner bad advice. They had done an inept job of research—which ultimately damaged Tagliabue's standing and made the league look foolish.

The NFL's declining an invitation to return to Baltimore came after long deliberation and was based on the commissioner's right to approve or disagree. In many ways, it was worse than what Irsay had done, because years of study and careful consideration had gone into the evaluation of Baltimore by Goodell, Ellis, Austrian, and Tagliabue. If the commissioner is going to be the Baltimore whipping boy, then his three assistants deserved equal treatment. They, too, were blind to the virtues of Baltimore, in the way they measured the expansion sites. Before the commissioner made his formal announcement of the selection of Jacksonville, a procession of club owners and league officials filed out of the meeting room, followed by Tagliabue. Although it was still unofficial, reliable word had again preceded the verdict: Jacksonville was in, Baltimore out. As Jay Moyer, an NFL vice president and legal counsel, who was raised in Westminster, Maryland, walked past, he reached over and patted me on the back. Weiss made the same gesture. They were to say later that the stunned look on my face conveyed to them—correctly—that I was in a state of shock. And so was all of Baltimore and Maryland.

The next morning, as I checked out of the hotel and headed across the lobby, I was depressed. Not for myself, but for Baltimore, the old hometown. One thought lingered in my mind. If only George Halas and Art Rooney were alive this never would have happened. They and their influence, plus the high regard both held for the city, would have led them to making sure Baltimore was back in the NFL. But Halas and Rooney had died, Rozelle was in retirement, and the league was never going to be the same. And Modell and Lerner? They had walked away and disappeared without so much as a single word of regret or explanation.

CHAPTER 4

# ACCEPT NO SUBSTITUTES

Baltimore, its self-esteem battered, was sprawled on the ground thumping the turf and groping for something to hold on to, much the way an infuriated and victimized empty-arms tackler looks after a ball-carrier runs over him and is on his way for a score. Charlotte and Jacksonville had crossed the goal line. How could the National Football League have denied Baltimore when it had so much to offer? Not only as a city that once had a famous football team but also as a way for the league to enhance itself. Wasn't the NFL's own heritage worth something? Or didn't it care about tradition? The answer was obvious. The people making the decisions were incapable of measuring the value of returning a team to Baltimore, where devotion to the game was beyond compare.

Baltimore continued to be knocked down but always got up one more time. This resiliency earned respect, even if it didn't lead to getting a football team. It was difficult for Schaefer, the old City College cheerleader, to accept the ongoing rejections. A somewhat similar treatment had been afforded Buffalo after the demise of the All-America Football Conference at the end of the 1949 season, when three cities were taken into the NFL. But Buffalo was excluded when, on paper, it had a better team and a home attendance record that surpassed Baltimore's, which was included in the historic merger.

Schaefer was livid over the way the NFL had acted. As they say in the country, he had been turned down more times than an old bedspread. He kept asking the NFL for the "next dance" and continued to be ignored. It was his opinion, not necessarily true but based on instinct, that the NFL held a bias against Baltimore that had its origin with Jack Kent Cooke, the irascible owner of the Washington Redskins, who hoped to build a stadium in Laurel, about halfway between Baltimore and Washington, so he could capitalize on rich sky-box buyers from both cities.

I never believed the conspiracy theory but felt, instead, that Tagliabue was playing the political game, as almost all commissioners must do, and trying to curry favor. Keeping Baltimore out of the expansion picture would, no doubt, have pleased Cooke, and the commissioner wanted to keep him happy. He much preferred to have Cooke on his side than to be glaring at him from the opposite corner waiting for the bell to ring. Remember the "beltway lawyer" criticism Cooke had leveled earlier? Tagliabue was trying to mend fences, so to speak, with the owner in Washington, a man he much preferred to develop into a friend rather than an enemy. He wasn't about to do anything that might be construed as hampering Cooke from doing what he wanted and thereby allowing him to achieve what he was after—total domination of the Maryland football marketplace.

It was Cooke's belief that Baltimore business and industry would buy sky-boxes to see the Redskins in Laurel, but his figuring was all wrong. He never got to the point of trying to sell them, but it would have been a losing proposition if he had. There was simply little Baltimore interest in the Redskins in a city thirty-eight miles away, something he would have difficulty believing because a man who started out playing music in his own dance band and selling encyclopedias in Canada had never, in a manner of speaking, knocked on any doors in Baltimore. His knowledge of Baltimore was zero.

Cooke isn't able to even remotely understand the mind-set and reasoning behind Baltimore's apathy—not hatred—towards the Redskins. A well-connected figure in the NFL had said earlier, without offering an explanation, that the success of the Orioles, of all things, had hurt Baltimore's football chances. This rather incredulous observation was presumably based on Cooke's thinking he could sweep in and use some of the baseball business the Orioles were doing in their new park at Camden Yards to fill his own cash register. He envisioned that customers supporting the Orioles could be tapped for buying tickets to the Redskins during football season. A cartoon, drawn by Mike Ricigliano and published in the Baltimore *Sun*, was hardly complimentary to Tagliabue. It was a take-off on "Nero" Tagliabue fiddling while the NFL burned. One of Cooke's sons was so taken with the cartoon that he wanted the original for a keepsake. That's how enamored the Cookes were of Mr. Commissioner.

The Cooke deal to put a stadium in Laurel, on the property owned by the race track, was similar in concept to when he constructed The Forum, which housed major league basketball and ice hockey, adjacent to Hollywood Park in California. If he made it work there then why not in Laurel? This, too, would be making use of land that was already served by suitable roads and had adequate parking areas.

Cooke, insulated from the world of realism by his untold millions, felt if he placed the Redskins in Laurel it would give Baltimore access to the NFL, which, of course, he would then control. It was throwing Baltimore a bone. This was not what Schaefer wanted nor was it acceptable to the citizens of Maryland. It would be advantageous only for him. And, of course, Cooke, a superb and eloquent speech-maker, with a marvelous command of the King's English, was totally condescending in presenting his rationale for why Laurel was such an ideal place for the Redskins to be. This was one time Baltimore looked a gift horse in the mouth and said no. It wasn't going to accept what Cooke was trying to "sell." The Laurel community also was something he knew little about. He completely misread how the proposal to move the Redskins to a midway point between Washington and Baltimore would be received. In a word, it was disdain.

Personally, I had felt for years, and told others repeatedly, that the Redskins could build a new stadium in downtown Baltimore—the gates could be opened for free-admission but the seats would remain empty. There just wasn't that much interest in anything the Redskins were doing. Certainly not in Baltimore, going all the way back to when the Colts came into being in 1947. George Young, general manager of the New York Giants and a native Baltimorean who never lost the love he holds for his city, insisted there was never a behind-the-curtain deal made with Cooke. "I can tell you in all honesty that nothing like this ever happened," he said. "Some people might think that's the case but, believe me, if anything like that was going on it would be the talk of the league, because secrets don't keep that well with so many teams and people involved."

Cooke, accustomed to getting his own way in almost everything, because that's the way it is when you are wealthy and powerfully connected, wasn't able to implement the Laurel deal he made with the track owner, Joe DeFrancis. It wasn't for any lack of effort. Oh, how he tried. The Laurel opposition, made up of working-class residents, screamed that having the stadium in their area would result in traffic problems and the crowds, coming and going on Sunday afternoons, would be a nuisance. Little neighborhood groups banded together under the banner of CATS, which translated to "Citizens Against the Stadium."

Jeanne Mignon and fellow taxpayers put pressure on the politicians and, in the end, prevailed. Score points for Jeannie and John Q. Public. They rallied a groundswell of support for their position and, because of their vigilance and persistence, put Cooke away. He had earlier tried to impose his will on Alexandria, Virginia, for the chance to develop waterfront property for a stadium, but the Virginia legislature killed the measure. The District of Columbia also refused to allow him to take over a public golf course for a stadium, and environmentalists were a force for stopping him when he eyed other tracts of land that had ecological implications. Cooke was 0-for-3, striking out on three stadium locations.

Finally, he retreated to a site near Landover in Prince George's County, where he got approval but, again, not without a battle. The state and county eventually agreed to build the infrastructure, such as roads and sewerage, at a cost of $70 million. Cooke would put up a $160-million stadium accommodating 78,600 that he would pay for with his own money. For that reason, Cooke, despite all his vanity, merited a 21-gun salute. Well, at least a drum roll. In an elaborate brochure he circulated to potential ticket buyers, Cooke also wrote, "Most important, I am happy to say the Redskins will not be charging personal seat licensing fees (PSLs) for the Redskins new stadium. Not now, nor as long as I am in charge." This was all to his credit, to the Redskins' fans and certainly the taxpayers who wouldn't have to be paying for the cost of a second stadium in Maryland. It was definitely going be more beneficial to the public coffers than the free ride Modell was getting in Baltimore.

So, after paying a large part of his own way towards building a stadium, the imaginative Cooke bore some resemblance to a sportsman, a once courtly reference that can no longer be used when applied to owners of sports teams. At least he was picking up part of the tab and not asking Marylanders to pay the entire bill. The stadium would not be placed in Landover per se, but at a new mailing address Cooke had personally created. It was to be called Raljon, Maryland, a name derived by merging parts of the names of two of his sons, Ralph and John. The postal service authorized the requested designation and the Redskins quickly had it printed on maps they circulated to ticket subscribers. At one time, Cooke owned a 16,000-acre ranch in California that he also called Raljon, but the stadium and this newly crafted Raljon was on property that had always been known as the Wilson Farm.

With all the Cooke controversy and after the NFL had eliminated Baltimore at two expansion meetings, a feeling of resignation and retrospective contemplation set in—that the city and state had done all it could to advance its cause. It had a far more impressive building plan for a stadium and the television market area was larger than Charlotte and more than *twice the size* of Jacksonville. Still, all Baltimore was getting was sympathy from the country-at-large and lip service from the NFL, which counted for nothing.

The death of Hugh Culverhouse, owner of the Tampa Bay Buccaneers, resulted in another strong effort being made to get a team—this time by

Peter Angelos, owner of the Orioles. Angelos wanted to buy the club and move it to Baltimore. Otherwise it held no appeal for him. He wasn't interested in the Buccaneers if he couldn't bring them to Baltimore. Angelos was so interested he made an offer of $210 million to the Culverhouse estate. However, he lost out to Malcolm Glazer, who bought the Bucs for $170 million, but promised, with conditions, he would keep the club in Tampa. That's what the Culverhouse family wanted and why the sale was consummated with the Glazers. But after one season, Malcolm said he would move if a new stadium wasn't approved.

Shortly after Baltimore was knocked down by the NFL in its expansion efforts, the city heard from Jim Speros, who paid a visit to Mayor Kurt Schmoke and talked about being a part of a Canadian Football League plan to enlarge. He explained how the CFL was older than the NFL and that it was expanding into the United States, south of its own borders, for the first time, much the way major league baseball had migrated north into Montreal and Toronto. Speros had been raised in Potomac, Maryland. His father, Leo, was a former running back at the University of Maryland, also at Bainbridge (Md.) Naval Training Station, and later operated a well-known restaurant called Normandy Farms. Young Jim, one of eight children, had played football at Clemson. He also had two brothers who had been college players at Penn State and Temple. Together, they made history by being the first family to have three boys playing with teams in three different bowl games in the same year.

Speros, outgoing and at times an impulsive talker, convinced Schmoke he could do what he promised—bring the CFL to Baltimore and play in Memorial Stadium, vacant after the Colts left in 1984 and the Orioles vacated for their new park at Camden Yards in 1992. It wasn't that Speros was a complete unknown. He had worked as an assistant coach for the Washington Redskins and Buffalo Bills and, obviously, his resume was impressive for one so young (thirty-five) considering, too, that he had dealt in commercial real estate and other ventures.

Suddenly, he was heading a franchise in Baltimore, returning professional football to a city that was desperate for the game. In conversation, he occasionally stretched the facts or got carried away with his own rhetoric—nothing of a serious nature but more inclined towards exaggeration or selling a proposition. He claimed he was a friend of the NFL commissioner, but Tagliabue didn't go quite that far. "He tells a lot of people he's a friend of mine," said Tagliabue, "and you might get the feeling he's as close to me as my brother-in-law or my next door neighbor. But, actually, I only remember meeting him once or twice and one of the times was while on an airplane trip from Washington to Atlanta."

Speros was open and approachable. The public liked his style, and there was every reason to believe he carried goodness in his heart. But in his pockets he had far from a heavy bankroll. He was available for interviews any time, day or night, held press conferences at the slightest provocation, invited the well-spoken Larry Smith, commissioner of the CFL, for visits, and hired a proven winner in coach Don Matthews, who, in turn, brought with him an excellent evaluator of talent in young Jim Popp.

The team was quickly under way, establishing its camp at Towson State University. Speros, meanwhile, went about rehabilitating Memorial Stadium as best he could—with a lot of courage and limited funds. He made trade-offs with various companies, getting Bruning Paint and Standard Carpet to utilize their products in making the Stadium interior more presentable. He hired Bob Leffler of the Leffler Agency, who knew Baltimore, to help market the new brand of football.

At the inaugural game, Speros and Smith, mounted on horseback, were introduced to the crowd in a unique sort of way. Speros bought new uniforms for the Colts' Band, and the members never looked or sounded better. He created a ring of fame, where former athletes and other Baltimore sports figures had their names erected in huge letters on the facade below the second deck. Old Colts were introduced on a regular basis.

Leonard "Big Wheel" Burrier came on the field and roamed the stands to lead cheers. Ticket prices were affordable at $7, $11, $14, $17, $19, $21, and $25. In his second year, the price scale was simplified to $15, $20, and $25. Memorial Stadium, like an aging gal with rouge on her face, didn't appear as old as its forty years of service might have been expected to make it look. But beyond the paint and carpet that Jim had spread, the place was still not what it should have been. Elevators, restrooms, and the press box were in functional, but shoddy, condition.

Speros was an absolute expert at bartering, getting services from hotels, automobile companies, sports medicine centers, soft drink firms, office supply houses, television distributors, and caterers—sometimes for merely mentioning their names. He signed a contract with Fine Host Corp. to handle all food and beverage services in the stadium for five years and received a $1 million check. He'd exchange tickets or give away billboards, or program advertising, or the right of a company to hold a contest. Time-outs in the game were sold, not only for commercials on the radio broadcast, but also for advertising gimmicks on the field. His principal financial backers, listed as limited partners, were Michael Gelfand, M.D., and Marv Stursa.

In the formative days, Speros hired Tom Matte as a vice president. Matte, a popular ex-Colt halfback, opened doors by dint of his name recognition and engaging personality. Just like that, Speros was in the football business, going full bore, operating the club, making decisions, riding a wave of popularity and being regarded as some kind of a messiah. He could always talk a good game—about football—and this was a constant. He dressed his team in royal blue, silver, white, and black uniforms, somewhat remindful of the slick Dallas Cowboys, and they made an impressive appearance—both before and after the ball was snapped. They became an instant winner and built a following.

The Canadian Football League (CFL) played on a longer and wider field and used twelve players. It was wide open; there was no such thing as backfield-in-motion or a fair catch. Teams only got three downs to make ten yards, and a first down, so the rapid exchange of the ball was reminiscent of basketball on the grass, except there was blocking and tackling. The CFL's regular schedule began the first week in July and closed with the Grey Cup the last Sunday in November.

Half the regular season was completed by Labor Day, which meant it was a hot weather sport in the United States. If you craved action, it was there—far more than in the NFL, which had become stereotyped with much of its once captivating appeal legislated away by rule changes, unimaginative play books, and cautious coaches. From an entertainment standpoint, the CFL was better to watch than the NFL except, of course, the quality of play wasn't being produced by the best talents in the business. A safe lead in the CFL was thirty-five points with two minutes to go. Action personified. If you went to a game for the sheer entertainment, it was money well spent.

Matthews could coach and wasn't afraid to make tough decisions on personnel. Players knew what they contributed last week was ancient history. If Matthews became disenchanted, then personal sentiment and past achievements meant nothing. He got his team to play hard. And it consistently won games—far and away the best record of any start-up Baltimore franchise or that of any new professional sports team in the United States.

Baltimore qualified for the Grey Cup championship in both its years, and that's the ultimate. A vast achievement for Speros, Matthews, Popp, and the players. The first season, 1994, the team played without a nickname. Just Baltimore. Again, as a historical distinction of sorts, it was the only pro club that used the name of a city and nothing more. Not a bad idea if you're looking to please the chamber of commerce. It wasn't that Speros wanted it that way.

After sampling public opinion, he wanted to call the club the Baltimore CFL Colts and did just that. Two months later, an irate NFL was suing for name and trademark infringements. In a case that went to a hearing in an Indianapolis court, the NFL showed how trifling and "small minded" it could be when it contested Speros's right to use the name CFL Colts. The NFL, with heavy legal guns, went all-out to beat Speros and it did. Actually, the name Colts belonged to Baltimore three years before its team even entered the NFL. So how could the league claim authorship?

The league had absolutely nothing to do with origination of the name since it was designed for the original All-America Football Conference club that represented Baltimore in 1947, 1948, and 1949. Still, the NFL usurped the rights to the name the same way that Irsay had taken the Colts away. For the NFL to believe it owned the name Colts was pure fiction, but it got away with it in court.

Fans at the CFL games were alive and enthusiastic, the only problem being there weren't enough of them. But it was by no means a disaster; when they screamed Baltimore, on cue from cheer-master "Big Wheel" Burrier, there would be a definitive pause and then the roar, "C-O-L-T-S." It was every spectator's way of vocalizing a belief that the Colts belonged in Baltimore. Visiting sportswriters were amused and interested. They'd look at each other and realize how proud the city was of a team that had been pulled out of that same stadium ten years before.

In its first year of existence, the no-name team, called in some headlines the CFLers, had a 14–7 record and was within one play of winning the Grey Cup in the magnificent indoor facility known as BC Place, in scenic Vancouver, before a crowd of 55,097. The Grey Cup celebration, Baltimore was to find out, was a northern version of a Mardi Gras with strolling bands and visitors showing up from all over the dominion. It was an event that attracted average fans and not the tent-type corporate leaders who infest the Super Bowl sites. James "Bucky" Ward, one of the tourists who made the trip to root for Baltimore, said, "I've been to all kinds of sporting events but I thought the Grey Cup captured the true feeling of what sports is supposed to be. We fans could relate to the players, many of them being paid in the range of from $30,000 to $60,000 for the season and working hard for their money, some playing two and three positions. Even though Baltimore lost in Vancouver, I believe the game ranked as a classic and one that won't be soon forgotten for the unbelievable excitement that unfolded."

It remained for a forty-year-old kicker, a soldier of the football wars, one Lui Passaglia, to swing his foot into a field goal from thirty-eight yards away that enabled the British Columbia Lions to win, 26–23, as the final gun sounded. It was a hometown victory by a native Canadian who put away America's first attempt to win the Grey Cup and thereby preserved a sense of pride throughout the provinces. Passaglia, however, who kicked four field goals in all and was the difference in the outcome, did not receive the game's most outstanding player award. It went, instead, to Baltimore cornerback Karl Anthony, who had scored a touchdown and intercepted a pass in the end zone. More importantly, the Grey Cup still belonged to Canada, for which it was thankful, but that was to change in the season that followed.

Baltimore came back stronger than before and this time had a nickname. If it couldn't be the Colts then Speros settled on remaining in the "horse family." He picked Stallions. Quarterback Tracy Ham, who combined running with passing, and runner Mike Pringle, a pickup from the Sacramento Gold Miners, led the offense. Pringle, deceptively strong, broke tackles and demonstrated an ability to find the end zone. He dealt punishment when taking on defenders and was as durable a ball carrier as any Baltimore team ever had, right up there with Lydell Mitchell.

The Stallions of 1995 went all the way to the Grey Cup again, a repeat, only this time they prevailed, beating the Calgary Stampeders and Doug Flutie, plus fifty-five-mile-per-hour winds, 37–20, in Regina, Saskatchewan. Overall, the Matthews team won 18, lost 3, giving Baltimore a total record of 32 and 10 in two CFL campaigns. For the first time in the history of the Grey Cup, the massive trophy traveled below the Canadian border to Baltimore, Maryland, U.S.A., but the unprecedented triumph didn't bring the exultation and satisfaction it might have because the city was caught in another kind of football frenzy. The Browns were coming to Baltimore, and there'd be no place for the Stallions. They were past-tense even if they didn't know it.

It seemed grossly unfair to a Stallions team that had tried so hard and performed with such splendor but, alas, that's how the cards had been dealt. The Stallions were in no position to control their fate. They wanted to stay in Baltimore but couldn't. Their future was decided for them by an unlikely source: Modell, owner of the Browns.

After only two years, and what Speros estimates as a loss of $1.6 million the first season and $800,000 the second time around, his team was out of business. "Like in any start-up operation, you are almost bound to lose money the first year," Speros explained, "I thought we were moving into position our third season to turn it around and get in the black." Any way you measure the performance, it was immensely successful although too brief a run. Two seasons, two championship games . . . a Grey Cup crown.

And if you think it wasn't a formidable force that Speros, Matthews, and Popp put together then reflect on these facts: Matthews was CFL coach of the year; thirteen Stallions made all-conference; nine were elected to the all-CFL team; Pringle became the league's most valuable player; and Mike Withycombe was voted the best offensive lineman, earning the same honor teammate Shar Pourdanesh had received the year before. The team also had cornered all-rookie honors for two years in a row: linebacker Matt Goodwin in 1994 and kick returner Chris Wright in 1995. The Stallions were so good that NFL teams signed sixteen of their players for 1996 tryouts. There would have been more, except some Stallions were tied to CFL multiple-year contracts that preempted any chance to go elsewhere.

Attendance figures were another matter. Speros gave away so many tickets the first year that it was difficult to get an accurate count of paid admissions. The largest home crowd announced was 42,116 versus Sacramento in 1994; the lowest, 21,040, came to see the Stallions in a playoff against the Winnipeg Blue Bombers in 1995—just two days before Modell made the news official that he was bringing the Cleveland franchise to Baltimore.

Mike Gathagan, the team's public relations director, who had left a sports producing position at WMAR-TV to take the job, was disappointed over the turn of events, but the NFL reports had been around for so long he said none of the Stallions' personnel could say they were surprised. "There wasn't any emotion or sadness expressed," he recalls. "We expected it to happen. Our staff included thirty-five full-time men and women. All of us had progressed in the way we were doing our jobs. They could all hold their heads high over the way they performed, just like the team on the field. We worked hard but that was easy to do when we saw the boss, Jim Speros, putting in some days when he was on the job from 12 to 15 hours."

While the Browns in Cleveland virtually took the rest of the season off when they heard Baltimore was to be their new residence and lost seven of their remaining eight games, the Stallions never "spit the bit," as they say at the race track. They didn't quit. Not for a second. Matthews showed his ability to maintain control and to stay the course as the Stallions won all three of their final outings, certainly a credit to his leadership and the character of the players. Part of his scheme was to emphasize a speed game, especially on defense where he had undersized ends and linebackers.

Their fast reflexes were supposed to overcome the size of the rival offensive lines by continually beating them to the point of attack. In two years there wasn't a team in the CFL that Baltimore didn't defeat at least once. Again, another tribute to Matthews, his leadership, and the personnel he commanded.

During his two-year stay, Speros often voiced a belief that the city would never return to the NFL so the CFL was what it was going to be.

He said sources continued to tell him as much. Could it have been Cooke? When November 6 arrived and Modell's press conference stamped the move to Baltimore as official, it was Speros who was forced to react. He was as good as out of business, pushed aside. He gave all employees two weeks' notice.

The Browns of the NFL had turned out the lights on the Stallions; the CFLers were forced to find a different home and take on another life. They were to head for Montreal and become the Alouettes, a replacement for a city that had been in the CFL but had abandoned its once-illustrious franchise in 1987. Partners Gelfand and Stursa were still with Speros. So was Popp, who was promoted to general manager in Montreal.

As for Matthews, he accepted the opportunity to take on another challenge, the immense task of coaching and directing the football operations of the Toronto Argonauts, a team that had fallen on lean times. Both Matthews and Speros wanted to hire Gathagan, but he wanted to stay close to home, suburban Baltimore. For others, it meant relocation: a handful going with the NFL club in Baltimore, a few to other pro teams, some to colleges and universities, and others to livelihoods outside of football. It had been a compact work force that fought an uphill fight to exist and lost in the end through no fault of its own. Speros's estimated total losses, he said, reached between $1.5 million and $2 million for the chance to operate in Baltimore.

While losing Baltimore as a franchise holder, the entire Canadian Football League also retreated in its expansion movement. Only three years earlier it had trumpeted its entrance into the United States, first in Sacramento, then Baltimore, Shreveport, Las Vegas, Memphis, Birmingham, and San Antonio. What looked to be an idea with vast potential, a viable entertainment option, and eventual competition for the NFL, if only in a small way, had come to an inglorious ending.

The CFL, which had moved too quickly, was giving up on its U.S. franchise experiment. America wasn't going to buy into what it couldn't be sure was a major league product. It was an assessment that wasn't fair because the CFL, despite its problems, was far better than what the average sports fan perceived. Serious money had been lost in the bold venture. All the CFL could do was take stock of itself and return to its roots. Speros, meanwhile, had serious financial woes in Montreal.

For Baltimore, it was a circumstance reminiscent of the U.S. Football League, which had gone out of business ten years before after a one-season association, in name only, with Baltimore. This meant, bottom line, as with the USFL, that the city owned another title it would never get a chance to defend.

CHAPTER 5

# THE FURY OF IT ALL

It took more than the press conference announcement by the principals, Modell, Glendening, and Moag, to fully guarantee the Browns were coming to Baltimore. Approval by the league was needed, which at first seemed assured. However, Cleveland was still hoping to rally sufficient support to aid its cause. Mayor Michael White quickly visited the commissioner's office in New York, held a press briefing in Baltimore, a rather extraordinary development, and instead of being on the defensive went about establishing his own method of attack.

For Cleveland, at that point, to have kept the Browns would be equivalent to pulling a rabbit out of a hat. The move was too far along, the breach too wide, to get Modell to turn back. He was a stubborn and emotional man who could see nothing wrong with his arbitrary decision. The possibility of prolonged litigation, tying up the league and the two cities, while a final legal solution was found, seemed a likelihood. Months or even years for appeals would surely further delay the process of determining the ultimate winner.

What followed, in the way of an enormous backlash of public criticism, couldn't have been predicted. Modell was catching heavy fire, blitzed from all sides, even by fellow owners in his league. He felt it necessary to travel with bodyguards. Some of the anticipated legal maneuvers that usually accompany the transfer of teams had already been implemented, as well as lawsuits, countersuits, and threats by Congressional members to stop the Browns' departure. Meanwhile, as a backdrop to what was going on, the national media offered an outpouring of unprecedented support for Cleveland. It was almost nonstop, consistent in its resentment over what Modell was doing. It wasn't that they didn't like him. Quite to the contrary. Arthur was almost always available and generally considered a favorite of sportswriters and broadcasters. But the heat continued unabated. At one point, after *Sports Illustrated* printed a caricature of Modell in the act of throwing a body blow at Cleveland fans on its cover, he was so bothered, according to Moag, that he left Baltimore for the hoped-for peace and quiet of his Florida retreat. It was understandable.

To take what he was seeing and hearing would have troubled any man. Modell was saying, defensively, that when all the facts were revealed his leaving Cleveland would be understood, and he'd be viewed in an entirely different light. He also said eventually the controversy would go away and time would again be the benevolent healer. He's right about that; however, while the rest of the country may forget, he'll never be forgiven in Cleveland. The Cleveland fans had offered the Browns all of their affection, showed Modell much respect and admiration, while allowing him to attain a life-style commensurate with the rich and famous.

A desperate battle to retain the Browns got under way, even though its chances for success were considered remote. If other NFL club owners, such as Al Davis, Bill Bidwill, Bob Irsay, and Georgia Frontier, had been able to move teams, then what was going to prevent Modell from taking advantage of the same freedom-of-franchise opportunity? A strange precedent was on his side, regardless of the public outcry. The charge of "foul" and accusations that he hadn't played the game in a fair and noble way drew the ire of America. The feeling, close to unanimous, was that Cleveland, after all it had done for the Browns and Modell, didn't deserve such rejection. Even men and women who didn't know the difference between Jim Thorpe and Jim Brown commiserated with one another over what a national disgrace it was to have the Browns leave Cleveland.

The story moved out of the sports sections of newspapers and bled over to the editorial pages. Even George Will commented. It wasn't where they were going, Baltimore, that was bothersome, but rather that Cleveland had been robbed of a team that had been a fixture since 1946, the year after the end of World War II.

The property belonged to Modell, and obviously the call was his. Unless NFL owners pulled an upset of their own and managed to chain Modell to Cleveland, there was actually little they could do, even if they disagreed with him, and some did. Initially, Modell said the franchise in Baltimore would carry the Browns' nickname—just as happened with the Raiders in Los Angeles, the Colts in Indianapolis, the Cardinals in Phoenix, and the Rams in St. Louis.

Yes, it appeared at last, after all this time, there would be a team called the Baltimore Browns, with apologies to the St. Louis Browns who came to Baltimore in 1954 but shed the Browns as a nickname and assumed the proud and established name of Orioles.

After Modell said he intended to bring the Browns' name and team colors with him, there was disagreement in both Baltimore and Cleveland. The public in neither place was enamored of the idea but realized it had no voice, or choice, in the matter. Baltimore didn't want to go quite so far as to assume the Browns' identity in name, colors, and uniforms. Guilt does have limitations. After all, Baltimore was getting Cleveland's team, courtesy of Modell. Either leave the name behind or else every time the team, dressed as the Browns and called the Browns, took the field, there would have been a pre-game reminder that what Baltimore had was previously Cleveland's property. Too bad Indianapolis hadn't offered the same consideration. If Baltimore was going to be the address for the next thirty years of a franchise that migrated from Cleveland, then why not a different color combination and a new nickname?

After a period of reflection, Modell said he would give back the name and also the colors of seal brown, orange, and white. The decision to appease the howling critics was significant to Baltimore but much more to Cleveland, which was ready to take any bone it was thrown, even from Modell. After all, the Browns' name was established in Cleveland sixteen years before he bought the club.

Later, the National Football League would issue a report that the Browns, under the guidelines of what constituted approval for allowing a team to transfer to another location, did not meet the specified and acceptable criteria. Modell wasn't happy to hear this and felt the league was being unfair to him; he believed he deserved special treatment because he was one of the "good ole boys" of the ownership fraternity. The NFL statement got little attention, coming when it did—after the fact, when the team was in the throes of removing itself from Cleveland. It served merely as an official on-the-record reminder that the owner failed to get permission under the agreed-upon league rules before making the switch. Modell was already in Baltimore. Had the league tried to penalize him, legal action would have ensued, instituted by Modell and Moag.

It represented the potential for more trouble and discontent. So the NFL, all things considered, wasn't about to attempt to enforce its own rules pertinent to franchises moving, and take a chance that Modell and Moag would have them in court for long and expensive trials. The threat was intimidating. Eventually, the league gave in to Modell without a fight, which he continually predicted would be the result. He was, of course, free to remain in Baltimore. There was never any doubt, he said, of it being any other way.

Modell, however, was miffed the league didn't do more for him in defending his position. He felt, as a veteran owner, true to the cause, that he deserved special consideration and his track record of being good for the NFL should have merited an easier exit from Cleveland and a softer landing in Baltimore. He couldn't understand, and probably never will, why it is that Cleveland continues to hold him in such disdain. A public enemy of sorts.

Meanwhile, he insisted he bore absolutely no responsibility, absolutely none at all, for what had taken place. The criticism and debasement of Modell went on for weeks, months, even to this day. NBC commentator Bob Trumpy, quoted in the publication *Inside Sports*, said "Art Modell's actions were criminal." An exaggeration, of course, but the same kind of a charge that might have been leveled at Irsay for a similar deed perpetrated twelve years before.

How Modell held up under the onslaught proved the inner strength of the man. In all my years as a sportswriter, going back to when I was a mere kid in 1945, I never witnessed such an unrelenting denunciation of any club owner, unless it was Walter O'Malley when he moved baseball's Brooklyn Dodgers to Los Angeles.

Back to the divergent and often complicated arguments advanced by both Modell and those he was leaving behind in Cleveland: It was Modell's contention he was for too long taken for granted, that a new park could be built for the baseball Indians and an arena for the basketball Cavaliers, but all he was getting were promises. He also was hit by some financial stress brought on by how radically the game was changing, poor judgment in the way the team was being operated, and bad personal investments he made outside of football.

When the Indians left for their own park, he lost the $700,000 rent and concession revenue baseball represented. Cleveland Stadium was important to Modell. If only one team was going to be playing there then the financial picture had to change. The immediate novelty of the Indians' new park resulted in almost one-quarter of the loge boxes being empty for Browns' games, which was a reversal of form for Cleveland. Some businesses and individual patrons weren't going to buy both, so they decided to go to the new facility to watch an exciting team, one that was challenging for the pennant. This caused more than passing concern. Baseball had made a comeback. Corporate subscribers, but certainly not all of them, were going where they felt they could get the best buy for their money. That meant the comfort and appeal of Jacobs Stadium.

Then, too, escalating player salaries and free agency had created myriad new problems within the NFL. It was costing an owner, be he Manny, Moe, or Jack, more money to operate in the NFL. Modell made personal calls to Cleveland businesses to ask that they remain loyal to the Browns and not give up their boxes. Roughly twenty years before,

Modell assumed management of that same stadium and two years later, in his own stated opinion, was responsible for the start of the Cleveland downtown renaissance. He helped save the bankrupt Cleveland Sheraton Hotel. If he was not the catalyst, he was certainly a serious player.

When the $425-million Gateway Project, a make-over for Cleveland, ultimately came along, Modell says he wasn't given an opportunity to participate, but others strongly contradict his contention. Invited or not, he showed a spirit of good fellowship and participation by writing a check for the necessary campaign fund that private business provided to get the advertising campaign off and running. An early attempt was made to build a combination stadium, accommodating both the Indians and Browns, but this meant Modell would have to share the revenues from loges with the baseball team.

He personally felt, and others around the country then agreed, that baseball didn't lend itself to corporate sky boxes as well as football did—an opinion that has been debunked by what has happened in baseball parks built in Baltimore and Cleveland, to name the two that are close to the heart of the story.

What Cleveland and Cuyahoga County had in mind was an intimate facility that seated 43,000 for baseball and could be enlarged by the flip of a switch, or switches, to roll in banks of seats that would increase capacity up to 69,000 for football. But Modell wasn't interested. It meant he would have had a seating ceiling that was 11,098 short of what he had in the old structure, meaning less income, and his role as his own landlord would have changed. Meanwhile, he remained in the "same old house," Cleveland Stadium, while Jacobs Field was built for the baseball Indians and Gund Arena for the basketball Cavaliers.

Modell had earlier proposed that the Browns and Indians, meaning owner Dick Jacobs, cooperate in a joint $130-million rehabilitation effort to update Cleveland Stadium, but the thought was discarded by Jacobs, who wanted a park to call his own, even if he wasn't paying for the construction. It's doubtful that Modell, as perceptive as he is, made a proper read on the success of the ambitious Gateway effort and the way the Indians would draw a multitude of fans. Being a championship contender didn't hurt them either.

In 1996, the Indians, astonishingly enough, sold every ticket for the entire season before the first game was played, an unprecedented testimonial to their ability and the way the customers were attracted to Jacobs Field. But 1995 was the year of decision for the Browns and, at the same time, the organization of a plot replete with signs of deception. Modell was weary, he said, of being put off and having no tangible result by way of definitive stadium plans in Cleveland. The administration, under Mayor Michael White, as in every other major city, was strapped for finances but was still making attempts to get help for improvements to Cleveland Stadium.

White talked about finding a way to spend $171 million on the sixty-five-year-old structure. The Browns' owner wasn't threatening to leave if it didn't happen, but Modell wondered when his turn would come. In 1994, White and Modell talked frequently but nothing materialized. In early 1995, White appointed a committee to pursue the stadium matter again. By this time, Modell was irritated by the delays while the Indians, simultaneously, were enjoying an exciting new life in their own park. Maybe, too, Baltimore was looking like the place he ought to be seriously considering. But secretly. Yes, the possibility was there.

By the time the Browns were in training for the 1995 season, Modell had already informed the world, including White, that he was instituting a moratorium on stadium discussions. He would not talk about the stadium matter while the season was in progress nor would he answer questions from reporters regarding the subject. The implication was that nothing should be allowed to detract from the Browns going to the Super Bowl, which had never happened. All concentration from his perspective had to be directed toward football and not building a new stadium or improving an old one.

What he was at least suggesting by establishing the moratorium was that the stadium issue could be dealt with at a more appropriate time in the future. White said he contacted Modell within two days of receiving his advisory on the moratorium and notified him he was going to proceed with getting $171 million in renovations anyhow—regardless of Art's desire to temporarily mute the matter.

A resumption of talks never came because Modell pulled the plug on the Browns in Cleveland—and the rug out from under White—before the moratorium, or even the regular season, expired. He was headed instead for Baltimore, after word broke in midseason that a deal had been signed with the Maryland Stadium Authority. Was this all a preconceived game plan? Yes. Could this have been a master plan of willful deception? Yes. Did Modell intentionally mislead Cleveland into a feeling of false security while he went behind the fans' backs to make a deal in Baltimore? Yes. Is there a "smoking gun" still to be uncovered? Maybe. Or was it a new kind of a "trap play," different, of course, from the kind Marion Motley used to run for the Browns when he took a handoff from Otto Graham and bolted up the middle for acres of yardage?

The painful deduction for Cleveland was that Modell put one over on them with tactics less befitting the man they perceived to be an honorable figure in their community. The word *moratorium*, certainly in Cleveland, took on a different meaning. Just like that, Modell was no longer role-model Modell. A hero had fallen.

It's especially revealing that Moag admits his first contact with Cleveland was in March of 1995, two months before the moratorium instituted by Modell. In January, Governor Glendening had appointed the young lawyer Moag, a member of the firm of Patton Boggs & Blow, to the chairmanship of the Maryland Stadium Authority. Moag was succeeding Herb Belgrad, who was originally named to the post by Governor Harry Hughes and who also was working for Patton Boggs & Blow after leaving the statehouse. Although at least one top advisor on the staff of the incoming governor, William Donald Schaefer, wanted Belgrad to be replaced on the basis that he was a Hughes choice, no change was made. Schaefer was obviously pleased with what Belgrad was doing and how he kept him apprised of all details in the quest for a team. What Belgrad knew, Schaefer knew.

Moag mentioned that after Glendening picked him for the nonpaid job his instructions were to "go at it hard" because the appropriated money for a new stadium for football was only going to be kept alive for probably another year. The State Legislature was getting restless, seeing the money held in limbo since 1987 with no sign of a team coming to play in a facility that wouldn't be built unless the NFL gave assurances a franchise was to be awarded. The funds couldn't be preserved forever. There were too many worthwhile needs waiting to be addressed.

"The governor told me, 'give it one more year,'" said Moag, who used that specific dictate to attach a sense of urgency to his negotiations. In ten months from that moment, playing hardball, Moag made the deal. Since the NFL had rejected expansion, Moag tried to tap into, or lure, an existing team. There was no desire on his part to plow the same ground Belgrad had already covered. Instead, he made a list of prospects and included Cleveland as a possibility but not, in his opinion, a realistic one.

In February, he contacted Frank Bramble, the able president of First National Bank. Bramble had once been associated with Lerner, Modell's friend, at Maryland National Bank before it was bought by NationsBank. They held each other in high regard. It was Bramble who was to play an important role as the vital go-between, sounding out Lerner, who, in turn, talked to Modell and relayed information pertinent to the effort Baltimore was making. Moag was to say, "My negotiations were through Al Lerner." None of the lead characters may have realized it at the time, but the process of transferring the Browns to Baltimore was moving into its formative stage. Moag and Lerner were making it happen and Modell only had to wait.

Modell's call to Mayor White for a moratorium on stadium talks was included in a letter of June 5. In seven weeks, Modell, via Lerner, a 5 percent owner of the Browns, was learning what was being offered to a potential team in Baltimore. The basic deal was the same as it had been two years before. The late July meeting in 1995 between Lerner and Moag was held near the private plane terminal at Baltimore-Washington International Airport but inside Lerner's jet aircraft. It was more than hello and goodbye. They talked for ninety minutes.

Lerner relayed the details to Modell when he returned to Cleveland, which was a week preceding the Browns' opening of their exhibition schedule at home against the New York Giants and five weeks before the regular season began. More was shaping up behind the scenes than anyone in Cleveland or Baltimore knew about. Moag was charged up emotionally over the interest expressed by Lerner, a two-fisted businessman who kept a low profile and didn't engage in puffery.

After they concluded their prolonged discussion, Moag intended to head for the beach to meet his family for vacation, but was so encouraged by what he heard from Lerner that he made a quick end run to Annapolis to visit the governor and provide an enthusiastic account of what had transpired. So even before the Browns kicked off the 1995 season, their future in Baltimore was being contemplated.

Two days later, like a boxer feinting one plan of attack while preparing to do something else, Moag wrote commissioner Tagliabue requesting the league pass a resolution promising Baltimore a franchise. The NFL was quickly asking questions about Moag, searching for background and somewhat more than casually concerned. Then, too, there had been an earlier meeting in Washington between Glendening, Moag, and Tagliabue so they knew each other. The Maryland officials came away without much hope for a franchise. Moag also had threatened legal action under the Sherman antitrust laws, charging the league with denying Baltimore a team because it was guarding the territory for the exclusive use of Jack Kent Cooke and the Redskins.

In Moag's message to Tagliabue, he cited the pressing fact that the appropriation of money to erect a stadium was only going to be good for the remainder of the year. Baltimore needed to hear something or he intended to haul the NFL into court. This got the attention of the league and even today there are observers who believe some type of a promise regarding a franchise was going to be forthcoming at a regularly scheduled NFL meeting on November 7. This all became moot when Modell made his move to Baltimore the day before.

Two other prime team prospects for relocation were on Moag's list, the Tampa Bay Buccaneers and the Phoenix Cardinals. He talked with both ownerships, found them eager to grasp the Baltimore offer, but he explained later, "It would have been easier to have gotten either one of those teams but, as it stands, we got one of the best ownership situations in the league [meaning Art Modell]."

As the Browns conversations continued, Moag also kept talking in similar tones to the Glazer family in Tampa Bay and to Bidwill in Phoenix, making trips to both places; this constituted more of a diversionary tactic. He didn't want Tampa Bay or Phoenix to lose interest because they could be options he might have to go to later. At the same time, this would help him with Modell, because if he heard about the Tampa Bay and Phoenix possibilities, it would send a message and give the impression he better not procrastinate or some other club would take the Baltimore offer. "I even heard from the Colts but didn't respond," Moag said. "We got quite far with Cincinnati but Mike Brown had a strong family relationship with Ohio. I could have signed Tampa Bay in a heartbeat. My secretary kept making up excuses about why I couldn't take their calls and get right back to them."

Mark the night of September 6 as an important one in the sports history of Baltimore . . . for the Orioles, for Cal Ripken, Jr., and—little did anyone else know—the future of pro football in both Baltimore and Cleveland. Lerner was in Baltimore attending the record-setting event when Ripken surpassed Lou Gehrig's "iron man" streak of playing in 2,130 consecutive major league games. Moag remembers telling Lerner, in an aside, that if Modell is serious "then we got to get to work."

Within twenty-four hours, Lerner, serving as a conduit, got back to Moag and a date was set to meet with Modell. Son David and Browns executive vice president Jim Bailey were included. It would be a fact-finding, get-acquainted session in New York at Lerner's office. Present from Baltimore were Moag; Bruce Hoffman, executive director of the stadium authority; and Alison Asti, the authority's general counsel. The conversation flowed and there were no apparent barriers standing in the way.

It was, however, Modell's call all the way. Moag mentioned he was against selling the stadium name to a corporation, a cheap stunt but one that could enhance the total revenue picture. And he says he didn't favor charging permanent seat licenses. So much for good intentions.

Modell didn't ask for a guaranteed number of seats sold per game, or a specified list of home sellouts. But permanent seat licenses would indeed play into his equation. It was first said the club could charge up to $74 million in PSLs, but the monies could only be used for paying off the three years remaining on Modell's lease in Cleveland—an odd thing for the fans of Baltimore to have to do—and to cover moving expenses, plus completing payments on the training complex left behind in Berea, Ohio, and the new one they planned to build in Maryland. Modell would utilize a $50-million line of credit from Bramble's bank until he got a cash flow established. The projected PSL income was accepted as collateral.

At the press conference, when the switch of cities was announced, Modell was to say, upon introducing Bramble, that he wanted the crowd to meet his new banker. And then, trying to draw a laugh, asked, where was his toaster, alluding to the way banks used to advertise free gifts for opening savings accounts. The team, as part of its rent-free contract, agreed to maintain the stadium and pay for cleanup expenses after events were held, which it was said would cost an estimated $4 million annually. This seemed a huge tab for picking up trash after only ten football games and keeping the grass mowed.

On the morning of October 27, again at BWI Airport, the final meeting, the document signing, was to be held. It would bring the franchise to Baltimore. Moag, Glendening, the Modells (father and son), and Lerner were there. They gathered in the rear of the plane. Modell said the matter of leaving Cleveland had bothered him. Then he looked at Moag and asked for the contract he was to sign. Moag watched and said later, "Yes, I recognized it as a historical moment." The team Modell owned for thirty-five of its forty-nine years in Cleveland was coming to Baltimore.

Despite agreements of confidentiality between all parties, with huge fines involved for any information leaks that might occur, there was just no way to keep the story under wraps. This forced the premature November 6 press conference at Camden Yards but, the day before, the Browns were scheduled to play at home. It was a foregone conclusion as the fans filed into the stadium that it was all over. Forty-nine years and now this.

Instead of having the season behind them before the move was disclosed, the Browns were going to have to play as a "lame duck" in Cleveland for four home games, plus four on the road. It was to become a public relations disaster for Modell. Teams will use any convenient excuse to let down and the Browns had one. They didn't "go in the tank," but the angry mood of Cleveland influenced their mental approach for that afternoon and the remainder of the schedule. Their focus was impaired. Modell met with the players on a quick visit to the practice site in Berea, saying he knew they were in a difficult situation as athletes but hoped they would give the maximum effort.

"I challenge you and appeal to your pride to play your rear ends off in the next seven games. We can make a statement to the whole country

Monday night in Pittsburgh. Do that for yourselves." As for what happened against the Steelers, the Browns were ineffective, losing 20–3. The season was a nightmare. A team that had a commendable 11 and 5 record in 1994, with hopes high, reversed itself to 5 and 11.

It was a sad ending to the long Modell chapters written in Cleveland, constituting thirty-five years of memories. He was vilified on radio shows and in newspapers. One station gave away "Go To Hell Modell" tee-shirts and played an insulting ode to Modell throughout the broadcast day. He was like a displaced person, fleeing Cleveland and never again watching the team play in the stadium which had been his Sunday afternoon home in the fall of the year since 1962. For the rest of the winter, he spent his time between Baltimore and West Palm Beach, Florida, but generally, when he was in public, it was in the company of bodyguards.

There was no end to the salvos of indignities directed towards him. Maybe he's overly sensitive, as friends say, but only a tough man could endure that kind of a pounding. In Cleveland, where he had been revered, he was quickly perceived as public enemy number one. It traumatized Cleveland to lose its team and Baltimore could understand why. The resentment against Modell continued, far surpassing what happened when Irsay exited Baltimore.

The Browns' fans, not just in Cleveland, but all over the country, reacted with bitterness. Modell's previous statements were used against him, as in 1989 when plans were being readied to build Gateway: "We will not move out of the existing facility to move to a dual-purpose facility in the Central Market. Tell the city fathers to try and do something for the Indians alone."

Then in 1990 he said, "The stadium has a lot of pluses and minuses. The pluses outweigh the minuses." And in 1993, he mentioned that if renovation to the stadium was rejected he could accept it. "A deal is a deal. We'll live with it." Another morsel from Modell, dated 1994: "You'll never hear me say, 'If I don't get this, I'm moving.' You can go to press on that one. I couldn't live with myself if I did that. I will say this—the Cleveland Browns as an organization will expect only fair treatment. There will be no demands made."

An interview that Baltimore broadcasters Ted Patterson and Phil Wood conducted with columnist Bill Livingston of *The* [Cleveland] *Plain Dealer* offered razor-sharp observations on Modell that cut deeply into how one of the most widely read sportswriters in Ohio felt about him. The writer said such things as, "He's the most despised man in the history of Cleveland sports; it's not even close . . . he's impulsive, temperamental, thin-skinned and good with a joke . . . if the Indians had lost 100 games in their new park, he would still be in Cleveland so it was an envy thing . . . there was a tremendous desire for retribution on Art Modell and that went unsatisfied because they didn't get him in court to see him sweat bullets."

From the ranks of the Browns' alumni, namely four Hall of Fame members, came the following comments: Jim Brown—"It's a terrible feeling. The only time I felt sadder on a field was when President Kennedy was shot." Otto Graham—"I feel sorry for the fans. It's a crying shame. The bottom line is money. I've always said the biggest problem with owners in pro sports is that the owners have tremendous egos." Dante Lavelli—"Modell has no credibility. His integrity is done. How'd he feel if the shoe was on the other foot? Does he think that's loyal to the people who helped him make money? The owners brought this on themselves through greed. If the owners don't vote against Modell, they have no guts." Lou (The Toe) Groza—"I'm kind of shocked he [Modell] would do such a thing. I'm more sad than anything because there is such a tradition. You've got the greatest fans in the country."

Thousands of those same Browns' followers united to send letters, faxes, and phone calls to every team owner and especially to Commissioner Tagliabue as reaction to Modell's actions. *The* [Baltimore] *Sun* received thousands of protests, most of them handwritten on brown-and-orange postcards, from fans all over Ohio. *USA Today* headlined: "Browns Fans Unleash Fax Flood." Often, such campaigns last a day or two and then trickle off to a silent ending. But not in this case. The drive was relentless.

Meanwhile, *Financial World* reported the Browns' total revenue in 1994 had reached $64 million, so it was difficult to believe Modell was going broke in Cleveland. The anti-Modell mood became ugly. Fans demonstrated outside his Florida condominium. A hired plane flew over his residence trailing a sign that read: "You Can Run But You Can't Hide. Woof. Woof." The "woof woof" was a silent message from the "Dawg Pound," the end-zone fraternity that was so identified with Browns' home games. Irate advertisers, who had paid for signs in Cleveland Stadium, asked that they be taken down.

Twenty of twenty-two sponsors pulled their spots off the radio play-by-play and a television station canceled three weekly shows devoted to the Browns. "Rover Cleveland," the aptly named mascot, refused to roam the field or wear his costume. A nationally known talk show host, Pete Franklin, who spent twenty years in Cleveland radio, said, "If I ran into Art Modell now, I'd have to look him in the eye and tell him that I no longer consider him a friend. Not after what he has done to Cleveland." And perhaps the most troubling of all statements about Art came from the former sports editor of *The* [Cleveland] *Plain*

*Dealer*, one Hal Lebovitz, who said, "For thirty-five years in Cleveland I was his friend and we regularly had lunch together. Because of what he did and how he did it, I'll never speak to him again."

A meeting of the owners in Atlanta was picketed by sign-carrying fans, many of whom came from Cleveland. The league and its club owners got the message. For the first time, the sports public had spoken with unmistakable clarity and, in a unified way, with a volume that couldn't be ignored. Baltimore didn't get hit with any of the flak but some citizens, wincing at the ranting and raving, felt what happened was starting to create a feeling of undeserved guilt for them.

Moag said it made for difficult times for his brother, who lived in Cleveland, and was subjected to unfair criticism because of the Browns' move, a fallout from the fact that lawyer Moag in Baltimore had initiated the deal. Finally, to quiet the uprising and settle the natives, the league realized it had to take special care of Cleveland. It entered into an unprecedented arrangement with the city, akin to a partnership, that would assist it in building a stadium. And, just as important, promised to provide a team for the season of 1999.

In a final approach to Modell, the league, mainly through Tagliabue and Austrian, presented a proposition that offered a perfect solution, one that would certainly have best suited the purposes of all concerned. Their plan was for Modell to sell the Browns to Cleveland interests, which would have softened the blow over the way he handled things and bailed him out of a public relations disaster. For doing this, Modell would then have exclusive ownership rights to an expansion team in Baltimore in two or three years. The offer would be put in writing and legally certified.

The league leaders were hopeful they could make such a deal, pressed for it, but the man they were giving a chance to escape, or ease away, from the line of hostile media fire said he wasn't interested in any such arrangement. He wouldn't go for it. Modell said he wanted to play now and not wait. He was emphatic.

Modell, throughout the slugfest, continued to insist when the truth emerged and all the facts were divulged, he would be vindicated of any criticism and the public would know where to place the blame. This was his way of trying to deflect the pounding he was taking. In a Modell manifesto released on January 17, 1996 at a league meeting in Atlanta, it was written into the record as follows:

> Cleveland's expensive and violent campaign against Browns' owner Art Modell is an effort by Mayor Michael White to cover the city's unwillingness or inability to deal with the team or the National

Football League, team representatives told the NFL today. Mr. Modell told fellow NFL owners that neither he nor his property would be held hostage by a mayor who for two years broke every promise to help the team. "If this league allows the mayor to hold the Browns hostage," Mr. Modell said, "then everyone of you are hostages too."

Modell added that: "No one in my 35 years in this league better fits the NFL guidelines on relocation." [Author's note: But the league was to dispute this, in writing, much later.] A review of Mayor White's broken promises in failed negotiations was presented to the owners by Robert Weber, Mr. Modell's attorney and partner of Jones, Day, Reeves, and Pogue. The Browns also explained the relationship between the city and Cleveland Stadium Corporation, which leases the Stadium from the city.

The relationship has allowed the operation of the Stadium without any taxpayer money for the past 22 years, while Mr. Modell's company has spent $44,984,775 maintaining the 64-year-old building, while Cleveland realized an additional $27,015,225 in taxes and savings to the city. The team also reported the recent history of the government and business development in downtown Cleveland, which includes $700 million invested without one dime being invested on the Browns and the NFL.

Also chronicled, with documented detail, were the failed negotiations with Mayor White, who, for nearly two years, promised a solution but never made an offer to the Browns until after they had signed a contract with Maryland. That's a total of 670 days since the mayor promised a stadium proposal. Mayor White first met with Mr. Modell in January of 1994 and promised a resolution to the stadium within 120 days, Mr. Weber said, adding:

"Mayor White also made another fateful promise: a promise to deliver the necessary political consensus . . . Mayor White demanded that the Browns deal only with the mayor and his representatives, and the Browns, to their manifest detriment, agreed."

More than 40 meetings were held and expensive studies were provided by the Browns, but there was no plan by May, or later by Labor Day, as the mayor had promised. In September of 1994, the Browns concluded the talks because the mayor did not have city council, county or state political support and ended negotiations. "But Mayor White did not tell the fans and public that negotiations had failed and that he had made no offer," Mr. Weber said. "Mayor White instead told *The Plain Dealer* that the city was close to finalizing a deal with the Browns even though no offer of any type had been made."

The Browns also told owners about the work of several task forces that dragged into 1995. "After over 40 formal meetings, after four studies of feasibility, after every deadline set by the city had passed, and after constant reminders from all politicians that proposed concepts were dead deals, Mr. Modell called time out," Weber said. Mayor White told Mr. Modell he would not honor his moratorium, Mr. Weber said, and urged County Commissioners to place an extension on the county's sin-tax on the November 1995 ballot.

"The ballot issue created the worst of all situations," Mr. Weber said, adding: "If it passed, the Browns still lost, because any goodwill of the voters would have been expended and adequate funding still was not there; and, if it failed, as the mayor and others had earlier predicted, the Browns and the NFL were dead in the water."

Mr. Modell then decided to meet with Maryland Stadium Authority representatives, which culminated 40 days later in the move to Baltimore, Mr. Weber added. "It took Maryland 40 days to do what Mayor White, over nearly two years, never did—put a deal on the table," he concluded.

Then in what was subtitled a "factual review," the attorney presented a dated twenty-eight-step chronology of Modell's association with the city relative to stadium business and discussions.

If there was an obvious blunder by Modell it came from clamping a moratorium on stadium talks in Cleveland while simultaneously going behind the backs of the most loyal fans any team ever had and making a secret agreement to head for Baltimore. Modell, in a network television interview after coming to Baltimore, said he wasn't appreciated in Cleveland and if the city had offered him the same terms as it promised a new team he would still be there. During the same show, he mentioned that if the late Art Rooney, the patriarch of Pittsburgh, had known his son Dan had voted against Modell's move, he would have been furious.

That's not the way I believe it would have happened and I knew Rooney for much longer than Modell. This was a man of substance and character, who held great affection for Cleveland, where his friend,

Arthur (Mickey) McBride had founded the Browns in 1946. Rooney had reprimanded Al Davis for leaving Oakland for Los Angeles and in my opinion would have felt the same about Modell pulling out of Cleveland.

After Moag scored his victory, he was honored by the Better Business Bureau of Greater Maryland. He said he pursued the Browns despite death threats that had been made against him. His further comments had to make the NFL happy since he referred to its operation as "one of the most dysfunctional entities you can imagine," and said the league had unfairly denied Baltimore a franchise. No doubt of that.

As for Lerner, who had an enormous influence on the decision, he backed away when the heavy criticism entrapped Modell. Instead of being Modell's game-day companion, Lerner withdrew from the line of fire—separating himself from the firestorm—and fading into the background. Modell took the full impact of the hit.

At no time, though, did Modell tell Cleveland, or allow the Browns' fans to realize, that the franchise was in jeopardy. Had he so informed them of any such possibility, there would have been offers to buy the team or public demands made that he be provided with a rehabilitated stadium or a new one—whatever his pleasure. The Browns meant that much to Cleveland.

CHAPTER 6

# HOW IT ALL BEGAN

Acknowledging Cleveland's long-proven allegiance to its beloved Browns, it is still difficult to believe that any city ever carried more intense passion for a team than Baltimore held for the Colts. Maybe Green Bay for the Packers, but that's different. How did the game get started in Baltimore?

The first franchise and the football it played with had life pumped into it by the best friend Baltimore ever had in Washington—political or otherwise. He was a tall, handsome man, Robert Ridgway Rodenberg, who had the daring, imagination, and faith to provide Baltimore with a team and then give it a perfect fit for a name: Colts. It was the beginning of a love affair that endures to this day.

The Colts of 1947 were the pioneers and for this reason are remembered with special affection when Baltimore's football past is examined. The fans in the stands were excited, not only by what they were watching on the field but by the long-desired chance to prove the city had major league capabilities. Rodenberg, a Harvard graduate, the son of an Illinois congressman who served twelve terms, had come home from World War II, after overseas assignment with the Office of Strategic Services, and decided he wanted to own a football team.

As an OSS agent, he served with guerrilla forces of the Kachin tribesmen in Burma behind enemy lines. A chance meeting in Calcutta, in the midst of the war, with Maury Nee, a friend from Washington who was working in Naval Intelligence, was an occasion for giving preliminary thought to the formation of a pro football team in Baltimore. Rodenberg said the two talked about the success of the Redskins and believed Baltimore was the perfect place to put a team once hostilities ended and the world regained some sense of normalcy.

Three years later, Bob got Nee, his brother Bill, and two other Washington friends, Herb Bryant and Karl Corby, to combine in a partnership that bought the bankrupt Miami Seahawks of the All-America Football Conference and gave them a home. For Baltimore connections, they took in Charles P. McCormick, R. C. "Jake" Embry, and Albert Wheltle for minimal investments.

The All-America Conference was originated by Arch Ward, sports editor of the *Chicago Tribune*, the same man who created the baseball all-star classic as a promotion for his newspaper and also a game that pitted the NFL champion against a selection of college all-stars in midsummer. The latter event became a mismatch and, mercifully, is no longer played.

The Seahawks had enormous trouble making any kind of an impression in Miami, where the fans were oriented to the college game. Miami never accepted the Seahawks and late in the season, the sheriff actually locked the gates of the Orange Bowl because they weren't paying their bills. One of the Seahawks' owners, Harvey Hester, said when the foreclosure came he hurried away in the team station wagon and "headed for the Georgia border as fast as I could."

It was a run of bad luck for the Seahawks. They had to schedule their home games on Monday nights and two of them were postponed because of hurricanes and the rains that soaked the Orange Bowl. The largest crowd for the pros in Miami was 9,700; the smallest, a mere 2,250, and that may have been an exaggeration arrived at by counting everyone twice. The AAFC had located other franchises in the following cities: Los Angeles, the Dons; San Francisco, the 49ers; Cleveland, the Browns; Chicago, the Rockets (later renamed the Hornets); New York, the Yankees; Brooklyn, the Dodgers; and Buffalo, the Bills.

It was a new and ambitious challenge going up against the National Football League, which was chartered in 1920 and had a twenty-six-year head start against any competitor that might come along. Because of a surplus of players, backlogged by being in the military during World War II, the AAFC had no trouble signing talent, plus it was offering bonuses and paying salaries the NFL never thought possible. Over a hundred players, more than a third on the rosters, deserted the NFL for the new and enterprising AAFC. Salaries were to escalate from 100 percent to 200 percent. AAFC Commissioner Jim Crowley, the former coach at Fordham and one of the celebrated "Four Horsemen" of Notre Dame, put the drastic change in football economics into a few rationed and rational words when he said, "Even if the two leagues decide on a common draft, they will never go back to the days when a good lineman played for only $100 or $150 a game."

The differences between the leagues seemed nothing more than a mere skirmish at first. Name-calling and insults—the NFL talking down the "new kids" in the business and contending they would never amount to much. Any hope they could coexist went out the window as they attempted to bid against each other for players. It escalated into what was finally an all-out war of checkbooks, one against the other.

Serious losses were to beset every club in both leagues, plus the animosity became deeply personal between NFL and AAFC rivals in New York, Chicago, and Los Angeles, where the battle became a bitter fight for survival. As the teams lost money the resentment increased.

There also was difficulty between the Redskins in Washington and the Colts in Baltimore. George Preston Marshall, owner of the Redskins, was anti-Baltimore for financial reasons. Marshall insisted the arrival of the Colts was partly the work of one of his foremost enemies, Shirley Povich, the extremely literate and hard-riding sports editor of *The Washington Post*. He believed Povich and some other Washington sportswriters had conspired against him by encouraging Rodenberg to go to Baltimore to set up a rival stand, hoping the availability of another football option on Sunday afternoons would damage the Redskins. Of course, Marshall blamed Povich for a lot of things, maybe even rain at kickoff time.

Before Rodenberg and the Colts arrived, the Redskins had over seven thousand season ticket holders in Maryland, most of them from the Baltimore area. The Redskins also had used Baltimore as a profitable location to play one or two annual exhibition games, usually in September, prior to opening their regular schedule. The exhibitions amounted to significant pay days for the teams, with crowds in the range of fifty thousand. Generally, they were promotions handled by the Variety Club that assisted their charitable purposes.

In coming to Baltimore with a franchise, Rodenberg had the remnants of the Seahawks as a nucleus and then added graduating college players and free agents gathered from other teams in both leagues. Its "name" players were end-halfback Lamar "Racehorse" Davis, the Colts being an appropriate connection for a former Georgia captain nicknamed "Racehorse"; end Hub Bechtol of Texas; halfback Billy Hillenbrand of Indiana; and an immobile quarterback, Wilson "Bud" Schwenk, formerly of Washington University, who could pass but couldn't run because of previous ankle injuries.

The new Baltimore team was off and running for its opener September 7, 1947, in Municipal Stadium against the Brooklyn Dodgers. A momentous occasion for Baltimore. It was a hot, humid day, known as a steamer on the Chesapeake. A light rain fell and the wooden structure, built in 1923, was little more than one-third filled with a crowd of 27,418 anticipating the start of something it didn't know much about—what it was going to be like to have its own pro football identity.

Baltimore kicked off to the Dodgers and no team anywhere ever experienced a more bizarre debut. Elmore Harris, a swift halfback from Morgan State College, now a university, located only two miles away, gathered in the ball for the visitors and came out to the twenty-five-yard line. He was hit hard by Bechtol, the All-American and later College Football Hall of Fame inductee.

The ball popped in the air and was recovered by a Dodger, guard Harry Buffington, formerly of the New York Giants, who was naturally unaccustomed to being a ball carrier. Buffington, pleased he had the ball, as any interior lineman would be, advanced to near midfield, where he was hit, turned around and temporarily lost his sense of direction. He then resumed his sprint for the goal line . . . except it turned out to be the wrong one, retracing his steps from whence he came.

It was comparable to Roy Riegels running the wrong way in the Rose Bowl of 1929, a celebrated 66-yard run that ended when one of his California teammates, Bennie Lom, pulled him down at the three yard line. A safety resulted on the next play and the two points were the difference in California's 8–7 loss to Georgia Tech. The incident remains one of the most unforgettable events in all of football history.

Now it was Buffington, in Baltimore, experiencing similar confusion, as he headed towards the end zone, only in the opposite direction from where he should have been going. He was about to score a touchdown for the Colts—while playing for the other team—but suddenly had the inspiration to free himself of any such ignominy. Quickly, in a sudden burst of realization, he threw the ball away and it found the arms of the Colts' Jim Castiglia, who stepped over the goal line and, for historical purposes, scored Baltimore's first touchdown. One kickoff, one score—but oh, so incredibly weird. What a way to baptize a franchise.

A former Castiglia teammate at Georgetown, guard Augie Lio, missed the point, but pro football in Baltimore was under way. And what happened, you may ask, to Harry Buffington? He played for another year with the Dodgers and eventually became a highly proficient scout in the NFL, one of the best at judging talent, and laughed about, but wanted to forget, what happened in Baltimore and the role he played on that long ago afternoon.

Years later, while I was sitting next to him watching a game in the Houston Astrodome, he said, "There's another part of the story I've never told anyone. The next night, Monday, we had our team meeting in Brooklyn and I was driving my car to get there. I got confused about where I was going, being in unfamiliar surroundings, and a policeman pulled me over. I had been driving the wrong way down a one-way street." So much for guards running with footballs!

With the second half kickoff from the Dodgers came another stunning score. Hillenbrand caught the ball and with deliberation, good blocking—little running speed—and what used to be referred to on the sports pages as "snake-hip" moves, rambled ninety-seven yards for a touchdown. Few runners could do more in the open field or handling a screen pass than Hillenbrand. Put a stopwatch on him and a coach would be so unimpressed he'd have his name on the waiver wire before the day was out.

So, against the Dodgers, thanks to Buffington, who played for the opposition, and Hillenbrand, both kickoffs turned into touchdowns. An extraordinary way for any city to begin a football life.

The Colts of '47, though, won only two games, tied one, lost 11. It wasn't a financial success, as the accountants determined, but it was a fun-filled year for Baltimore having its own team and getting the game established. The Colts practiced in a public park, Clifton, because there was no place else to work out.

The founding father of the team, the high-spirited Rodenberg, who at 6-foot-5 looked as if he ought to be playing forward on a basketball team, was a joy to be around. He was an engaging personality, an extrovert, with a desire to frolic. He made friends all hours of the day and night, was invariably up to boyish mischief, and never took himself too seriously. He once told N. P. "Swami" Clark of the then-*News-Post*, "You know, Norman, there must be something wrong with me." Yeah, what's that, Clark wanted to know. "Well," continued Bob, "every girl I see I want to ask out on a date." Clark advised Rodenberg that wasn't so unusual; he was merely a typical American boy.

It was Rodenberg who realized Baltimore deserved a football identity and so provided it. The only previous experience the city had with anything professional was the Dixie League, a minor operation that played in old Oriole Park, where the field ran from the right field bleachers to the third base line, in the late 1930s. The team's name was the Bluebirds but, out of habit, the team was often called the Orioles. Rodenberg's entrance, after paying $50,000 to the AAFC for the franchise and players from the defunct Miami club, was a first-rate operation from the day he opened the doors of the team office at 6 South Howard Street.

He hired Jack Espey of the Washington Redskins to be his general manager. The head coach signed by Rodenberg was a familiar football name: Cecil Isbell, part of the great pass-catch combination of the Green Bay Packers, who, along with receiver Don Hutson, represented a potent force for producing touchdowns. Kind of an earlier day Unitas-to-Berry connection or Montana-to-Rice.

When Rodenberg engaged Isbell, he was at Purdue, his alma mater, as head coach. He was a master of the passing offense, conversant with its complexities and regarded with the utmost respect by quarterbacks. He talked their language. Bringing Isbell to Baltimore provided credibility to the upstart team since his reputation was recognizable throughout football. Despite winning only two games its first season, Baltimore was alive with enthusiasm. It was the post-war period and returning servicemen and their families, settling in for what they hoped would be a more passive way of life, quickly adopted the Colts.

Baltimore had only one college playing football, Johns Hopkins University, where it didn't cost anything to attend the games. Hopkins was playing for fun, not finance, in the personification of pure amateurism against such foes as Western Maryland, Swarthmore, and Haverford. Meantime, the University of Maryland, on its way to becoming an intercollegiate power under its ambitious president and former football coach, H. C. "Curly" Byrd, made only rare appearances in Baltimore since its home games were played on campus or, occasionally, at Washington's Griffith Stadium. The Naval Academy was a national force at the time and usually agreed to host an annual game in Baltimore, which was treated as a highlight of the year. Newspapers couldn't wait to publicize the name of the team Navy would be playing and the fans responded accordingly.

The arrival of pro football appeared to offer no serious threat to the popularity of the Midshipmen, since they had been a Baltimore staple since 1924, playing some of the best competition in the land at what was then called Baltimore Municipal Stadium. Notre Dame was a frequent visitor, usually every other year, plus such standouts as Ohio State, Michigan, Wisconsin, Duke, Southern California, Yale, Harvard, Purdue, Dartmouth, Cornell, and Princeton.

What benefited the Colts immeasurably and got them off to a popular start is that the team was recognized and embraced as a surrogate alma mater for thousands of Baltimoreans, some with colleges behind their names and other working-class citizens who never had the opportunity to extend their educations beyond high school. The Colts, then wearing green and silver uniforms, became every Baltimorean's "school" to cheer for on Sunday afternoons. There was, without a doubt, more of what has come to be known as old-fashioned college spirit than in some college stadiums.

Rodenberg, hoping to add to the prestige of his new club, hired broadcaster Ted Husing, one of the nation's best, to handle radio play-by-play. He was reported to be making $1,000 per game, which was then regarded as an unusually high talent fee. Husing brought a distinctive professional voice, marvelous resonance, and style but, unfortunately, was ill-prepared on game days. He obviously spent more time getting ready for his college assignments on Saturday afternoons than doing the Colts the next day.

Again, it was Rodenberg making every effort to do what was best for his team in establishing a big league persona. A band was organized, yes, the same one that survives to this day. It included pipe fitters, school teachers, doctors, students, and truck drivers, all volunteers. The majorettes, captained by Doris Snyder in 1947 and then joined by her sister, Margaret, the next year, were so outstanding, they were featured in national magazines and network television shows. Although the city was to lose its team twice, in 1951 and 1984, the band played on, bringing pleasure to the audience and distinction to itself, all the while becoming a Baltimore institution. Rodenberg, through publicity director Tommy Dukehart, had the song, "Fight On You Baltimore Colts" written and produced. Dukehart merely had to walk around the corner from where the Colts' office was located to meet with Jo Lombardi, conductor, and Benjamin Klasmer, lead violinist, of the Hippodrome Theater house band on Eutaw Street to have the composition worked on and refined. The result met with applause, a popularity that has perpetuated itself for all this time. Official credits for the song and lyrics go to Lombardi and Klasmer, with Dukehart playing the role of the Colts' in-house contributor, since he frequently wrote poetry and even had a daily column in the *News-Post* that highlighted the day's sports happenings in rhyme.

It was pro bono; they never got paid for it, a contribution to their city. John Ziemann, who has been devoted to the band and heads its current operation, says, "To me, it's the Maryland professional football fight song. When we'd go out of town for games and parades, the spectators let us know what the song meant to them. That really made us feel good." A prominent teacher of music at a midwestern college, critiquing what bands were playing at football games, both college and pro, put the Colts' song in the lead category, up there with *On Wisconsin* and the *Notre Dame Fight Song*. It has stood the test of time, fifty years of enjoyment and excitement within the walls of stadiums everywhere the Colts' Band appeared, including, at Modell's invitation, Cleveland.

With the Colts, winning or losing at home, Rodenberg became known for hosting lavish after-game receptions, held in the administration building of the old stadium. When it got dark and the party ended, the survivors often adjourned to the bar at the Belvedere Hotel to continue celebrating a victory or drowning their sorrows, whatever the case might be. Morris "Moe" Siegel, a legendary Washington newspaperman of exceptional ability and wit, joked that the worse the Colts played, the better the parties. Rodenberg's outgoing personality, and the way he enjoyed entertaining, absolutely guaranteed that a good time was had by all.

Once, returning from New York, and another losing effort, the Baltimore broadcast crew paused in the bar at Pennsylvania Station to await the scheduled departure of their train. Bailey Goss, a popular on-air personality, said they had a few drinks as they idled away the time and verbally replayed the game. Rodenberg, noting it was a Sunday and remembering that blue laws were still observed in Pennsylvania, realized the train's bar car would shut down during that part of its passage, the miles between New Jersey and Delaware. He decided to improvise, telling the bartender in the station to let him have two fifths of whiskey to take with him. To do this was against the law, the man said, because he wasn't allowed to sell liquor by the bottle, only by the drink. It was a bar, not a package store.

That didn't deter the still-thirsty Rodenberg, who found a convenient but expensive way to circumvent the problem. Bob merely instructed the barkeep to pour enough out of two bottles, via individual shots, into as many large paper cups as needed and then to charge him on a per-drink basis. The group later walked through the concourse of the station carrying a load of beverages which supplied the traveling party with adequate refreshments for the ride home. It was expensive to buy that much poured liquor, but Bob never let money stand in the way of a good time. He was a man's man, a gracious host in any circumstance.

I once met Bob for an interview at the Mayflower Hotel in Washington, long after his one-year association with the Colts. It became an unforgettable afternoon. Trying to demonstrate that I could somehow keep up with Rodenberg, drink for drink, after a light lunch, was a contest I was destined to lose. It wasn't the best of times. The dining room began to spin.

Finally, I tried to walk a straight line out of the hotel, hailed a cab, but had the presence of mind not to head for Griffith Stadium, where a close Baltimore friend, Lou Sleater, was a pitcher for the Detroit Tigers and playing that night against the Washington Senators. We had agreed to meet when the game was over and ride home to Baltimore. After the session with Rodenberg ended, the plan had to be revised. Sleater, since he was with the visiting Detroit club, had a room where the team was staying, the Woodner Hotel, so that's where I headed with a befogged mind and befuddled equilibrium. In short, I was drunk. Certainly in no shape to watch nine innings of baseball.

At the hotel registration desk, I said my name was Sleater. Could I please have the key to the room, where I ultimately found the bed and flattened out. One of Sleater's teammates and roommate, Steve Boros, then a newly signed rookie, later told Lou that some strange fellow was sleeping in his bed. After two hours of rest and recuperation, I awakened refreshed and ready to go to Griffith Stadium, where I rode back to Baltimore with Sleater. I told him of the shape I had been in, only hours before. He expressed disbelief but, upon hearing the details, knew it was a legitimate account of what had happened. Moral of the story: Being with Rodenberg was a total joy; drinking with him a near-certain disaster.

That was far from a typical afternoon for a young sportswriter. Bob was a more seasoned imbiber; I was in over my head. A gentleman at all times, who was colorful and interesting, Rodenberg had served a turn as a reporter for the *Washington Herald* and as a foreign correspondent. At times, when he became excited, a slight speech impediment occurred, which leads to another anecdote.

The lead columnist at the *Herald*, later to be a giant for William Randolph Hearst's Los Angeles *Examiner*, was Vincent X. Flaherty, who had a more serious stammering problem than Rodenberg. When they first met in the city room of the paper, Rodenberg and Flaherty each believed the other was trying to mimic him. The two got over that tentative misunderstanding, becoming good friends and drinking companions for the rest of their lives. When Rodenberg was in the process of starting his team in Baltimore, Flaherty reported getting an early morning telephone call from Rodenberg that awakened him from a sound sleep. He was informed by Bob that a name had been picked for the just-born team, and he wanted his pal to be the first to know. Flaherty, taking the bait, asked what suggestion had finally been approved?

After a long-distance pause, he was given the surprising news that the team was to be known as the Baltimore Whirlaways. The what? Whirlaways. What kind of a name was that? Rodenberg explained that since Whirlaway had won the Preakness at Pimlico in 1941 it made for a natural association in Baltimore, considering the city's time-honored link to horse racing. Flaherty, of course, was baffled. Actually, Rodenberg was merely engaging in some late night/early morning leg-pulling from three thousand miles away.

The grand name Colts, not Whirlaways, actually emerged from a contest. Again, the idea to do it that way was instigated by the imaginative mind of Rodenberg. A total of 1,887 suggestions were received. A committee comprising broadcasters Nelson Baker, Nick Campofreda, and Eddie Fenton; business leaders Sam Hammerman, Ed Finnerty, and Bob Swindell; plus sportswriter N. P. "Swami" Clark, decided on the winning name. The Sunpapers, for reasons known only to the editors, wouldn't allow any of its reporters to participate in the selection of a name for the hometown team. How times change. In 1996, the paper sponsored the contest naming the Ravens.

The group agreeing to make the decision in 1947 didn't need any help. Colts was presented several times, but the accompanying letter from Charles Evans of Middle River, Maryland, offered sound reasons why it should be selected, citing Maryland's love of the horse and the four-and-a-half letter units that the Colts name comprised, which made it a breeze for headline writers. Being declared the winner meant Evans received a visit from Rodenberg, who presented him with an autographed football, a floor lamp, a radio-phonograph console, a $50 savings bond, and two season tickets. He and his family still have the ball, but the names are fading away with time, like many of the coaches and players who signed the ball as members of that first Baltimore major league football team.

One more Flaherty recollection of Rodenberg: "It was when things were going sour for the Colts and they were taking some bad beatings," he recalled. "Rodenberg called me from the Belvedere Hotel in Baltimore. 'It's all your fault,' he said. 'I want you to know I am lying here on the bed with a bottle of acetylsalicylic acid and I've already taken half of it.' Then I heard the receiver fall. In sheer panic, I telephoned the hotel back in Baltimore and told them to rush upstairs; there wasn't an instant to lose. A half-hour later, the phone rang again and Rodenberg, still breathing, was on the other end. 'I just wanted to find out if you really didn't like me,' he said. How was I to know that acetylsalicylic acid is just another name for aspirin." Maybe all that was wrong with Bob was a hangover but he had this wonderful sense of humor and enjoyed orchestrating pranks.

Bob died in 1994 at age eighty-four, "leaving beautiful memories," as they say in the old country song. I listened with amusement while seated in a pew behind Ben Bradlee, the executive editor of *The Washington Post*. A nephew of Bob's got up to recount how enjoyable it was to be around him, even though there was a vast difference in their ages. He recounted the story of the water battle. It was what kids do all the time. Two boys had water pistols and were shooting at each other in front of one of their houses. They didn't realize Bob was upstairs, watching out the window and preparing to make his presence known. As the two chums squirted each other, Bob was overhead quietly waiting until they came within range. When they did, a sudden splash of water cascaded over their heads, tossed from the second-story window by Uncle Bob. He didn't have a water pistol, but he did have a basin of

Art Modell, the man who made the call. He took the Cleveland Browns to Baltimore and renamed the team the Ravens, in the most controversial move in National Football League history. (Courtesy Pro Football Hall of Fame)⇒

⇓ An aerial view of Cleveland Stadium, where the Browns played for 49 seasons. It was the fourth largest stadium in the NFL, with an enormous seating capacity of 78,512. A new facility will be erected on the site. (Courtesy Pro Football Hall of Fame)

⇑ The last road trip for the Baltimore Colts. A moving van departs the training complex in Owings Mills on the snowy and sleet-filled morning of March 28, 1984, for the infamous defection to Indianapolis.

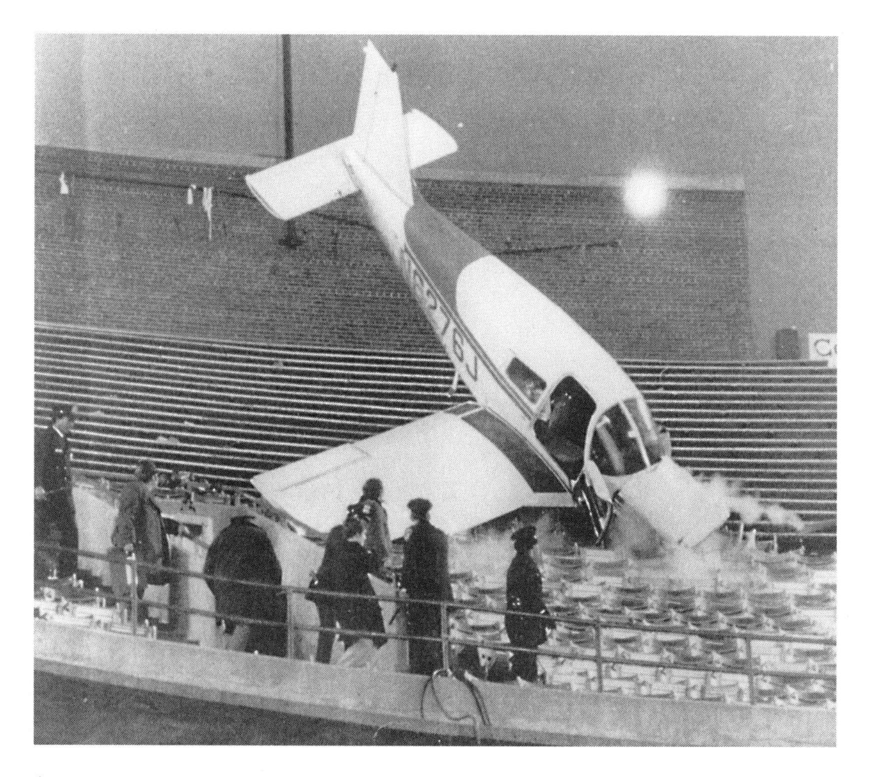

⇑ The picture published around the world—the crash of an airplane in the top deck of Memorial Stadium after the Colts-Pittsburgh Steelers playoff in 1976. Miraculously, no one was killed or seriously injured.

⇑ Billy Stone *(far left)* returns a kickoff against the New York Yankees in a 1949 exhibition game. Wendell Williams (No. 53) and Paul Page (No. 88) lead the convoy. The Yankees No. 26 is Len "Tuffy" McCormick, a former Colt.

⇑ President Harry S. Truman receives a season pass to watch the 1948 Colts. In the presentation photo are *(left to right)* R. C. "Jake" Embry, Colts official; O. O. Kessing, All-America Football Conference commissioner; and Walter Driskill, Colts general manager. Truman never availed himself of the invitation to come watch the Colts. He had more important things to do.

⇑ An early version of the Colts Band, 1947–1948, led by drum major Bob Cissin. The musicians wore green and silver uniforms, the same colors as the team, and "beanie" caps. Fifty years removed, the band is still playing.

⇓ From running with the ball to chasing criminals (for TV purposes) has been the saga of Herman Wedemeyer, a Colts halfback in 1949. After his playing career, Wedemeyer returned to his native Honolulu, where he served in the state legislature and later played the role of "Duke" on the long-running television series *Hawaii-Five-O.*

⇑ Colts general manager Walter Driskill *(left)*, and chairman of the team's board of directors Charles P. McCormick. Driskill had been told he would have to assume coaching duties after the firing of Cecil Isbell early in the 1949 season.

⇓ Fullback John "Red" Wright, a Baltimore-born product of the University of Maryland, signs with the Colts in 1947 as president Bob Rodenberg *(left)* and coach Cecil Isbell look on.

⇑ Billy Hillenbrand, coach Cecil Isbell, and Y. A. Tittle in a jubilant 1948 locker-room scene.

⇓ Touchdown Baltimore. Jim Mutscheller jumps high to make a scoring catch against Val Joe Walker (No. 47) and the Green Bay Packers.

⇑ Head coach Weeb Ewbank and assistant Frank Lauterbur on the sidelines. Team doctor Erwin Mayer (wearing hat) is in the background.

⇓ Baltimore Police Boys' Club members *(left to right)* Sonny Augustyniak, Butch Kotowski, Jim Galloway, and John Randall meet Colts Alan "The Horse" Ameche and Claude "Buddy" Young in a training camp visit.

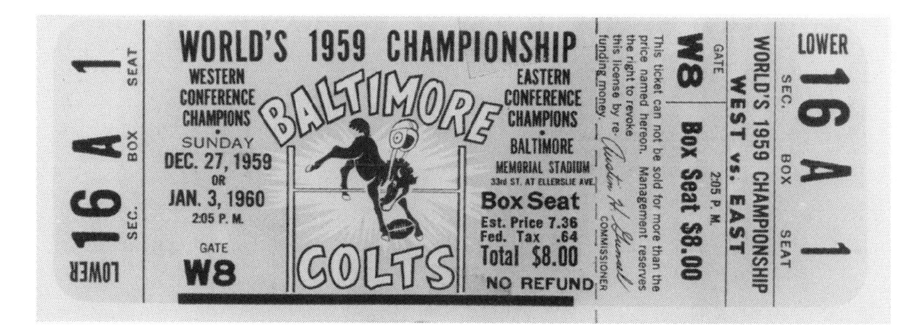


⥣ A ticket from the only world championship played in Baltimore.

⥣ Breakfast in Milwaukee before a game against the Packers. Coach Weeb Ewbank, Carl Taseff, Don Joyce, and Art Donovan are seated in the hotel coffee shop. Two hours later they had their pregame meal.

⇐ Bruce Livie *(left)*, a minority owner of the Colts, and head coach Keith Molesworth, a former Oriole shortstop and Chicago Bear, meet at a preseason outing in 1953.

⇐ The author talked Claude "Buddy" Young into racing a live colt as a preview to an intrasquad game. Young, a former national sprint champion, whipped the Colts' mascot, ridden by Allan Zimmerman, in a 40-yard dash.

⇓ Colts' defensive front in 1953. *Left to right:* Barney Poole, Alex Agase, Tom Finnin, Sisto Averno, Art Donovan, Ed Sharkey, and Art Spinney.

⇑ Native American Euchee Indian Jack Bighead, a wide receiver and part-time movie actor, surveys the field in this publicity shot.

⇑ Don Shula, Colts defensive back, tries his helmet on a young fan, four-year-old Bobby West, after a training camp practice in Westminster, 1956.

⇐ Friends and teammates Claude "Buddy" Young and Zollie Toth also became roommates in 1953, the first black and white players to room together in the NFL.

⇑ Aspiring quarterback/punter Dick Horn in a practice field critique with coach Weeb Ewbank on the importance of extending the arm before delivering a pass.

⇓ Coaching staff of 1953: head coach Keith Molesworth, assistants Nick Wasylik, Ray Richards, and Otis Douglas *(seated)*. Douglas also doubled as the team trainer, which was an economy move.

⇑ Colts Dick Chorovich (No. 78) and Alan "The Horse" Ameche (No. 35) greet Jim Mutscheller after his "miracle" touchdown against the Washington Redskins in 1956. Mutscheller's catch and run saved the job of Weeb Ewbank, who might otherwise have been fired by owner Carroll Rosenbloom.

⇑ Raymond Berry, the Colts' premier pass receiver, pulls the ball to his chest after making a catch. He rarely dropped a ball or fumbled it away. (Courtesy Pro Football Hall of Fame)

Bert Rechichar, one of the Colts' ⇒ early heroes. He kicked a 56-yard field goal the first time he ever tried—an achievement that made Ripley's "Believe It or Not" syndicated newspaper feature.

⇐ Defensive linemen Art Donovan *(left)* and Joe Campanella watch intently from the bench as the offensive unit goes to work. Note the Colts horseshoe design on the back of Donovan's helmet, later moved to the sides of the headgear.

⇓ Congratulations go to team-name contest winners Charles Evans, Mrs. Maxine Cox, and Jerry McDade. Evans was selected as the grand winner because the letter of explanation accompanying his entry was judged the best. Team owner Bob Rodenberg *(far left)* makes the presentations.

⇑ With an all-out rush, Eugene Lipscomb, otherwise known as "Big Daddy," exerts pressure on Y. A. Tittle. Lipscomb, 6-foot-6, 282 pounds, came to the Colts for a $100 waiver claim after being released by the Los Angeles Rams.

⇓ The NFL's first cheerleading squad originated with the 1954 Colts. Pictured are *(front row, left to right):* Eleanor Dudley, Barbara Ortt, Janice Lambdin, Marian Cholewczynski, Mary Lou Kelso, Joyce Woodham. Back row *(left to right):* Doris Metcalfe, Joan Johns, Pat Pinkowski, Thelma Mack (founder and organizer), Alma Vitek, Rosemary Stafford.

⇑ Colts officials make plans for resumption of pro football in Baltimore for 1953. *Left to right:* attorney William Macmillan, general manager Don Kellett, and owners Carroll Rosenbloom, Bruce Livie, and Zanvyl Krieger. Two other owners, Bill Hilgenberg and Tom Mullan, weren't available for the meeting.

⇓ Colts officials R. C. "Jake" Embry *(left)* and Abraham "Shorty" Watner were deeply involved in the city's football machinations. Watner sold the franchise to the NFL for a total of $50,000 after the 1950 season and was hit with a lawsuit.

⇑ Fans George Kelch, Jean Luckabaught, and Hurst “Loudy” Loudenslager make arrangments to honor John Unitas at the 1977 Preakness.

⇓ Ex-Colt Y. A. Tittle was so admired by Baltimore fans that they literally tore his jersey off when he returned with the San Francisco 49ers in 1953. Baltimore police had to “rescue” him from the overly friendly crowd.

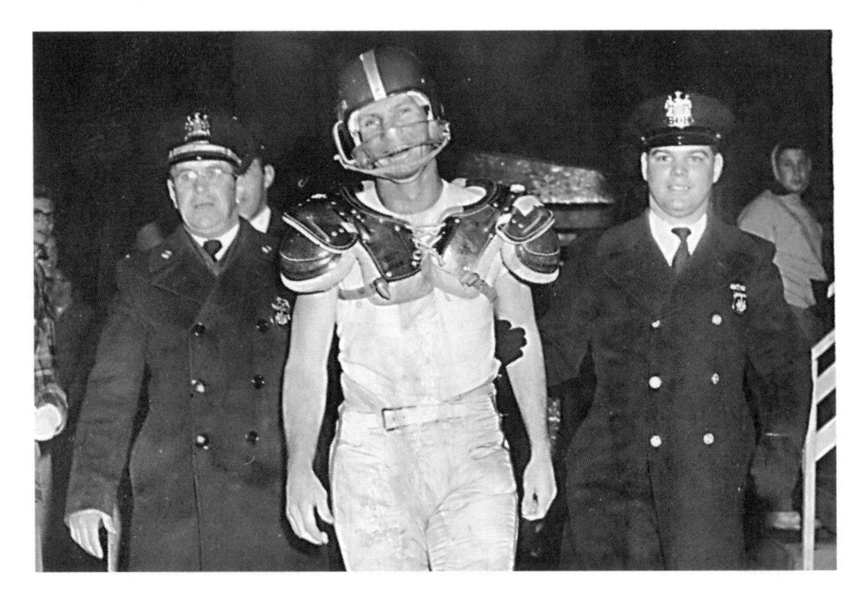

water. When they confronted him, it was his insistence they must have been caught in a cloud burst. Just Bob Rodenberg getting in on the fun.

Another time, with a new Cadillac, he gave the same nephew a test ride in the car. He told the boy to watch this—then the radio came on. He quickly signaled with his hand, whipping it toward the radio and it stopped playing. Then he pointed his hand again and it came back on. The lad was mystified that Uncle Bob had such magical prowess. It wasn't until much later that the child realized that near the accelerator, on the floor, was an "on" and "off" button that Uncle Bob was tripping with his foot. Doesn't it make you regret that more men with the basic fun-filled outlook of Rodenberg don't own sports teams today?

When he had the Colts, a wild scene and much discontent erupted during a game in Buffalo against the Bills. "Racehorse" Davis appeared to have scored but the officials denied it. Players then began to push and shove, even throwing punches. The fans were screaming and Rodenberg somehow came down from the stands and appeared in the middle of the fracas. A policeman collared Rodenberg and was leading him off the field. No doubt, the officer was preparing to bring charges or at least escort him from the premises.

George Zorich, a Colts' guard, seeing what was going on, rushed up and hollered, "Take your hands off that man. You can't arrest him." "Who says I can't," answered the policeman. "I says you can't," Zorich screams. "I just passed my law exam at Northwestern and I'm this man's lawyer."

With all the good times, the Rodenberg regime ended too quickly. For seven home games, crowds totaled 199,661 and on the road the Colts drew 157,980. But the year before, in Miami, the Seahawks attracted only 50,151 for an entire season in the Orange Bowl. Had there been television money, the Colts would have been rolling in clover, but in those times TV hadn't become what it is today. Few people had sets and sports telecasts were rare during those pioneering days of the medium.

In fact, Rodenberg once made a television deal. But only as an experiment. A Baltimore station paid him $100 for the rights to carry one game; then another $50 for the authority to show the signal in Washington. After the Colts' maiden season, Rodenberg said he thought the team was going to make a "little money" and then, in a few days, revised that statement by downgrading it to "we may break even." The final accounting showed a loss of between $165,000 and $250,000, depending upon the way the figures were calculated, brought on by the start-up costs that go with any new business. That's not much by today's football standards, but it was then.

It was close to impossible for a franchise to make a profit, not with a football war going on and the continuing battle to sign players. The breakdown on their personal football investments showed Rodenberg and Bryant lost $70,750; Corby and Bill Rodenberg, $37,500; Nee, $25,000; McCormick, $5,000; Embry, $2,500; and Wheltle, $1,000.

On the fortieth anniversary of the formation of the Colts, I had lunch with Rodenberg in Bethesda to toast the event, no doubt the only gathering (this was a twosome) ever held to note such a modest but exciting undertaking as a football team for Baltimore. Asked if he felt disappointed over not being given much credit for putting up the seed and feed money to get the Colts started, he replied, "Naturally, I was a little hurt. Then again, I don't give a damn. You can't live in the past. I know that if I continued to own the Colts, I would have had a lot of fun. And I always liked to believe if I was having fun everybody else would be having fun, too."

What a spirited way to look at football and life, kind of an all-around Rodenberg philosophy. He simply ran out of funds but it was fun while it lasted—a one year run, over and done. A good time, though, was had by all, which unfortunately doesn't happen much in today's grim world of sports.

CHAPTER 7

# TO THE RESCUE

Baltimore had tasted from the football water bucket—certainly not champagne—at best a cold beer. The rookie year for the team had been pleasing, encouraging, but far from satisfying. Would Rodenberg be able to get the Colts back on their financial feet? He said he could have raised new money but it would have meant persuading other men to come into the venture and he didn't want to do that. "I made mistakes," he admitted. "Plenty of them. But I don't regret anything that happened. I got forced out of the Colts picture in 1948 when it was reorganized. I wanted to be part of it. But the truth is I 'got the business.' Let's let it go at that."

As a going-away present, Rodenberg left a future Hall of Fame quarterback for the Colts. Y. A. Tittle, a rifle-armed passer and one of the purest of all throwers, was gift wrapped by the Cleveland Browns and handed over to the Colts. After all, Coach Paul Brown had Otto Graham as his incumbent quarterback and knew he couldn't use Tittle. He merely gave him to Rodenberg and to Baltimore in an effort to help bolster the weakest franchise in a league, the All-America Football Conference, that was going all-out in its battle with the NFL. What was an ominous development for the league is that this franchise, first in Miami and then in Baltimore, had run out of funds in each of its first two years. It was 0-for-2 in profit and loss.

In Baltimore, it was going to take more than Tittle, but he helped immeasurably. The Colts, as a matter of necessity, were going to have to be refinanced, so a group of Baltimore business leaders, championed by Mayor Thomas D'Alesandro, Jr., called an emergency meeting at City Hall. They were up against it. Either they must make a commitment or Baltimore was going to wind up on the junk pile of failed franchises, the same as the Seahawks in Miami the year before. Of course, the Colts had drawn much better at the box office and were considered worthy of continuing if a way could be found to administer a financial transfusion.

A "Save The Colts" committee was formed, headed by Howard Busick, who operated the Lord Baltimore Hotel, now the Radisson Plaza Lord Baltimore Hotel. With Busick was a lineup of spirited and effective businessmen, including Bill Hilgenberg, Charles P. McCormick, R. C. "Jake" Embry, Zanvyl Krieger, Francis McNamara, Sam Hoffberger, Tom Mullan, Jeff Miller, William Callahan, Leiter FitzSimons, George Langenfelder, Charles B. Hart, Louis J. Smith, Elmer Free, Victor Skruck, James M. Kennedy, and Maurice Nee. McCormick was picked to head the group as chairman of the board. Embry was the president and Krieger and Hilgenberg the vice presidents.

Its pledged assets were $200,000, and the public was invited to buy common stock at $1 per share. Each of the new incorporates, generally agreed to be fifteen, would put up $10,000. Not more than 5 percent of the capital stock, or $25,000 (whichever was greater) could be owned by any one individual.

In a review of the minutes of the reorganizational meetings held through the early months of 1948, it is apparent that Busick, Hoffberger, Embry, and Krieger were major players in the direction Baltimore was moving. It was interesting to note, then and now, that four of the investors were men with family brewery ownership connections—Hoffberger with National, Krieger with Gunther, FitzSimons with American, and McNamara with Arrow. Being involved in sports sponsorships, broadcasts, or billboards was important to the beer "barons," but this does not mean they weren't motivated by an awareness of civic responsibility to save a major league team because, after all, only one brewery was going to get broadcast rights.

Embry agreed to serve as president for a year, citing personal obligations with radio station WITH, the presidency of the Baltimore Bullets basketball team, and involvement in other civic affairs. It was at this point that the Baltimore football neophytes screamed in unified voice: "Help." They were trying to rescue themselves from a sea of red ink and, realizing the playing personnel needed to be improved, wanted the stronger teams in the AAFC to share some of their talent. Out on the streets it's called begging.

Commissioner Jonas Ingram, a retired admiral, who had succeeded Crowley as the league leader, visited Baltimore with coach–general manager Paul Brown of the Cleveland Browns and owner Ben Lindheimer of the Los Angeles Dons. They listened as the Baltimore officials made their appeal. It was unheard of in competitive professional sports to help out the opposition by giving up players but that's precisely what occurred.

The Colts' new owners were given the right to buy guard Dick Barwegen of the New York Yanks, tackle Ernie Blandin of the Cleveland

Browns, tackle Pete Berezney of the Los Angeles Dons, and tackle Fred Land of the San Francisco 49ers. In talking about Blandin, and this is a quote from the transcribed notes of the meeting, Brown said, "I have already agreed to let Ernie Blandin come with you. But I want to make this clear to you gentlemen: I don't give anyone unless I get what I want. In the case of Blandin, I haven't got the guts to tell him, and I have gotten the Admiral's promise [meaning Ingram] to tell him, saying that it is the Admiral's decree that he come to Baltimore. Blandin is one of my best men."

Several weeks later, the Colts forged a similar deal to acquire the contract of quarterback Charlie O'Rourke of the Los Angeles Dons and, eventually, a crashing end, Bob Nowaskey, who became a crowd favorite because of the aggressive way he played. Isbell was retained as coach for two years for the same salary he was getting from Rodenberg, $18,500, and then the search was on for a general manager. At one meeting, Paul Brown was asked if a sportswriter could do the job. It was likely if he had answered in the affirmative the group would have turned to Paul Menton, sports editor of *The Evening Sun*, who thought like a businessman, knew how to manage money, and was a college game official. But Brown replied that he was doubtful a sportswriter was qualified and the only one he could think of who had made such a switch was Jimmy Gallagher of baseball's Chicago Cubs.

Walter Driskill, who had been brought to the University of Maryland by Jim Tatum when he left the University of Oklahoma to be his athletic director, was suggested. Driskill, though, after only a year at Maryland, had returned to Oklahoma to be an assistant coach for Bud Wilkinson. He was immediately lured back to Maryland, not to the university but to the Colts, for a salary of $12,000, where he remained for all of 1948, 1949, and the start of 1950.

At one of the reorganizational meetings, when finances were being reviewed, Embry related to members an interesting conversation he had with "Mr. Abe Watner who asked that the committee consider his underwriting the balance [of what the subscribers had raised and what the final goal might be] provided he was made president and director of the corporation." The significance of Watner's name being mentioned is that two years later the same group turned to him in a desperation move that blew up in their collective faces. It resulted in the loss of the team.

The Colts had draft rights to Bobby Layne, graduating from the University of Texas, and Isbell was optimistic he could be signed for the 1948 season. However, it would be a competitive battle with the Chicago Bears, who had drafted him in the NFL. The Bears, though, already had Sid Luckman and Johnny Lujack. What could they do with Layne? Not much, except to prevent him from going to the rival league, the AAFC. That was their intention and exactly the way it evolved. Isbell had visited Layne and offered him a three-year deal that graduated in salary from $20,000 to $22,000 to $25,000. Then he reached in his pocket and pulled out $10,000 in cash, a promised bonus, that he put on the bedspread in the hotel room where they were meeting. Layne promised he would sign the contract the next day at 11 A.M. But overnight, his college coach directed him toward the Bears, saying the Colts had no rating in Dun & Bradstreet and that the Bears were well established. When a disappointed Isbell returned to Baltimore all he could say was, "Our league wanted Layne. I wanted Layne. And I know the people of Baltimore wanted Layne." In Chicago the Bears billed Luckman, Lujack, and Layne as the three "Ls."

For the 1948 season, the Colts had the most scenic of all training camp settings. They went to Sun Valley, Idaho, with a roster bolstered by the veterans they had received from the stronger AAFC clubs. There were training camp diversions being in a vacation resort. Hospitality abounded. The Colts worked out, fittingly enough, on a rodeo field while a galaxy of pretty waitresses from the lodge frequently looked on at practice. Equipment manager John Sanborne said the young ladies were taking T-shirts and athletic supporters off the clothesline when he put out the laundry to dry at night, and were crocheting their names on the material. It was a different way to flirt.

Although the quarterback staff included the veteran O'Rourke; promising rookie Dick Working, a Baltimore product who had distinguished himself at Washington & Lee; and Rex Olson of Brigham Young University, it was evident Tittle had excited the entire camp with the power and accuracy of his throwing arm. Coaches and players knew right away he was something special.

"I roomed with Y. A. that year in Sun Valley," said Working. "All he talked about was football. I liked him a lot as an individual, [he was] sincere and considerate. A country boy from Marshall, Texas. One way or another, either in person or on television, I have seen all the great passers of the last fifty years. I rank him with Sammy Baugh, who I watched play as a kid, as the most effortless thrower of a football I ever saw. I can tell you that he made me feel I ought try to change over and become a defensive back. His ability was just so natural and so enormous."

When the Colts came home to open the season against a difficult foe, the New York Yanks, Tittle got the nod from Isbell. He was only twenty-one years old, the youngest player on the roster, leading teammates who were all older and opposing more experienced players, many of them veterans of the fighting in World War II. It's doubtful if any rookie in any sport, especially a first-time quarterback at any level of professional football, put on such an overwhelming show in his debut. He completed 11 of 21 passes for 346 yards, three touchdowns, and scored one himself while leading the Colts to a 45–28 win over the favored Yanks. He drew rave reviews.

Baltimore, with Tittle throwing and Davis, Hillenbrand, and John North catching, had reached a level of early excellence and, admittedly, the team was going to be competitive. After jolting the Yanks, they added wins in six more games, finishing with a record of seven and seven, good enough to tie the Buffalo Bills for the division title. Then came another crisis.

The players suddenly weren't sure they wanted to play the Bills unless they collected a share of the playoff monies, but Embry and Driskill told them the tie-breaking contest was considered part of their contract obligation and they'd be paid their normal game salary. Finally, Embry called their bluff when he said if team members didn't want to play then they should just consider the season closed. All could go home—which would mean the Colts had forfeited to the Bills. The players would then be faced with explaining to the public what happened. Of course, they decided to play. What took place on the field added to the controversy.

A questionable call on a pass play altered the outcome. It may have been one of the most legitimate complaints any Baltimore team ever had, comparable, in a way, to losing to the Green Bay Packers in 1965 on a disputed field goal. The Colts deserved to beat the Bills and were ahead, 17–14, when Bills' quarterback George Ratterman passed to halfback Chet Mutryn.

I was seated in the stands watching the play, had a reasonably good angle, and it appeared that after Mutryn caught the ball he took three steps laterally to his left and fumbled after being tackled by Barwegen and Sam Vacanti. The ball squirted loose and was retrieved by another Colt, John Mellus. However, head linesman Tommy Whelan ruled Mutryn never had control of the ball. It was a tough call for Whelan but, from the Baltimore perspective, a bad one. Had the Colts been awarded possession at that stage, late in the game, they would have been in position to hold on, to use up the clock, and win the playoff.

Instead the Bills got six more plays and scored on a 26-yard pass from Ratterman to Alton Baldwin with only 2 minutes and 30 seconds left to play to move in front, 21–17. A desperation pass by the Colts from their own ten yard line was picked off by Ed "Buckets" Hirsch and returned for a score. An apparent Baltimore victory had ended in bitter defeat. The Colts had 24 first downs to 11 for the Bills, a total yardage of 394 to 297.

The Colts' 1948 season was at an end. But before the stadium emptied, a wild scene, like none I had ever witnessed, in Baltimore or anywhere, erupted. A sizable part of the crowd of 27,327, estimated to be as many as 10,000, and looking the part of a giant tidal wave, rolled across the stadium field—all intent on inflicting bodily harm on Whelan. It was frightening and unforgettable to see a mob so out of control, demonstrating an emotional frenzy that approached insanity. It was a sad sight, like a pack of barking dogs treeing a helpless raccoon.

More than twenty-five years later, on a hot summer night, the phone rang in the *News-Post* sports department. I answered and the caller identified himself as a priest who had just returned from decades of service in a foreign mission. He said he wanted to relate something he had never forgotten and, incredulously, proceeded to talk about the Bills-Colts playoff and the ugliness of what followed.

The priest explained that as a child he lived near the stadium and was there the day the crowd invaded the field when the game was over. "I was just a little boy and my brother, who was with me, was only a couple years older," he recounted. "We both ran down on the field when we saw the crowd. I guess we knew something was going on and wanted to be there. You know how kids are. I somehow got shoved to the front row, looking directly at the official, who was being protected by the police and some players. I have never forgotten the terrified look in his eyes. It is an experience that has stayed with me forever. The fans were trying to attack him by throwing bottles and screaming all kinds of things. I hate to think what might have happened had the crowd gotten to the official. I'm back in Baltimore for a visit and wanted to tell you the story. Did you happen to be there?"

I also remembered what it looked like to see the makings of a riot—a crowd incensed over the difference of opinion in something as irrelevant as a football game. The ground was scattered with bottles of all shapes and sizes. Whelan had a swollen eye and a torn shirt. Finally the police got matters under control, and most of the angry crowd dispersed.

Still, some fans wouldn't leave. They wanted to get their hands on Whelan and congregated outside the administration building, where the dressing rooms were located, in an effort to make another attempt to settle a score with the official. They were screaming, "Let's Get Whelan . . . Let's Get Whelan." The Bills, after showering and dressing, finally left the stadium with Whelan accompanying them. He looked as inconspicuous as a coach, carrying his small equipment bag. The Bills escorted him to their team bus and secreted him away. City police were commended for their handling of the situation and two Colts' players, Aubrey Fowler and Len "Tuffy" McCormick, were praised for coming to the aid of the besieged official. The play Whelan had was difficult and every time I see one similar to it I never fail to quietly remind myself of the unsavory situation it created in Baltimore on that Sunday playoff afternoon in 1948.

Another member of the officiating crew was the father of Fay Vincent, who later became the commissioner of baseball. Young Fay was at the game, a mere lad, and frequently talked about the incident when the subject of crowd control was introduced in conversation. If you were there, it made an unfavorable impression, to say the least, to last a lifetime. Years later, when I got to know Mutryn on a personal basis, he would never admit it was a bad decision by Whelan. But he wouldn't say it was the right one, either. Other Buffalo players weren't so evasive. They admitted Baltimore should have been awarded the ball after making the recovery and that the Colts truly deserved a victory they didn't get.

Coming that close to a divisional title excited Baltimore. Hopes were high for 1949. Tittle had made a quick impression, and people thought he'd be better the second time around. Instead, the Colts had a disastrous year, which proved to be their third and last season in the All-America Football Conference. Peace talks were held between the NFL and AAFC and there was even an attempt at a merger, but Baltimore wasn't going to be included in the projected plan.

Only Cleveland and San Francisco would be joining the NFL and, had it happened that way, Baltimore would have been in position to bring suit under the Sherman Antitrust Act, it was so advised by John Henry Lewin, acknowledged to be one of the country's foremost authorities on antitrust legislation. Lewin of the prestigious firm of Venable, Baetjer and Howard made it clear to the Colts that if they were in accord with the league constitution and had the funds to continue, they couldn't be forced out of business. On the other hand, George Marshall, Baltimore's nemesis in Washington, was to accuse the Colts of holding up the settlement between the leagues and costing every team thousands of dollars that didn't need to be spent.

The 1949 Colts, in what was the last year of the All-America Conference, had a brutal time of it. Much of their undoing came with the way the schedule had been arranged. It called for Baltimore to be on the road four straight weeks, meaning they would be in San Francisco, Los Angeles, Cleveland, and Chicago before coming home to play. The only game they won all year was a storybook kind of finish, against, oddly enough, the Bills in Buffalo's Civic Stadium. It was Tittle firing to North for a 79-yard touchdown to tie the game and then in the last 24 seconds Y. A. made connection with Billy Stone on a 53-yard shuttle to win it, 35–28. The winning coach was Driskill, not Isbell, who had been fired, prematurely, after the team lost its first four games.

I was there for the two opening losses of the season, played on the road. I was serving as a fill-in reporter for N. P. "Swami" Clark, who called from home to tell the sports editor, Rodger H. Pippen, he couldn't make the trip. Clark's son, Dennis, had been stricken with a case of infantile paralysis. Fortunately, the attack was of short duration and Clark, in two weeks, was back with the team. I was just a young sportswriter in the office that morning when Pippen asked, "Are you afraid to fly in airplanes?" "No sir," I said, "but I've never been in one." He told me to go home, pack clothes, and meet the team for its flight to California that evening from Harbor Field.

At age twenty-two and with little experience, I walked self-consciously over to introduce myself to Isbell, a great name in football. Teams were wary of a new reporter, even one there on a temporary basis, and Isbell said, "You know, as you came over here I noticed you have kind of a funny walk." This was the coach's way of getting on the offense from the start and reminding a rookie that he shouldn't be too critical of the team he was going to be with for only two games. It was easy to find fault, he was telling me, as demonstrated by the way I walked.

On my inaugural flight, I noticed that veteran players insisted on being in the circular seats which were then built into the rear of the commercial airliners. They said if the plane went down that part of the aircraft had a better chance of sustaining less damage in a crash. They might come away as survivors, not casualties.

Before and after the season-opening loss to the 49ers in San Francisco, the team was quartered at what was known as the Old Hearst Ranch, one of many owned by the newspaper czar, near Pleasanton, California. The facility had a swimming pool, golf course, and all the trappings of a first-class dude ranch. Not exactly the kind of environment suited to get a team thinking about football. Be that as it may, the Colts were beaten soundly by the 49ers and returned to Pleasanton to await a later trip to Los Angeles to meet the Dons. On Monday, the team worked out lightly and, for the fun of it, played a touch football game called "two hand tap."

We asked Isbell, since they weren't hitting or wearing heavy equipment, if he minded if I played. He said that would be fine and to see John Sanborne, the equipment manager, for a sweatsuit and a pair of shoes. So I was able to catch passes from Tittle, lateral the ball to Davis, and have the kind of a good time reporters of today would never have the opportunity to enjoy because the league has become wary of sportswriters and prefers to keep them as far away as possible.

Isbell didn't get to finish the season because, after the four opening losses in 1949, he was fired under circumstances that were not entirely honorable. The Colts' new board of directors held a meeting at the home of Charles P. McCormick and invited the three sports editors, Paul Menton of *The Evening Sun*, Jesse Linthicum of the morning *Sun* and Pippen of the *News-Post* and *Sunday American*, to be with them. They talked about doing something to give the team a lift and discussed changing coaches.

It was agreed that everything said would be off-the-record. Menton, Linthicum, and Pippen were in accord. But in a morning edition of the *Sun*, Linthicum's column made reference to drastic action being taken if the team didn't turn around and get back on the winning track. When Pippen arrived at the office, he was livid. He said, "Jesse double-crossed us." He immediately told Clark to write that Isbell was being sacked as the Colts' coach, and then called Menton at *The Evening Sun* to tell him what he was doing.

Menton and Pippen, although rivals, understood one another's problems since they were in charge of afternoon sports sections and cooperated on numerous occasions in regard to the timing of P.M. news releases. This was one time they were creating their own news story. Menton, with Pippen going full blast on the Isbell angle, had no alternative but to handle it the same way, telling *Evening Sun* reporter Jim Ellis to put a story together that said the same thing—Isbell was being fired. Meanwhile, the Colts' directors were having another meeting when the first edition of the afternoon newspapers hit the street and headlines screamed that Isbell had been fired. Actually, he hadn't been terminated; it was only one of the possibilities they were considering. After the "news" broke, however, they felt there was no alternative but to confirm that Isbell was out, a classic case of overreacting or giving in to the power of the press, which was unfortunate. In a manner of speaking, Pippen and Menton literally fired Isbell—which was a terrible mistake.

The replacement for Isbell was a reluctant Walter Driskill, the general manager. That was the last thing he wanted to do . . . to take over for a man he regarded as a friend under such ambiguous and stressful circumstances. Driskill knew he had to go meet the team, so he was driven to the Clifton Park practice site by A. Hungerford (Hunky) LaMotte, Sr., who was president of the Colts Associates, a group of businessmen who supported the team with volunteer efforts. LaMotte said Driskill was so emotionally upset "he had tears in his eyes" and, as he stepped out of the car to talk to the team and try to explain what had happened, said, "This is the last thing I ever wanted to do."

Under Driskill, the team won only the game against Buffalo, but gave a creditable account of itself most other times. It was competitive and didn't embarrass itself on the scoreboard, although a loss is a loss and the Colts lost 11 times and won only once.

McCormick, the chairman of the board, said the club would take financial hits that would come to between $80,000 and $100,000. So, again, Baltimore had to contend with a dollar crisis. The owners weren't going to put up any more money so, as politicians have been doing since time immemorial, they decided to hold a fund-raiser. Not a bull or oyster roast or even a crab feast; this was to be an exhibition game played where all tickets would be sold for $5 with the revenue being used to assist the team treasury. Mayor D'Alesandro was again the catalyst, saying to an audience, "You want to save the Colts. I want to save Baltimore's face. And I need people like you to help me do it."

Driskill made a statement, too, explaining, "A small group of men saved the Colts two years ago. These men have already been taxed enough. They can't be asked to give the money we need now. No self-respecting community could expect them to contribute more. Now the future of the Colts is up to all of us—every citizen of Baltimore." The idea wasn't popular and, besides, it was getting to be an almost end-of-the-season ritual, the team in need of fresh money. All clubs in both leagues were taking a beating.

It wasn't just Baltimore. In Green Bay, solicitors went door-to-door raising funds. For a $25 contribution you got a certificate attesting to the fact you were a "Packer Backer," but that was all, no dividends or the right to vote at stockholders' meetings. In fact, the Packers were in such bad shape they played an intra-squad game on Thanksgiving morning in Green Bay, with the regular season still on, to raise money. It also helped when their training camp burned down and the club received an insurance settlement. Football times were tough.

Baltimore's effort to raise $250,000 by selling the 50,000 tickets at $5 each barely reached the halfway point when the inevitable happened. The AAFC decided to fold or, to put it more politely, to merge with the NFL. The story was broken by Hugh Trader, Jr., in the *News-Post*, and it had national impact. Actually, Trader got the tip that the merger was imminent while covering the minor league baseball meetings that were held in Baltimore in December of 1949. Six hours after his exclusive lit up the news wires, it was confirmed by Commissioner Bert Bell of the NFL. Peace was at hand. Baltimore, San Francisco, and Cleveland would be joining the new alignment, under the National Football League banner, and players from the other teams would be divided in a common draft, after the New York Giants and Cleveland Browns got special privileges to select the best players from the rosters of the New York Yanks and Buffalo Bills, including such talents as Arnie Weinmeister, Tom Landry, John Kissell, Abe Gibron, Otto Schnellbacker, and Rex Bumgardner.

The teams that desperately needed help were Baltimore and Green Bay, but they didn't receive the type of charity that was bestowed upon the Browns and Giants. There was shock in Buffalo that the Bills weren't included. And they should have been. After all, they had a better record on the field and at the gate than Baltimore, but were left out in the cold, the NFL saying it wasn't interested in Buffalo.

This meant that for 1950, there would no longer be an All-America Football Conference and the NFL would have thirteen teams—the thirteenth being Baltimore. The number was an unlucky omen. The Colts were to be known as the "swing team," meaning they would not have a home and home series but would play every club in the league one game. Things would be different: pro football was now unified. Salaries also would be held in check. But the Colts, as an organization, had problems. Money was still in short supply.

The campaign to sell $5 tickets to an exhibition lost its momentum when it was announced Baltimore was becoming a member of the NFL. It was as if the public considered the effort wasn't needed now that a merger had been approved and the financial fight for players would be lessened. Some of the Colts' directors would have made another investment but the majority of the owners had exhausted their patience and said they weren't interested. It was at this point that Embry, always alert to the possibilities of making a deal, remembered that a fellow officer of the Advertising Club, one Abraham "Shorty" Watner, had only two years before expressed a desire to own a pro football team. Embry and Hoffberger met with Watner. They agreed, Hoffberger quite reluctantly, that Watner would assume operation of the team for a period of two years.

"The contract he first signed," said Embry, "was tough. In fact, it was actually brutal but he agreed to it. He was responsible for lots of things. Simon Sobeloff, his attorney, met with us. Sobeloff, former Solicitor General of the United States and later a judge, said Watner had signed the agreement before realizing all the entanglements. But it was Watner or no football. It was as simple as that. The directors relented, which was the only thing they could do, and let Watner out of the two-year pact. A revised contract was written for one year—1950."

Not much was known about Watner but it didn't take Baltimore and its football team long to find out. Watner had received a splash of publicity in 1943 when all the Baltimore newspapers reported that $10,600 had blown out the window of his office in the American Oil building at Baltimore and South streets, floating down upon the heads of happy pedestrians. He said he was talking on the telephone at the time with George Preston Marshall, owner of the Redskins, when a breeze came up and carried the money off to the four winds.

From Watner's accounting and reporting, only $200 was recovered in this "manna from heaven" incident. With that kind of a history, he was deemed ready for pro football; the perfect angel, as they used to call backers of sports franchises and Broadway shows. Watner was obviously enamored of all the attention that came with owning a team; but it soon became obvious that he had zero understanding of football and how it operated. He did have a sense of humor that came forth at the first meeting of the NFL after its amalgamation with the AAFC. Marshall was dominating the session, held in Philadelphia's Bellevue-Stratford Hotel and making numerous proposals. Almost automatically, puppetlike, Watner would raise his hand to "second the motion." It got to be expected. Marshall would make a point and right behind him would come Watner offering support to what Marshall had just recommended.

On the matter of Baltimore becoming a "swing team," Marshall said it would be "suicide" but Watner, for the first time, disagreed. Marshall left the room in a mild huff and said in disgust to a group of reporters, "Watner has been in the league for two days and he thinks he knows more than I do and I have been here for eighteen years." At a recess, Watner was told what Marshall said. Then, as the meeting resumed, Watner signaled to Commissioner Bert Bell and called for the floor. Amidst what was one of the most significant gatherings in pro football history, Watner announced, "I want to make a correction in something Mr. Marshall said about me. He said, 'I have only been in the league for two days.' That's wrong, I have been in pro football for four weeks, four days, and 23 minutes."

Watner had a sense of humor, no doubt, but didn't belong in football. His knowledge of the game could have been put in a thimble but that wasn't what made him undesirable. He just wasn't equipped with the basic awareness of how a team should be operated, and he became suspicious of everyone, including general managers and coaches when they tried to help him. After the Browns and Giants dipped into the now defunct AAFC for many of the standout players, before the Colts and the other clubs had a chance to draft, the new coach, Clem Crowe, who had been with the Bills, expressed disgust over how Baltimore was being shortchanged. "Don't worry, Clem," Watner said, "we'll beat the Browns and the Rams even if I have to kick the extra-points." And then, in front of Crowe and this reporter, he demonstrated his kicking style, without a football, right there on the mezzanine level of the hotel. Owners of football teams don't usually act that way. At the outset of his administration, Watner was providing a lot of reason to laugh, but that all soon changed.

Marshall, his friendly antagonist in D.C., was declaring openly that the Colts weren't going to make the grade, that their time was limited. To this, Watner countered by insisting, "George says the Colts are dead. We are going to operate. I told him that a Colt was a frisky animal . . . ." It was suddenly reported and later confirmed that for the Colts to play in Baltimore Watner had to pay $150,000 to Marshall in tribute money, a licensing fee, so to speak.

The indemnification was at Marshall's insistence, claiming the Baltimore area fell within the seventy-five-mile territorial rights of the Redskins. This didn't make anyone in Baltimore happy but the first of three $50,000 installments was paid. Driskill was pleased to be back exclusively as a general manager, leaving the coaching problems for Crowe. But working for Watner was far from a joy and in May, realizing how hopeless it was going to be for a general manager, Driskill resigned to join McCormick & Co., under the former Colts' chairman, Charles P. McCormick. Driskill's replacement was Al Ennis, who had worked in the NFL office and had once been publicity director and general manager of the Philadelphia Eagles. Ennis tried but was in over his head, spending most of his time trying to appease Watner and rarely making a decision.

In training camp, the Colts had over a hundred players come and go. Rookies named Adrian Burk, Leon Campbell, Don Colo, Art Donovan, Herb Rich, Sisto Averno, and Art Spinney were impressive. Overall, though, there wasn't much in the way of talent. Watner, ever the optimist, came to a workout at Western Maryland College and, not having a football background, said to Jim Ellis and me, as we watched from the sidelines, "You know, those boys are such great players that you could put them up against any college team in the country—even Notre Dame—and they would win easily." That's what Abe reckoned but it was doubtful. Played-out veterans and woeful free agents were on the field. Far from an imposing lineup of talent.

One rookie billed himself as a former end at the University of West Virginia, but inquiry proved he had been working at a gas station since he graduated from the eighth grade. This tired and undermanned team was facing a horrendous exhibition schedule of seven games with three of them to be played, if you can imagine, in the space of six days, the 49ers in Baltimore, the Rams in San Antonio, and the Yanks in Shreveport, Louisiana. The Colts lost all three and four others—making it 0-for-7 in the preseason grind.

Oh, yes, don't forget the "Save The Colts" exhibition. All of the seats were sold on an unreserved basis. Five dollars each and sit where you wanted. Only days before the game against the Pittsburgh Steelers, Watner decided to recall all the tickets and reissue them as reserved. It created a logistical problem for ticket manager Herb Wright and was a headache for the public. Only 22,000, far less than the projected 50,000, showed up to see the single-wing-formation Pittsburgh Steelers deal the Colts a 30–27 defeat.

In a disgraceful exhibition at San Antonio, the Colts lost to the Rams, 70–21. Only weeks before the Rams had made a coaching change, firing Clark Shaughnessy and replacing him with Joe Stydahar. An embarrassed Shaughnessy, one of the most innovative but certainly complicated coaches in the sport, was so miffed that he took a shot at his successor by saying, "Let Stydahar spend a couple weeks with the Rams and I'll be able to take a high school team and beat them."

Surprisingly, when the Colts arrived at their hotel in San Antonio, they found Shaughnessy waiting to greet them. He knew one of Crowe's assistants, Wayne Millner, who introduced him all around. Millner, Crowe, Shaughnessy, and, amazingly, this reporter went to a room where Shaughnessy gave the Colts a complete scouting report, even describing how the Rams' check-off system worked at the line of scrimmage. He wanted to see the Rams go down to defeat and tried to help Baltimore do it.

Before leaving, Shaughnessy left this thought: "Try to score on this team early and the Rams will fall apart." But the final score told it all: Rams, 70, Colts, 21. A complete rout. The Rams were pressing so hard that after their final touchdown, with only seconds left, they attempted an on-side kick with a 49-point lead. The humiliation was too much for Crowe, who told Stydahar, when they met at the middle of the field after the final gun, what he thought of him for pouring it on an outclassed foe in an exhibition game.

Crowe, introverted and rarely given to vulgarity, used a derogatory term. Stydahar turned to Bob Nowaskey, a teammate when they were both with the Bears and then a Colts' linebacker, and said, "Did you hear what Crowe called me?" Nowaskey nodded in agreement and then said, "Yes, Joe, and it goes for me, too."

Watner said he expected the Colts would beat the Rams. "I wanted the Colts to win so much that I called upon my Maker and asked Him to intercede," he explained. "That night I went to bed and had a dream. It came to me just as clearly, Colts 21; Rams, 0. I thought this was one dream that would surely come true. I felt so sure about it that I sent a telegram back to Baltimore to a friend. By gosh, the Colts were going to win, I told him. But then when the game was over, I looked up at the scoreboard and saw the result. It was Rams, 70; Colts, 21. I thought to myself that the Good Lord had slipped me a seven."

In desperation, at 2 A.M., following another beating in Shreveport, 42–17 to the Yanks, the Colts decided to trade for player help. They took on the master dealer, George Halas, who was happy to accommodate them. He wanted guard Dick Barwegen for the Bears and also tackle Dub Garrett, who hadn't bothered to report to camp. Halas got both by giving the Colts quarterback George Blanda, halfbacks Bob Perina and Ernie Zalejski, guard Jimmy "Tank" Crawford, and end Bob Jensen.

It was an atrocious deal, compounded by the fact Halas got Blanda back after one game when the Colts attempted to trade him to Green Bay. Since Halas had to meet the Packers, a bitter rival, twice during the season he didn't want to chance Blanda going against him. He claimed he had a provision in the transaction that if the Colts couldn't use him (they had Tittle and Burk at quarterback), then he had the right to insist he be returned to Chicago. That's exactly what happened—Blanda went on to become a durable quarterback, a great competitor, and a superb field goal kicker, eventually making the Pro Football Hall of Fame.

It became obvious that the Colts were a poor excuse for a professional operation. Barwegen started for the Bears and so did Garrett while the Colts got virtually nothing from the Bears in return, except players who would no doubt have been placed on waivers within a week. Halas had to be pinching himself and wondering how long such "pigeons" had been around? Welcome to the NFL. Earlier, Halas traded them a fullback, Jim Spavital, who wouldn't report, but he relented and finally joined the squad, costing the Colts their No. 1 draft choice for 1951. It was highway robbery, Halas taking advantage of all the confusion in Baltimore, even talking them out of their first-round choice for Spavital, who had a bone spur in his foot. Yes, Virginia, he could have said to his daughter Virginia, there really is a Santa Claus and he's in Baltimore.

Watner was starting to realize he had entered a costly business, especially one that he didn't remotely understand. The team used a heavy supply of adhesive tape, as all clubs do, and also put out chewing gum for the players. After seeing that twenty cases of gum had been ordered for the season, he suggested to trainer Mickey McClernon that he ought to consider breaking the sticks in half. Adhesive is a football essential, since every player has his ankles taped before all practices and games, but he never understood why they needed to use so much.

Once, while the team was working out in Egg Harbor, Wisconsin, before an exhibition with the Packers, and another loss, Abe found a small roll of narrow-width adhesive on a golf course, worth about a dime. It was the kind golfers might use to tape a blister on a finger. He picked it up and gave it to trainer McClernon but it was of no use in the training room and was quickly discarded.

The players only rarely came in contact with Watner. They knew who he was and realized from talking with others that he lacked even elementary football knowledge, but that was all. Once, in training camp, they asked about being paid for preseason games. After all, they were going to be playing seven of them for the benefit of the team, not themselves. Their salaries didn't start until the opening of the regular schedule. Watner finally agreed to give each member of the squad $25 and when they got the money personalized notes were enclosed. To center Joel Williams, he wrote, "You're in the center of things." To end Bob Oristaglio: "That tall majorette would like to have a date with you." To halfback Herb Rich: "You've already made a hit with the crowd." To fullback Leon Campbell: "Let's make up for the Bears (meaning an earlier loss) and go hunting." It was a strange scene on the plane as the players compared notes but they also were happy to be getting the $25 stipend. Most of them were broke. On one occasion, Watner pointed to Sisto Averno, a Colt rookie, and said, "That boy played a fine game. He got five yards every time he carried the ball." The only problem was Averno happened to be a guard and it wasn't in his domain to run with the football.

It's doubtful if any team ever had a worse season than the Colts that year, certainly not in my experience. One would be hard-pressed to find a team as bad as they were. Art Donovan agrees.

In midseason, Watner called a press conference to announce his plans for improving the Colts. He was elated to note that the team had just acquired a defensive halfback, Achille "Chick" Maggioli, a veteran who had been around and proved to be far better than anything the Colts had in their secondary with the exception of the young, flashy Rich. But Watner made it sound as if the acquisition of Maggioli, who had been released by the Detroit Lions, was going to be the difference between finishing last and winning a championship.

At the same time, Abe said he'd like to get Marion Motley to play center and Frankie Albert from the Pittsburgh Steelers. The only problem: Motley was on his way to the Hall of Fame as the crunching fullback for the Browns and Albert was with the 49ers. In midseason, the situation became too difficult for Eddie Adams, the publicity man, so he resigned, the same as Driskill had done months before.

At one point, with the team continuing to lose and crowds falling off, Watner took to the streets of downtown Baltimore and tried to give tickets away. He was lucky enough to find some takers but others walked on by, too busy to find out what it was he was handing out. Maybe it was a cough drop sample, or a half a stick of gum, and they just weren't interested. Later in the season, Watner signed quarterback Frank Filchock, who had been barred from the NFL in 1946 for failure to report a bribe offer while with the New York Giants. Filchock had been playing in Canada and I always felt Bell, the commissioner, felt badly that he had to discipline the player to such an extent.

Bell was a man of immense compassion and probably urged the Colts to sign him in what would be an effort to clear his name. At least in getting back to the NFL, Filchock accomplished that. Crowe didn't know he was getting Filchock until Watner told him. The old pro was around for three games but only took part in six plays. His arm was obviously shot. It was a pity to see him take the snap from center, make his pivot, set up and try to throw with not much more on the ball than the signature of the commissioner.

What beatings the Colts took! They went to Los Angeles and were ripped by the Rams again, 70 to 28. The Colts were at least gaining on them; they were a touchdown better than in the exhibition season. The Rams were naturally gifted, loaded with talent, and able to strike from any place on the field. Their quarterbacks, namely Bob Waterfield and Norm Van Brocklin, had championship qualifications. Both were destined to be elected to the Hall of Fame. For the Colts, 1950 was another year where they lost 11 and won only once.

Their upset of the Packers in Baltimore ended an eighteen-game losing streak, going back to the previous season and including the exhibition experience of 1950, plus league games. Spavital had a career day, running for 176 yards. When it was over, Watner descended on the dressing room and he couldn't contain himself. He literally danced around the locker room, embracing Crowe, and was totally carried away. Later, when the quiet, reserved Crowe was asked about it, he said, "I never saw anything in my life to equal that display of exuberance by Abe. He almost went berserk." Too bad the team couldn't have won more often. It might have saved much of the pain that was to follow.

In the final game, played against the Yanks in Yankee Stadium, with space for 67,000, only 5,003 fans showed up. The Colts were in danger of having to forfeit. They dressed the bare minimum of players, only twenty-five. One less and they would have been obliged to concede without lining up for the kickoff. Obviously, Abe was interested in cutting his losses. He set a maximum on what the players could order for their after-game meal on the train ride home from New York. Crowe, though, told them "to order what you want from the menu." A season of torture had ended.

CHAPTER 8

# DOWN AND OUT

Speculation was rampant about the future of the franchise. What was going to happen? Watner added to the problem. One day he was going to continue, the next morning it was a different story.

It became so confusing that an exasperated Harry Clark, managing editor of the *News-Post*, ordered the sports editor, Pippen, to find out from Watner, one way or the other, what he was going to do. A simple suggestion, but there was no assurance an answer would be forthcoming, considering the personality of the man. I knew it was going to be a hopeless mission to get him to define his intentions. With Pippen on an extension phone, I talked to Watner and told him the call was being made on instructions from the managing editor, who wanted an answer that would clarify the nebulous outlook once and for all. Watner listened and, after a typical pause and with slow-motion enunciation, declared himself: "I won't say yes and I won't say no."

At the NFL meeting on January 18, 1951, held at the Blackstone Hotel in Chicago, Watner finally made a decision. He was giving up the franchise. First, he asked for player help from the other teams but socialized football wasn't their game. These team owners were in a tough competitive business, and it was every team for itself—a free enterprise system, except for the draft. NFL owners, as a parting gesture, voted Watner $50,000 for his assets, meaning all the players on the Colts' active and reserve rosters.

They, in turn, were put into the draft with the regular graduating college seniors so it made for a bumper crop of prospects, proven pros of a sort mixed in with the collegians. However, only twenty-eight of the Colts were considered good enough to draft; the rest were left on the counter as free agents much the way you would pick around in a going-out-of-business sale in a dry-goods store. For instance, Spinney, Donovan, and Averno went to the Cleveland Browns, Eddie King to the New York Yanks, Burk to the Philadelphia Eagles, Paul Salata and Barry

French to the Pittsburgh Steelers, Billy Stone and Leon Campbell to the Bears, and Y. A. Tittle to the San Francisco 49ers.

Crowe went to the Chicago meetings as the head coach of the Colts but when Watner checked in he was with Wayne Millner, a former assistant, who was now ostensibly the head coach. It was all rather confusing for Crowe, who hadn't been informed and still had another year left on his contract. In another twenty-four hours, Millner would be out as coach, too, probably the shortest "reign" in NFL history. If there wasn't going to be a team then there was no need for a coach.

Crowe hadn't been paid in a month and was up against it. He had ten children on the farm in Eden, New York, and bills to pay. I had an extra bed in my hotel room so that's where Crowe stayed the rest of the week. His meals were paid for by his friend from Notre Dame, Buck Shaw, coach of the 49ers. Crowe, of course, reciprocated and helped Shaw with his evaluation of the Colts' personnel who had been abandoned but would now be a part of a draft that was suddenly thrown out of kilter because of the availability of the professionals.

What Crowe had to offer was inside information. Since the other clubs had played the Colts only once during the season they weren't too well versed on the ability of Colts' players, except for the obvious ones. The 49ers had the first draft pick and originally intended to take Bob Williams, the Cumberland-born but Baltimore-raised quarterback from Notre Dame. But Crowe, who also liked Williams, insisted Tittle was a gem. He had heard the old tired criticism that Tittle was a slow learner. This was unfounded, a bum rap. Crowe learned to admire Tittle through their tough season together and knew he was a thoroughbred. So it was Shaw turning to Crowe for an opinion he respected. On Crowe's advice, he made Tittle his choice. Williams went high in the draft but to the Bears—where Halas exercised use of the Colts' first-round choice he had obtained in the Spavital trade.

After Watner tossed in the towel in Chicago, I was on the telephone dictating a story to Neal Eskridge in the *News-Post* sports department. Jesse Linthicum was doing the same for the Sunpapers. After the sellout of the Colts, I asked Watner if he realized what he had done to a great city and to its public. And how do you feel, I wanted to know? "Just like crying," was his answer. It was pitiful to see it end that way. Abe didn't intend to hurt anyone; he was just in the wrong business.

That night there was a verbal confrontation between Watner and Crowe. The story I wrote for the *News-Post* might best describe what happened:

> CHICAGO, Jan. 19—When a man decides to walk up and say just what he thinks there isn't much you can do but listen. And Clem

Crowe, Colts' coach, poured out his every thought here last night in a stormy good-bye to Abe Watner, who had just put the Baltimore team on the scrap pile.

THE BACKGROUND —

Crowe had been at the NFL meeting for 28 hours and Watner ignored him completely. Here was Crowe, the head coach, being passed up for an assistant and a confused general manager.

It cut him. It broke his spirit.

But he found out in a hurry who his friends were—fellow leaders like Buck Shaw, Gene Ronzani, John Michelosen, Blanton Collier, Joel Hunt, one of his own aides; and football people from every other walk of life—Vince McNally, Art Rooney and many others.

THE ACTION —

Crowe located Watner, and, after debating with himself, says before a large audience: "Well, Mr. Watner, you got $50,000 for the players. Are you going to pay the money you owe the coaches?"

*Watner*: "I paid you as long as I was obligated—to Dec. 10."

*Crowe*: "Mr. Watner, you have treated me like a dog. I can't imagine why you would want to do such a thing. I worked hard for you and so did Joel Hunt (pointing to Hunt, who was at his side) and the rest of the coaches. I never said a critical word about you. I kept my thoughts to myself. And to think you wind up doing this to me."

*Watner*, somewhat aghast: "There are two sides to every story, remember."

*Crowe*: "I have coached for 25 years, but never have I ever heard of such a thing. The day after Christmas I came back to Baltimore to work on the draft. All the material had been taken care of. It just had to be dated up. You told me to look for a job. Why didn't you tell me then you weren't going to pay me? You just cut me off."

*Watner*: "Well, I offered to settle with you. Did you get the letter I sent you where I offered to pay you for the rest of December?" [Note: In that particular message, Watner reportedly wanted Crowe to take two weeks' pay and forget about the $12,000 salary he had due him for 1951 if the team operated.]

*Crowe*: "Getting your salary cut off like this isn't easy, you know."

*Watner*: "Clem, I have never said a bad word about you. And you should know that. Ask Steadman. He was always asking me what I was going to do with your contract."

*Crowe*: "But why would you want to treat me like this?"

*Watner*: "Truthfully, Clem, you never had a heart-to-heart talk with me like this. You always came in the office and walked up and down like you were so nervous that you never told me much."

*Crowe*: "You paid me to coach the team. I can't help it if I'm a football coach and act that way. But why did you want to treat me so lousy?"

*Watner*: "Well, you went to Philadelphia to see Bell over my head and you had lunch with Zan Krieger."

*Crowe*: "You want to know why I went to Philadelphia. Because Al Ennis asked me. I asked Bert what my status would be if the team folded and I didn't say anything I'm not ready to admit. And I had lunch with Mr. Krieger and called Mr. Hilgenberg, the chairman of the board, to find out the story."

*Watner*: "The reason I didn't pay you was because my obligation ended and Wayne and I were taking care of the draft."

*Crowe*: "I gave Millner a job when he was out on the street. You didn't do any work on the draft. I had it all set up, had the scouts and all the machinery ready, just like in Buffalo when Red Dawson [the head coach] went away. It was understood that it was my duty to keep things up to date."

*Watner*: "Why don't we go eat."

The wrangling continued, after which Watner and Crowe finally entered the dining room.

> Watner, according to Crowe, said he regretted the messy thing had to be exposed. Crowe, who had kept all this inside of him, was now relieved and relaxed. Watner couldn't believe what had taken place.
>
> As irony would have it, Watner was at Crowe's right. On Crowe's other side was Cecil Isbell. Remember him? He offered Crowe a sympathetic hand. He didn't say much. But he understood as only a coach can who has been through it.

When Watner returned to Baltimore, he didn't exactly receive a hero's welcome. He went off to Florida, a retreat Modell used years later after leaving Cleveland. It was obvious to all that this was a man who had absolutely no ability to run a football team. He started out with good intentions but when the losses came, on the field and at the box office, he panicked and didn't know which direction to turn. He was completely out of his element.

The fans were embittered, as was to be expected. On two occasions, he had his house in Pikesville vandalized. First it was streaked with green and silver paint, the team colors. Another time, a Liederkranz cheese bomb was thrown through a window. When it exploded, a room was speckled with bits of cheese and an aroma emerged that wasn't exactly reminiscent of a rose garden. N. P. "Swami" Clark of the *News-Post* talked to Watner after he reported the act to the police. "They painted a lot of obscene words," he said. "What I can't understand is that if they loved the Colts why would they want to —— them?"

Jim Ellis of *The Evening Sun* reported that Watner told him, "This was attempted arson and the law says that arson is punishable by death." The night raiders were never apprehended and to this day there has never been a clue to their identities. Not that they're subject to the death penalty. The statute of limitations has expired.

Baltimore wasn't about to take Watner's surrender of the Colts without reacting in the courts. Only five days after the team was disbanded, the team's board of directors held an emergency meeting. Attending the wake were Howard Busick, R. C. "Jake" Embry, Victor Frenkil, Leiter FitzSimons, William Hilgenberg, Zanvyl Krieger, George Langenfelder, Thomas Mullan, Charles P. McCormick, Francis McNamara, Vic Skruck, and Louis J. Smith. Hilgenberg, who was board chairman, stated his opinion and that of fellow members quite emphatically: "We have the interests of 202 stockholders and the fans of Baltimore to think about, but particularly the fans. It's one thing when Mr. Watner sells out the board. I was willing to go along with him as long as he was going to keep football here. But when he sold out the city, well, that's another thing."

Each man on the board agreed to contribute $500 to form a legal fund to pursue recovery of the franchise. Those who couldn't make the financial commitment were covered by Krieger. Always a man of exceptional decency and civic awareness, he detested what Watner had done and called it "inappropriate and inconceivable." Mainly through Krieger's direction, the Colts' directors engaged William D. Macmillan, a whimsical, astute attorney with the firm of Semmes, Bowen & Semmes to handle their case. Still, it seemed a desperation move. Teams and their fans don't often win sports disputes in a court of law.

The thought of retribution was appealing but few if any followers expressed confidence that a victory would be achieved. The Colts were gone, the players distributed to other clubs. Still, Macmillan needed to be equipped with background and found a lode of information in the comprehensive scrapbooks that had been kept by John Sanborne, the equipment manager who was out of a job when the Colts were scuttled. Sanborne went so far as to buy the first and last editions of the daily newspapers to make sure he never missed a mention of the team because he knew some stories would change as the day progressed and he didn't want something being printed that he didn't have in his books. What he had assembled was a work of art. There was no need to have law clerks squinting through endless hours of research at a public library.

Sanborne had it all and Macmillan was moving quickly. Within three weeks, he said the Colts had a strong case against the league for allowing the franchise to dissolve. Watner lacked authority to negotiate or give up the franchise and the league was an accomplice in the deed. What Watner was specifically hired to do was to run the team and guarantee losses. There was nothing in the contract that he had signed to abrogate the agreement and turn the club over to the league, whether it was for $5,000, $50,000, $500,000, or $50,000,000. He had made the wrong move and the league also was responsible for the part it played, according to Macmillan's opinion—one that also was shared by the attorneys for the league.

In less than two months, Macmillan was meeting with Commissioner Bert Bell and they got along famously. They were of the same build, short, squat, constructed along the lines of animated pillboxes, the kind they built during the war, and had outgoing dispositions. They knew how to laugh and didn't take themselves all that seriously.

At one early juncture in the talks, Bell said, "the league is considering your demands." The three sports editors, in a unified front, Pippen, Menton, and Linthicum, went to Philadelphia to meet with Bell at an informal luncheon. Bell admitted the league acted in haste in permitting the Baltimore club to withdraw without giving the Colts' corporation, the one Watner was representing, an opportunity to vote on its own future.

In a momentous concession, Bell, trying to extract himself from the perilous legal bind he was in, actually said the team could be revived and made that promise. He stipulated, however, that all team debts had to be cleared; $200,000 put up as an immediate operating fund; that one man had to be vested with authority to make decisions and run the club.

As part of its obligation, Bell said the league would return all original Colts' players to Baltimore and grant the team first choice in every round of the draft. He imposed an October 1, 1951, deadline for all this to happen. But Macmillan and his clients, the Colts' owners, wanted more. Contending that the team would still be weak, Macmillan asked that each club, as part of the agreement, name its "top five" players and then allow Baltimore the right to pick one player from the remainder of the twelve squads. This wasn't going to happen; the league would go only so far. Its willingness to bail itself out of a bad situation stopped right there. Turmoil continued.

Finally, the sparring stopped and real fighting began. On November 1, 1951, almost ten months after the club had folded, Macmillan filed suit in circuit court against Watner and the NFL. At the January 1952 league meeting in New York, the Colts were back to negotiating but not pulling away from their legal battle. The New York Yanks, once a talented team, had fallen on hard times and owner Ted Collins, who was both a television performer and a theatrical agent, notably for singer Kate Smith and her classic song "When the Moon Comes Over the Mountain," wanted to get out of football.

He had started in Boston with the Yanks, came to New York with a franchise that was renamed the Bulldogs, and then resumed the Yanks name with such talented performers as Buddy Young, George Ratterman, George Taliaferro, Zollie Toth, Barney Poole, and Dan Edwards. Crowds were sparse and he wanted out. Instead of dealing with Baltimore, after saying he'd consider its proposal, he sold the club to Dallas and the Yanks became the Texans for the 1952 season—but not for the entire schedule because they, too, were destined to fall on hard times.

Macmillan got to court but only for a hearing on the motions. It was held before Chief Judge W. Conwell Smith. Everything went in Baltimore's favor. Macmillan got to call Watner to the witness stand for questioning; he thought he would have a bit of fun toying with him. Nothing more than whimsy. Watner, among his interests, had owned Meadowridge Memorial Park, a cemetery near Laurel; a transfer company; and the Wisconsin Central Railway.

When Watner was asked his business in court, he mentioned Meadowridge. "What's that?" Macmillan asked, tongue-in-cheek, "Is it a race track?" Without changing expression, Watner replied: "No. It's a development of underground bungalows." The court erupted in laughter. Watner had tilted Macmillan, who was so gifted on his feet, off balance, and the man who enjoyed the exchange the most, even though Watner scored heavily, was Macmillan.

Regarding his cemetery investment, I once heard Watner say, "It's the only business I know of where you buy ground by the acre and sell it by the inch." Another time Watner talked about owning a Geiger counter that he was using to find golf balls at his country club. Just as an experiment, he took the equipment to Meadowridge: ". . .down there we have a real hard rock that is known as 'neger rock.' Well, I took the Geiger counter near that rock and you know what it detected? It showed a vein of gold. Of course, it wasn't enough to mine, but it was gold all right." Abe Watner, the only man who could discover gold in a cemetery or let $10,600 blow out an open window at his downtown office, was indeed an intriguing study.

The suit against Watner and the league could have resulted in a huge financial award had it proceeded in court, or gone to the next legal step after Judge Smith's hearing on the motions. But Macmillan insisted the idea was to get compensated with a franchise, not money. "All we want is a football team," he said. "Fans can't come out to the stadium to watch us count a cash settlement. It's a team we're after." But they didn't know where one was coming from. The move to Dallas by the Yanks, bypassing Baltimore, was distressing.

Within the league and its teams, except the wise Art Rooney in Pittsburgh, there was belief that taking pro football to Texas was going to be a bonanza, like striking oil or robbing a bank. The other teams were fighting to get there to play the Texans and wanted to be booked for early visits to the Cotton Bowl, where home games were to be played. Originally, the team was to be called the Rangers but switched to Texans for what it thought was a more identifiable name.

Rooney, all alone in his opinion, kept supporting Baltimore and wasn't impressed with the Dallas possibilities. He thought it was a mistake for the league to be there and not in Baltimore. For their opening game, the visiting Giants were expected to attract a capacity crowd, not only because pro football would be making its introduction but also because of the presence of two Southern Methodist University heroes, Fred Benners and Kyle Rote, whose performance against Notre Dame had been voted the most significant athletic achievement during the first half of the twentieth century in all of Texas. Two days before the game, the size of the expected crowd was downgraded to 35,000, but then only half that number showed.

The Texans weren't exactly a household word. At the Texas State Fair, some players asked visitors if they were coming to the game. And the answer they got? "What game? We ain't never heard of any team down here except SMU, Texas, and TCU." That was about the way it was. The Texans in Texas made no impact.

All the players were given ten-gallon hats, a gesture of hospitality. Art Donovan didn't like the idea of being a Bronx cowboy and never wore his. One of the Texans' owners, believed to be Colonel "Dry Hole" Byrd, said, "Oh, that's okay. If he doesn't like Texas we'll trade him to the Green Bay Packers." As it turned out, Donovan was destined to come back to Baltimore, play at a high level of efficiency, and take the high road to the Hall of Fame as the first Colt so selected.

En route to the Texans' 1952 training camp, Donovan and Don Colo stopped by the News-Post building. We had our picture taken, the three of us, and I still have it. I asked Donovan and Colo for a favor. "A young player from Baltimore is going to be there trying to make the team," I said. "Please look out for him if you can. His name is George Young. He was at Calvert Hall with my brother Tom and was a Little All-America at Bucknell."

When they arrived in Kerrville, Texas, for camp one of the first players they met was Young. Donovan said, "He was so big he filled out the whole door when he walked into the room." Donovan looked at Colo and suggested, "Maybe he's the one who should be looking out for us."

The Texans, like the Colts in 1950, were disorganized from the outset. The only redeeming quality was the humor of the head coach, a man named James Michael Phelan who was handsome, well-dressed, silver-tongued, and possessed of enormous wit. The equipment manager was an owner of a tortilla stand, one Willie Garcia, who had never seen a game of football but was somehow hired for the job. He had an artificial leg and anytime a ball bounced, or was kicked into a nearby field, where the grass was high and snakes abounded, it was Garcia who had to go retrieve it. "We figured," remarked Donovan in his inimitable way, "that he had a 50 percent less chance of being bitten by the snakes than any of the rest of us." Willie had been presented a homburg by Colo and wore it everywhere, even though it wasn't the normal headpiece you'd see or wear in Texas.

The only fan of the Texans I ever talked with, who actually saw three of their games in the Cotton Bowl, was Raymond Berry, who was going to Southern Methodist at the time and had a rooting interest since he was from Paris, Texas, and was thrilled that pro football was in his home state. "The main reason pro football didn't go over was because of a super-saturation of high school, junior college, and college football in the area," he said—a fact that wasn't true about Baltimore, where the market was wide open. Giles and Conell Miller, sons of the founder of the Texas Textile Mills, headed the ownership group but couldn't make it successful. After four home games, the Millers and their associates gave up.

It was Phelan's understanding they could have completed the two remaining home games for an additional funding of $50,000 but obviously felt they had a loser on their hands. On November 12, the directors admitted they could no longer finance the team and turned it back to the league for operation. They had even cut ticket prices in an effort to get people in the seats. Some reserved locations were scaled at $1.80 and children could buy general admission for 60 cents. The season ticket base reached only 5,200 and the Texans played to less than a total of 50,000 fans in four games at the Cotton Bowl. It was a disaster.

Once, while at an afternoon workout, Phelan sounded his whistle, called the players together, and said the pay envelopes had arrived. "They just sent the checks," he added, "and it might be a good idea if I gave 'em to you. I'm not saying these checks aren't any good but the banks close in half an hour. Once around the field, up the chute, and run for the bank." That was the Phelan humor at work. Another time while preparing for a game, Phelan abruptly halted practice to declare, "We better quit. We're looking so good we might beat the Rams." When they played, it was a runaway, the Rams winning 42 to 20.

Phelan even resurrected the stratosphere pass that he had used at St. Mary's College during World War II and which other coaches still call on when the occasion presents itself. Three or four receivers go deep to a predetermined location and the passer lofts the ball high in the air to resemble a pop fly. When it comes down, as all thrown balls will, they jump to make the catch or bat it back up in the air and then fight for it like basketball players pushing for a rebound. In the Rams' game, Gino Marchetti came down with the ball. Touchdown Texans. When Marchetti got back to the bench, Phelan checked the scoreboard and, with all seriousness, quipped, "We got 'em on the run." It might have been a long year for the Texans but it was never boring.

The league didn't have much of an alternative once the Texans surrendered ownership. Instructions from NFL headquarters to the Texans advised them from that day on they would be playing all their remaining games in cities away from Dallas. A team that had such high hopes when it went to Dallas was now nothing more than a road show. A football version of the touring Harlem Globetrotters.

On Thanksgiving Day, November 27, 1952, the Texans were considered for a Baltimore visit to play the Chicago Bears. The game, featuring two teams from elsewhere, would have counted in the standings; it would not be an exhibition. Bell wanted to put them in Baltimore but found out Memorial Stadium was taken—Calvert Hall and Loyola in the morning, City and Poly in the afternoon. He wouldn't attempt to dislodge two traditional high school football games so he looked for another place to accommodate the Bears and Texans. They went to the Akron (Ohio) Rubber Bowl and played before a lonesome gathering of 3,000. Only hours before, two Ohio high school teams had drawn 14,800 on the same field. There was no motivation for the Texans, this wandering group of football minstrels.

Phelan, viewing the few fans in the audience, told the team in his prekickoff remarks, "Boys, the crowd is so small today we are going to dispense with the formal introductions over the PA system and go up in the stands and meet everybody personally." The players roared. It was Jimmy at his best. And in an astonishing upset, the Texans won their only game of the year, shocking themselves and the Bears, 27-23. Halas was so infuriated that a bonus he promised the Bears for beating the Lions the week before might now not be forthcoming.

Some players on the sidelines who had missed coverages were physically kicked in the pants by Halas. This old coaching reaction was used in the NFL and even in some colleges and high schools. Boot 'em in the butt so as to embarrass them before teammates, the opposition, and the crowd. That would never happen today. The player would be filing suit for abuse. The Texans' meeting with the Bears was one of their two "home" games. The other was in Detroit, where Ray Pelfrey, a talented wide receiver and punter, punched one of the Lions and then ran toward the bench screaming he needed police protection.

In Philadelphia against the Eagles, the pass from center flew over quarterback Bob Celeri's head as he prepared to punt. Celeri tried to run out of trouble, zigzagging, dipping, and avoiding tacklers but dropping back and giving up yardage. Mike Jarmoluk of the Eagles finally got him in his sights at the seven yard line, where Celeri, going down, tried to rid himself of the ball. It went, instead, directly into the hands of another Eagles' tackle, Vic Sears, who scored the first touchdown of his then-twelve-year career.

As the bedraggled Texans came off the field, the impish Pelfrey sidled up to Celeri and playfully said, "Gee, Bob, I knew if you kept throwing you would hit for six." Celeri was trying to forget the interception but Pelfrey's comment irritated Celeri so much he chased Pelfrey to the bench. In the previous Bears game, Pelfrey got into a squabble with

George Connor. It was going to be a mismatch. As Connor squared off to fight, Pelfrey looked him in the eye and wisecracked, "You would, wouldn't you." Then he was off and running again.

The future of the Texans was up in the air, but sources in the league said Bell had something in mind: He was going to place the Texans in Baltimore for the 1953 season. The source was so good I wrote about it without confirmation. It broke as a page one story in the *Sunday American* on November 30, 1952, saying, without qualification, that Baltimore was back in the NFL. *The Sunday Sun* wasn't too happy to find a front page headline in the other newspaper reading: "City Returns to Pro Football."

In those times, if a reporter did a good job he received more than just a slap on the back. A bonus of $25 came my way, and I used it to throw a shrimp party at my mother's house for all the boys and men in the sports department. You could buy a ton of shrimp in those times for $25. There was an ironical twist to it all. When the year-end pay statement was handed out, the extra $25 put me in the next higher tax bracket so the bonus actually cost me money. But nothing comparing to the estimated $600,000 lost in the first four years of Baltimore's unrelenting football struggles.

Between games, the road-traveling Texans billeted in Hershey, Pennsylvania, where they practiced briefly in the afternoons and partied long into the nights. One old pro, Chubby Grigg, by actual count, consumed seventeen "grasshoppers." He got off the bar stool and hollered, "All you girls who can't swim head for the roof" and then threatened to relieve himself in public. More sober heads prevailed and led him to the men's room. Another lineman was so intoxicated at closing time he couldn't move, so some of his teammates borrowed a sled from a nearby house porch and slid him back to the Community Inn on the light snow covering the streets that morning.

There was no incentive to train because teams on the bottom in all sports are inclined to tell each other, "We're merely playing out the string." They fought among themselves and even with other drunks they met in the bars. At one Hershey saloon, where they frequently drowned their sorrows, the Texans estimated that collectively they spent $3,500 in ten days, or nights, of drinking. The players weren't concerned about what next year was going to bring, where they might be, or what was going to happen. This was an army of men put in a no-win situation and all they wanted to do was survive, forget their problems, get out alive, and maybe make it to another season.

At one point, I went to Hershey to visit a practice. The players were so worn physically that Phelan wasn't asking them to do much. They took calisthenics and worked on punting, extra points, and field goals. Then the squad split into four equal units and went to opposite ends of the field to play under the goalposts. They were competing in, of all things, their own version of volleyball, using the cross bar as the top of the net and batting a football over it. At that stage, life with the Texans was a ball day and night. Next stop Baltimore.

CHAPTER 9

# NEW LIFE

Since the Texans were available and Baltimore was holding a legal bomb it could drop at any time, it was a natural solution for the league to solve both problems at once—simply assign the Texans to Baltimore and end the lawsuit. That's precisely what happened.

The league also had been paying the bills for the team after the Dallas debacle and wanted to get out of any further obligation. So it was on to Baltimore for the Texans. The NFL was back in a city it had wrongfully left and an enthusiastic audience awaited.

Meanwhile, the commissioner, deBenneville Bell, otherwise plain old Bert, whose forefathers came over on the Mayflower (the ship, not the vans), but who never bragged about it, had another idea he wanted to put into motion. Something of a trick play, or a "gadget," to use the modern terminology. It touched on blackmail.

Bell conceded that, yes, Baltimore had a team awarded but only tentatively. The former Dallas Texans would be Baltimore's property, to have and to hold, but only if 15,000 season tickets were sold. Not pledges but checks and cash. The three sports editors offered their particular views. Linthicum said it was a fair proposal and could be met. Menton wasn't so sure. Pippen told Bell he didn't think much of the season ticket tie-in because it was strapping the public. "You're like a guy buying a girl a Coca-Cola and then trying to caress her," he told the commissioner. Bell appeared at an Advertising Club luncheon on December 3, 1952, and spelled out the ultimatum: either buy the tickets or no team. But, apart from the maneuvering and the preseason ticket demand, where was the league going to place a team if it wasn't in Baltimore?

The suspicion is that Bell had no city interested in taking the orphaned Texans team, although Buffalo was always a possibility. What Bell was doing was staging a colossal bluff but, at the same time, also positioning Baltimore to get off to a well-financed resumption of its football business. Meanwhile, the commissioner was also brokering his way out of the litigation dilemma the league had created for itself. Bell and the club owners had almost led Watner by the hand in getting him to abandon the franchise in 1951. At the same time, Bell was making Baltimore buy enough season tickets to fund the entire comeback. Simple as that. The program had a Bell-imposed deadline of six and a half weeks. Almost in the middle came Christmas, not exactly a time when John and Jean Q. Fan had extra money to lavish on a football season that was ten months away. But the drive became an overwhelming success, winding down before the forty-nine-day selling period had run its course.

Macmillan's law office was overwhelmed with checks and mailed requests for tickets. Bruce Livie, an automobile dealer who owned Bobanet Racing Stable, was recruited to head the campaign, when Busick, who had been an earlier Colts' investor, told him that a man with a recognizable name was needed to be out front as the spokesman and cheerleader. The team set up a temporary office on the second floor of the stadium administration building. Herb Wright came back from service with the navy during the Korean War to again serve as ticket manager and Harry Thompson, who worked for Livie in the automobile business, helped refine the details. Lou Staab and Bill Keneally argued about who deserved the honor of being the first ticket buyer. They were among the early subscribers, no doubt, but Wright's records showed the distinction belonged to Emanuel L. Hymen, who bought seats 7 to 12 in section 11 and wrote a check to cover the cost for $118.80. Football was more of an affordable commodity in those days.

With the team assured of solvency ($300,000 was raised from the advance sale by the fans), there was no need for any incoming owner to put up money. Too bad the actual ticket buyers didn't get stock options because they, indeed, made the return of the Colts possible. For the owners, it was going to be an easy ride. It's doubtful if any of them had to contribute anything more than their time. Hilgenberg, Krieger, and Embry had the financial means but, after all the hassling to keep the game alive in Baltimore, continued to tell themselves they weren't interested under any circumstances in being involved with any new team.

They had surely done their part. A state of fatigue, more like mental weariness, had set in, and they agreed it was time to take a walk. In making the early arrangements with Bell for the Texans to be placed in Baltimore, they told him it was his responsibility to find the owner, president, general manager, and coach. With the club close to being reestablished, they clearly wanted to withdraw from all football matters.

Even though the $300,000 raised from ticket sales was in the bank, Bell still didn't have an owner. He had an idea. When he coached the backfield at the University of Pennsylvania in the late 1920s, one of the halfbacks was Carroll Rosenbloom, a Baltimore native who also was one of his summertime neighbors in Margate, New Jersey. Rosenbloom had gone to work for his father in the shirt manufacturing business and was such a success as a salesman that he retired at age thirty-three and moved to the Eastern Shore of Maryland. But any retirement was sure to be short-lived, considering that World War II was on the horizon and the country was preparing to defend itself.

Quickly, Rosenbloom quit the farm and returned to work for his father, who had held the Marlboro Shirt Company together during the difficult times of the depression and was now in a better position to lift it to an even higher level. Carroll's foremost interest, though, was the Blue Ridge Manufacturing Company, which turned out overalls, dungarees, and also the bulk of blue denim used for military work uniforms. Under his guidance, Blue Ridge became a multimillion-dollar operation as its production lines accelerated.

The Colts, cost-free, were about to be wrapped up in a blue-and-silver ribbon and placed in the lap of Rosenbloom. For a time he didn't want them; he dodged the issue and avoided inquiries from the media. His brother was saying that "what happened to Watner" could be a replay for him. At one point, Bell said he didn't believe Rosenbloom was interested, "but he sure would make the ideal man." If it were not Rosenbloom, then perhaps one of the other names mentioned: Bill Veeck, Arthur Godfrey, Sid Luckman, Louis Wolfson, Gene Tunney, Jack Dempsey, Bob Rodenberg (the original owner), and John B. Kelly, president of Atlantic City Race Track and father of an Olympic participant son and an actress daughter who became Princess Grace of Monaco.

During a period of procrastination, when Rosenbloom was believed to be making up his mind, I tried to contact him sixteen times by telephone but failed to connect, trying him in New York; Margate, New Jersey; Palm Beach, Florida; Roanoke, Virginia; and Baltimore. Finding Elvis today would have been easier. Rosenbloom obviously wasn't ready to make a commitment. He was avoiding calls. Finally, on January 10, 1953, he gave a calculated "yes," but only on the condition he wouldn't be compelled to personally operate the team. The next day, a Sunday, Rosenbloom invited Krieger, Hilgenberg, Busick, Embry, Mullan, Livie, and Macmillan to meet with him. None had ever met Rosenbloom.

Although Baltimore-born, Rosenbloom wasn't involved in the business or social life of the city. Those invited to the meeting were skeptical but kept an open mind. I called Hilgenberg and told him too much was at stake to make a mistake. He agreed. "I'm not doing anything unless we have complete knowledge of what's going to happen," he commented. "But don't worry. This is too important. We aren't going to blunder."

The meeting with Rosenbloom, as described by Hilgenberg, was a delightful experience. Carroll made it so by giving them a grand reception and creating a momentous first impression. He also told them the only way he would accept the offer to take charge of the Colts was if they joined him in the effort. They didn't want to do it, were vehemently opposed to the idea, but Rosenbloom knew how to sell himself and also an idea. Busick decided he had had enough of pro football, regardless of the circumstances, and Embry was told that since he was affiliated with a radio station he wouldn't be eligible to join the group—something about conflict of interest if he entered into a bid for the team's broadcast rights.

The banishment of Embry, though, smacked of a powerful maneuver by Marshall, the Redskins' owner, but that couldn't be proven. It didn't need to be. Marshall had feuded with Embry during the war between the leagues and the animosity festered. He undoubtedly got to Bell and had him conveniently create a "policy" that would freeze Embry out of the picture. Livie didn't expect to be included but was invited and accepted. They all shook hands and walked away with a deal. The Colts were ready to play again.

The terms specified that Rosenbloom would get 51 percent of ownership with the other 49 percent to be shared by Hilgenberg, Mullan, Krieger, and Livie. Purchase price of the franchise was announced at $200,000 with $25,000 to be paid immediately.

It's likely that all the money came from the ticket receipts, not from the pockets of Rosenbloom and his new-found partners. Rosenbloom put up $13,000 and the other four minority partners contributed $3,000 each, making a total of $25,000. When I wrote an earlier book, *The Baltimore Colts Story*, Rosenbloom questioned why I used the figures, but never questioned their accuracy. This indicated to me that he was unhappy over the disclosure that his financial part had been so minuscule; because public belief then, as it is now, was that it took an immense investment to buy into football. To this day the funding of the Colts in 1953 remains one of the most spectacular buys in the history of sports, right next to Tim Mara buying an NFL franchise for New York for $500 in 1925.

The unpaid $100,000 still owed Marshall for territorial invasion was not paid directly to him but to the league, which handed off to George on an end-around. This meant the Colts could say they weren't paying

Marshall anything. True. They were merely giving it to the league office as a go-between and, in turn, Marshall was being paid "out the back door." The Colts' other payments to the league, similar to a mortgage, were spread over eight years, but Baltimore's cash flow was so healthy it paid off the entire indebtedness after only three seasons.

Hilgenberg said the Rosenbloom charm won them over when the former directors met him for the first time. "We walked up to Rosenbloom's house and he met us at the door in his shirtsleeves. Instead of acting the part of a 'big-shot,' he was very much a down-to-earth type of fellow, the kind of man we all liked right away." But as the years went by they didn't continue to hold to that belief. He was slick, featuring a soft-sounding voice that almost sang a song when he talked.

Bell had completed one part of his agreement in finding the owner. Now he needed a general manager and a coach. He picked a winner in Don Kellett, who had captained three sports at Penn and was a graduate of the Wharton School of Finance. Kellett was signed off the campus, after graduation, by the Boston Red Sox in the depression year of 1934 for a $5,000 bonus. He played briefly in the majors, going hitless in nine games, and spent time in the minors before turning to coaching at Ursinus and then at his alma mater. This ultimately led to a position as general manager of WFIL radio in Philadelphia and then the TV station owned by the same company. So, from a background standpoint, Kellett had it all—an athlete, he also understood the complexities of finance, had coached, knew the broadcasting industry, and had executive ability.

Kellett came to Bell's attention when the Texans were homeless, and Kellett called on him with an innovative idea. He wanted Bell to let him take over the Texans and use them as a team for television. They would be renamed the All-Americans and play in a different nonleague city each Saturday night for a game that would be presented nationally on the then-Dumont network. It sounded good to Bell but he told Kellett his desire was for the Texans to go to Baltimore, where they would, of course, play under a new name. But the Kellett idea had merit and still does.

For a Baltimore coach, Bell came up with a former National Football League halfback in Keith Molesworth, who had played for the Chicago Bears in the era of Bronko Nagurski. Helping make it a natural fit was the fact Molesworth had played the infield for the Baltimore Orioles of the International League and also had coached three sports at the Naval Academy. He was well liked and certainly not a stranger to Baltimore. By coincidence, Molesworth and Kellett had been the double-play combination when both were with the Syracuse Chiefs, also of the International League.

Kellett, in coming to Baltimore, walked into a difficult position. When they first met him the players weren't sure they liked what they heard. Kellett referred to the Texans as malcontents, which was an erroneous assessment. But Kellett wasn't talking from experience. At that early juncture, he didn't know the players on a personal basis. He leaned heavily on Bell for advice in the early going. When he wasn't certain which direction to go, or how to handle a problem, he called Bell to avail himself of the commissioner's counseling. Kellett also had to open a Baltimore office, hire a staff, prepare for the draft, sign players, and make training camp preparations. He also lost the first-round draft choice, Heisman Trophy winner Billy Vessels of Oklahoma to the Edmonton Eskimos of the Canadian Football League and the second pick, Bernie Flowers of Purdue. He, too, ignored the Colts and went to Canada, signing with the Ottawa Rough Riders.

It wasn't what could be termed a spectacular beginning for the new franchise. Memorial Stadium was in the throes of being rebuilt and the Colts were actually playing there while the work progressed. Capacities increased for every game as the contractors added new seats each week. A visit by the Detroit Lions was said to be sold out on three different occasions. Even then, more seats were found, in of all places, the men's room, which was being used for storage. Tickets for these seats also went on sale.

There was a chance the Colts could have had another name going into their year of rebirth. A meeting of the Colts' directors was held at the Gunther Brewery Tap Room, which was open for neighborhood and civic gatherings, and the idea was introduced that maybe what Baltimore needed was a new name to go with its new start. That was nonsense. I was just a kid, maybe the youngest in the room, but I raised my hand rather tentatively and was recognized. Although not sure of myself when it came to speaking in public, I reminded the men what the NFL had done to Baltimore and that to put another name on the team coming in would be eradicating the past and giving in to a silly idea that was only in the interest of the league clearing its conscience. My counterpart, Jim Ellis, of *The Evening Sun*, added, "I agree 100 percent." The Colts' directors were impressed and said, after looking at the issue from that angle, the name would remain the same.

For their first season the Colts went 3 and 9. Two victories came against Molesworth's old coach and team, Halas and the Bears; the other at the expense of the Washington Redskins. The Colts opened at home, feeding off the enthusiasm of the crowd, and shocked the Bears, thanks to an immense performance by Bert Rechichar, who even kicked a record 56-yard field goal in his first attempt. He had gone to the

University of Tennessee and had never been given a chance to kick. Actually, it was an afterthought that he was called on in Baltimore. With only seconds left in the first half, he came off the field as regular kicking specialist Buck McPhail lined up from fifty-six yards away.

At that moment assistant coach Otis Douglas remembered that Rechichar had a powerful leg and hollered for him to go in after he had made an early start for the locker room. Bert turned around and bluntly answered, "What the —— do you want?" Getting the hurry-up sign from Douglas, he ran onto the field to replace McPhail. The kick, with Ken Jackson snapping and Tom Keane holding, traveled on a low line and sailed not only over the cross bar but out of the end zone. The Colts' second victory over the Bears, another thriller, and a surprise, came in Chicago as Buddy Young made a jumping catch of a Fred Eke pass for a touchdown that was a classic reception. At that moment the Colts were three-for-three against the Bears, going back to the previous season when they upset them as the woeful Dallas Texans.

Kellett, after first appearing to be difficult, modified his relationships with the players as the season wore on and became extremely popular. Actually, it was Hilgenberg who got to him and said he felt it necessary that he project a more friendly presence. Hilgenberg, no doubt, was alerted to Kellett's early aloofness by Dick Barwegen, a Colt guard, whom Hilgenberg had assisted in helping open a seafood supply outlet—the same kind of wholesale business Hilgenberg had been in for years.

For players, Kellett was always eager to trade. His involvement in one deal remains the largest in NFL history, a ten-for-five swap with the Browns. General manager-coach Paul Brown came to Baltimore to hammer out the details. The trade that had involved so many players, a blockbuster, helped both Baltimore and Cleveland. Baltimore gave up tackle Don Colo of Brown University, linebacker Tom Catlin of Oklahoma, guard Herschel Forester of Baylor, tackle Mike McCormack of Kansas (a future Hall of Fame lineman, later to be head coach of the Colts), and halfback John Petitbon of Notre Dame. The players coming to Baltimore were end Art Spinney of Boston College, guard Ed Sharkey of Duke, end Gern Nagler of Santa Clara, tackle Stu Sheets of Penn State, guard Elmer Willhoite of Southern California, tackle Dick Batten of College of Pacific, halfbacks Don Shula and Carl Taseff of John Carroll, and Rechichar of Tennessee. Also included in the deal were negotiating rights to quarterback Harry Agganis of Boston University, who had signed as a bonus first baseman with the Boston Red Sox.

The Colts would talk with Agganis every few months. In fact, it was one of my assignments with the Colts, to meet him when he came to

Baltimore. The idea was to keep reminding him, in a subtle way, that pro football was an option if he became discouraged in baseball. Before anything substantial developed, Agganis was stricken with pneumonia and died in the summer of 1955 at age twenty-six.

As for Molesworth, believe it or not, he was almost fired before he opened the season, which would have been a monumental disgrace. To even think about it showed how little Kellett and Rosenbloom knew about running a team at that early stage. They were merely becoming acclimated. Kellett was disenchanted with Molesworth's coaching, but he was dead wrong. The team was showing progress and Baltimore was schooled in patience. No miracles were expected. While the team was practicing in Hershey, Pennsylvania, after playing out the exhibition schedule, Rosenbloom, because of Kellett's negative opinion of Molesworth, was ready to let him go. It was a case of an owner and general manager, both new to the game, acting without reason or foresight.

The Sunpapers didn't bother to have reporters in Hershey so I had the story to myself. There was not the slightest indication on radio or in any newspaper that a firing was imminent but it almost happened. I wrote and filed the story overnight from Hershey that Molesworth was about to be terminated. The next morning, when Pippen and his assistant, Art Janney, read the copy they were astounded. How could this be? Pippen decided to call Hilgenberg and read him the story. It was then that Hilgenberg asked that it not be used.

Pippen called me from the office and explained what had happened. Hilgenberg also phoned and apologized for helping to kill the story. Neither man denied that it could take place but felt, as I did, that it was the wrong thing to do at that time—before the Colts even played a regular game.

Later in the day, Kellett and Rosenbloom asked me to meet with them. I walked from the Community Inn where I was staying with the coaches and players to the Hershey Hotel where Kellett was already in the living room of Rosenbloom's suite. They wanted to know if I had any thoughts on what could be done to improve the situation. It was no secret that the coaching staff wasn't pulling in the same direction but that wasn't Molesworth's fault. I told the owner and general manager that from my viewpoint the situation wasn't that difficult. All that needed to be done to create harmony was to divide some of the responsibilities among the assistants. Define what they had to do and tell them what was expected, meaning assistant coaches Ray Richards, Nick Wasylik, and Otis Douglas, who also functioned as the team trainer to save a salary. That's precisely the way it worked out.

Kellett was at first embarrassed, then relieved. Rosenbloom later said he was grateful for the suggestion and admitted that had he acted in haste it would have been a mistake, since the Colts didn't figure, under any circumstance, to make a run at the divisional title. The coach, even if his name was Rockne, wasn't going to be that important to the Colts of 1953. The Colts, since they replaced Dallas, were assigned to the Western Division.

It was all rather incongruous that a team as far east as Baltimore was playing western opponents. The Colts were using some of the Texans' practice equipment and also their traveling trunks, plus adopting their blue, silver, and white colors. To make use of the heavy winter sideline capes, and in the interest of economy, they had a tailor stitch a patch over the Texas' name to make it read Colts. They wore them for years.

The NFL wasn't always as affluent as it is now.

Rosenbloom admitted he had never seen the old Colts play so this was a new experience; he really was a rookie owner feeling his way. He wanted to win and in the second game of the season, with the Colts leading the Detroit Lions, he visited the locker room and said there would be an extra $300 for each player if they won. The obvious question: was he betting? I don't know. At the time, he didn't realize such offers were against league rules. Alex Agase, a linebacker and later a head coach at Northwestern and Purdue, said the suggestion of a bonus didn't cause any undue pressure. "Sure we were amazed an owner would make such an offer but we wanted to beat the Lions before Carroll appeared in the locker room. The way we looked at it was that if we couldn't finish the job on the Lions then we didn't deserve to win or get extra money. The money had nothing to do with Yale Lary running that kick back on us for a score which opened the gates."

Late in the season, as a nice touch, Rosenbloom had one of his factories design casual coats for the players, coaches, and newspapermen to wear when traveling. Then at Christmastime, each coach and player received a $500 check from management.

After the season, Rosenbloom made a key move. He said Molesworth would become head of scouting and personnel, where the Colts were totally lacking. This meant a new coach had to be found. Possible candidates were Eddie Erdelatz of Navy, Buck Shaw and Red Strader of the 49ers, and Steve Owen of the Giants. First choice was Blanton Collier, long-time assistant of the Cleveland Browns, and for a time, it appeared Collier was Baltimore-bound. Then he asked to be dropped from consideration.

Collier had a reputation for being the best defensive teacher in the game and held a strong allegiance to Paul Brown, who signed him at Great Lakes Naval Station after seeing this lonely sailor peering through the fence watching the Bluejacket team at practice. It turned out that

Collier had been a high school coach in Kentucky and was an astute student of the game. That casual meeting with Brown at Great Lakes led to Collier's going to Cleveland with him when the war was over. Strangely enough, a month later, after pulling out of talks with the Colts, Collier became head coach at the University of Kentucky, a move that Brown no doubt approved. Meanwhile, one of the owners of the Browns, club president Dave Jones, got word to Rosenbloom that another Browns assistant he had probably never heard about, one Wilbur Ewbank, would make a better choice than Collier.

Rosenbloom became interested. Ewbank was nicknamed "Weeb" because a baby brother couldn't pronounce Wilbur. Odd, but the only one I ever heard call him Wilbur was Brown, who was visibly and vocally upset with Ewbank when he left for Baltimore. At the Senior Bowl in Mobile, Brown said Ewbank showed up late for the all-star game, well after it started. Brown was head coach of one of the teams and Ewbank was there as an assistant. For a coach to show up after the game has begun, except in a family emergency, just never happened. "I've been talking to Don Kellett about the Baltimore job," Brown quoted Ewbank as telling him right there on the sidelines after he asked him to explain his tardiness.

For Ewbank to leave the Browns' staff—at least to Brown—was tantamount to violating a sacred trust. He figured he gave assistant coaches a chance to be a part of a great organization and he didn't want them taking his system someplace else and making it work for a team the Browns were going to have to play. Ewbank, in a matter of weeks, was hired in Baltimore, much to the continuing consternation of Brown. Since Weeb handled the draft for the Browns, amassing all the information compiled from scouting reports and then grading it, Brown insisted the new Colts' coach not be allowed to have input into the Baltimore drafting. But he did. On the sly.

The Colts made choices they otherwise wouldn't have made. Ewbank even had a courier carrying notes to Molesworth, leaking information, as the draft slowly proceeded through its ponderous thirty rounds with all twelve teams taking part. Even though Ewbank wasn't calling all the shots on what players the Colts should take, he was most assuredly influencing the selections. His appointment as Colts' coach was to last nine years, before giving way to Don Shula. Ewbank duplicated the way the Browns had operated, instituted classroom sessions before every on-field workout, and graded each play in every game on a 1-to-5 point system.

Players such as Taseff, Rechichar, Donovan, Pellington, and Shula, all former Browns, said training camp procedures and the review and grading of game films were exactly what they knew under Brown. So was the playbook. Ewbank, strong-willed but yielding at times, knew what he wanted and got it. He mentioned to some players that if they didn't want to conform, "we'll put up with you for a period of time, or until we can get something better." Rechichar muttered, "Listen, Weeb, I knew you when you used to hold kicks for Lou Groza in practice." Ewbank, intent on details, found that the Colts' blue helmet didn't lend itself to sharp visibility on films, when the coaches and players reviewed them, so he changed to a white headgear. The addition of a horseshoe design on the side of the helmets was the suggestion of Sam Banks, the team's public relations director in 1953 and 1954. Baltimore, thus, followed the Rams and Eagles with logos on their headgear. The horseshoe was distinctive and supplanted the original logo of a horse jumping over the goalpost. A Baltimore first had to do with the formation of a cheerleading unit. Other teams had probably tried it but in 1954, at the suggestion of Thelma Mack, twelve young ladies, paying for their own uniforms, became the first successful cheerleading squad in all of football—long before the Dallas Cowboys were even organized as a franchise.

In the early stages of the Colts' return to Baltimore, Rosenbloom functioned as a game-day fan rather than as a club official. Kellett was making most of the decisions and he ran a tight ship. He kept the office staff at a minimum, and I once heard him say, "I don't believe in too many people having assistants. When that happens nothing gets done."

Kellett was an exceptional administrator, something his secretary, Margaret Madigan Banks, could attest to in the way he established his daily schedule of office procedures. He had a system of follow-up files for just about every matter of business so little was left to chance, even something like supplying an autographed football for a father-son banquet. As the Colts began to show progress, it became apparent that Rosenbloom was going to be taking a more active part. It's possible, too, that Kellett was gaining too much notoriety and popularity to please Rosenbloom.

Being human, Rosenbloom wanted some of the credit, but since he wasn't around that often the feeling among the masses was that he was an absentee owner. Suddenly, he began to have a stronger identity with the team. He was still spending most of his time in New York, Margate, and Palm Beach. Ewbank once asked him if he had any reservations about drafting "name" players, to which Rosenbloom told him, "Listen, Weeb, I don't care how much they cost. Your job is to win. Get the men you want."

After Baltimore's first year back in the NFL, which was a moneymaker, Kellett was in position to exercise an option to get a 25 percent share of the profits, which in some ways explained to the players why he was keeping a close watch on expenses. His other option was to take stock in the corporation. Kellett preferred the stock, but passed up the consideration after listening to Rosenbloom convince him that he shouldn't do it.

Rosenbloom said if Kellett accepted the stock plan then he'd possibly become a rival of his in percentage of ownership. "I let Carroll talk me into something I shouldn't have let happen," Kellett said later. "He told me, 'Don, you know as long as I'm here you are going to be taken care of.' My mother was to tell me later that of all the decisions I ever made she disagreed with that more than anything I had ever done." Kellett lived to regret it, saying on numerous occasions, "I never should have let Carroll soft-talk me out of the chance to own a piece of the team."

Kellett and Rosenbloom got along but had moments when things were anything but amicable. While I worked for both men, I was once ordered by Rosenbloom to accompany Kellett to a meeting in New York. We had no idea what awaited. But Rosenbloom launched into a denunciation of Kellett and humiliated him in front of me. It was not a pleasant morning. Coming back on the afternoon train, Kellett kept saying, "Can you believe what we just heard." It was as if Carroll was trying to embarrass him. If so, he succeeded. It was painful to see Kellett put so much importance on what had been said, which I remember as a trivial matter.

There was no questioning Kellett's vast capabilities and his loyalty. He was, by any measuring stick, an outstanding general manager, maybe one of the most competent any sport has ever known. He watched over the team budget, established a good rapport with the players and press, was a superb after-dinner speaker, and a consummate gentleman. He worked at his job, frequently cleaning up the business at hand by noon and, especially in spring and early summer, going to Baltimore Country Club to play golf. But there were times when Rosenbloom would stop speaking to Kellett and for days, or even weeks, would circumvent the general manager by telling me to do things that were in the province of Kellett.

Once, when the team was in San Francisco to play the 49ers over Thanksgiving, a dinner was arranged for the team and the entire traveling party. Rosenbloom ordered business manager Ben Small to make all the preparations but to make sure Kellett wasn't invited. So Kellett, Chuck Thompson, and Bob Robertson went out to eat on their own, while the rest of the team, plus newspapermen and broadcasters, were treated to a Thanksgiving extravaganza hosted by the club. I later hailed a cab and searched for restaurants in downtown San Francisco that were open. I soon found the "uninvited" Kellett and had dinner with him, Thompson, and Robertson. For a holiday like Thanksgiving it was difficult enough to be away from the family, but Rosenbloom showed Kellett a new way to be hurt and humiliated.

"I have no idea what I have done to offend him," Kellett would say. Actually, it was probably nothing more than getting his picture in the newspaper once too often. Then, almost as quickly as Rosenbloom shut him off, communication would resume and things would return to normal until the next time Rosenbloom became disenchanted for reasons known only to himself. It was a side of working for the Colts I didn't like and wondered if similar things went on in other organizations. When I was hired away from the newspaper to the Colts organization, Rosenbloom and Kellett kept telling me I was being groomed to become the general manager. I'm sure that was their intent. They knew I didn't leave the newspaper to become a career assistant general manager and publicity director. But, after making the change, I wasn't sure that's what I wanted to do.

Kellett often said if the Steelers wanted to get organized that "Arthur (meaning Rooney) ought to hire you to straighten them out." That wasn't necessarily true but it was nice to hear and even if such a possibility had come to pass, I doubt I would have agreed to go, although working for Rooney would have indeed been one of the true pleasures of life, as anyone familiar with the man would admit. On more than one occasion, Kellett, who rarely used profanity, said, "John, as soon as I get these girls [meaning his two daughters] through school, I'm going to tell off that dirty SOB." But he never did.

When the youngest, Dee, graduated from college, I reminded him that now he had the chance to assert himself and fulfill his oft-repeated threat to leave Rosenbloom. But, again, he backed away. Money has a powerful way of talking because Kellett, no doubt, wanted to protect his well-paid position, even if it was a hellish existence at times. He just wasn't about to challenge the owner because he realized what the outcome would be. Another time, talking about Rosenbloom, Kellett said, "He's the greatest prevaricator I have ever known. If he's caught in a lie and backed into a corner, he'll tell another lie to escape."

When it came time to make trades or sign free agents, even those cut from other clubs, Kellett would consult with Ewbank and Molesworth. The meetings were never prolonged; he would just ask do you want this halfback or not. Kellett was quick to move after he sounded out the other two. In 1953, he had acquired Fred Enke and John "Hurricane" Huzvar from the Eagles for the $100 waiver price. Bert Bell was taking such an interest in the Colts that some of his friends in the league were facetiously referring to the team as "Bell's Colts" and even told that to the commissioner. He no doubt was helping them all he could but within the constraints of his job. It was the belief of other teams in the league that he wanted the Colts to do well and was favoring them when he could.

In 1953, Kellett, apart from the 10-for-5 trade with the Browns, which provided instant help, made other moves. He dealt guard Bill Lange for tackle-end Don Joyce of the Chicago Cardinals; receiver Ray (Wrong Way) Pelfrey to the New York Giants for tackle Tom Finnin; and a tenth-round draft pick to the Los Angeles Rams for quarterback Gary Kerkorian, later a judge in Northern California. In signing mere names off waiver lists, he came up with John Unitas, Bill Pellington, Buzz Nutter, and Milt Davis. As other free agents he signed Doug Eggers, Bob Langas, and Royce Womble.

With Davis, the Colts broke a gentleman's agreement in the league by signing him away from the Detroit Lions. Davis had been on the Lions' "band" or "taxi" squad, meaning he was a player who practiced with the team and received a weekly wage but wasn't signed to a contract. Kellett swooped in and snagged him. Later the Lions paid back the Colts by snatching a similar practice player off their bench, in midseason, another defensive back, Dick LeBeau. The Lions had played a game in Baltimore but when they left to go home took LeBeau with them on the plane, much to the chagrin of the Colts.

Some trades went awry, such as giving up a fourth-round pick for Jim Winkler of the Rams. When he arrived they found he had both physical and mental problems and before a game against the Rams, the team that turned him away, he said he didn't want to play. Why not? "I don't want to hurt any of my old buddies," he answered. The Colts gave a similar pick, a fourth-round choice, to the Green Bay Packers for quarterback Dick Flowers. Another bad move on a player came in 1957, a year the Colts might well have won the division, when they took a defensive back named Henry Moore from the Giants, again for a fourth-round choice, and released Don Shula to accommodate Moore's arrival.

Moore missed a coverage against the Packers in a game they lost. Had they won, Baltimore would have earned the divisional crown in 1957. The veteran Colts were saying if they had kept Shula, he never would have gotten confused in that type of a defense. Maybe beaten on a play, as happens to every defender, but certainly not to "blow" the coverage by being so completely out of position.

Rosenbloom was creating a reputation as a "player's owner." He was giving team members extra money at the end of the season, much to the annoyance of other clubs; this made it especially difficult for those owners who were struggling to pay their bills.

When the subject of a players' union surfaced in the early 1950s, the owners acted as if they wanted to go off and hide. One of the first organizers was Creighton Miller, a former Notre Dame All-American and a Cleveland lawyer. In fact, Miller was the first general manager of the Browns and he signed Paul Brown to a contract to coach the new team of the proposed All-America Football Conference. Miller also was an assistant coach for the Browns in 1946, and therein is an interesting tale that reflects on the bitterness Brown could demonstrate when he held an opposite view.

When Miller was attempting to get the players' union, or association, started, Brown took the 1946 team picture off the wall of his office and sent it out to be "doctored." He had Miller "air-brushed" out of the photograph, as if he had never existed. Miller, in the photo, truly became an invisible man. Brown was vehemently opposed to the union in any shape or form, the same as he was to agents. He resented any condition or influence that could come between the coach and the player, one that might challenge or lessen his authority.

In my three years with the Colts, 1955–57, vital years in the growth of the franchise, I attended all league meetings and represented the team in executive sessions with Rosenbloom and Kellett. I watched and listened—intently. Brown and George Preston Marshall of the Redskins were lined up against the union. But Edwin Anderson of the Lions, Art Rooney of the Steelers, and Rosenbloom were advocates who believed a union's time had come.

"Look, I'm from a union town [Pittsburgh]," Rooney said, "and you have to accept the fact they are going to be in football." Rosenbloom delivered a spellbinding speech, telling the other owners he found in his various businesses that unions could be beneficial to the employer as well as the employee and they, meaning the NFL, might just as well get ready to accept them at some future date.

Vital to the success the Colts were to enjoy, which made them a contending team, was the 1955 player draft. It was their best ever. The Colts weren't spending much money on scouting reports, certainly nothing comparable to the Rams. Some clubs would draft out of the Street & Smith preseason football magazine. The majority of the teams, the Colts included, hired an assistant coach in most major college conferences to give them a list of players who impressed them—on their own squad and for the opposition. For this annual report, they were paid $50. Molesworth suggested that Rosenbloom's company also supply the scouts with gift sport shirts and that was done.

When the Colts concluded their 1954 season, a road game in Los Angeles, Kellett thought it would be a positive idea if the team had a representative stay on the West Coast to scout the East-West game and the Rose Bowl. This would mean, he said, that one of the assistants wouldn't get to come home for Christmas and New Year's. The Colts' only coaching bachelor, Joe Thomas, said he was willing to stay to cover the practices of the college teams. It became one of the most profitable moves for the Colts, as belated as it was. Meanwhile, in Baltimore, Ewbank and Molesworth were putting together the vast amount of information they had received in written reports. The organization didn't own a computer then, nor did any other team.

They also conducted mock drafts in the Baltimore office, trying to evaluate how the players might be taken. Heading for the draft meeting in New York, the Colts, having first choice, were dismayed to learn that the player they wanted to take, quarterback Bobby Freeman of Auburn, had signed with the Winnipeg Blue Bombers of the Canadian League. They next focused on linebacker Larry Morris of Georgia Tech. He was going to be their choice now that Freeman had signed elsewhere. But the night before, in a session held in Rosenbloom's suite, Thomas pleaded that since the Colts needed offensive help they should take either fullback Alan "The Horse" Ameche of Wisconsin or one of two quarterbacks: George Shaw of Oregon or Ralph Guglielmi of Notre Dame. By being true to himself and the team, Thomas changed the line of thinking. Later that night, when we talked, Thomas said, "I may have put myself in a bad position. I don't know if Weeb liked the way I spoke out. Assistant coaches aren't supposed to do that." But what Thomas suggested in revising their plan was exactly the way the Colts reacted when the draft got under way the next morning.

The first player taken, preceding the draft proper, was called the "bonus choice." This was a gimmick suggested by Halas and adopted, years before, to give teams that were consistent contenders a chance to get a "name" player, since the routine of the draft had been created by Bell on the premise that the weak teams drew first and the stronger clubs came later. Once a team won the "bonus choice," it was eliminated from future grab-bag selections. Baltimore won the "bonus choice" and got the first two players in the 1955 draft. The Colts took Shaw as the "bonus" and then followed with Ameche as their first choice. Whether the reach into the hat and pulling out the name of a team was truly dependent on the luck of the draw is difficult to judge. But I wonder.

Years later, Fred Schubach, Jr., who as a high school kid worked for the Eagles, then came to the Colts as equipment manager, and later was promoted to personnel director under Thomas, said that in 1949 it was a foregone conclusion the Eagles were going to get Chuck Bednarik, one of the great talents to come out of any draft. The war with the AAFC was on at the time and Bednarik played at Penn, in Philadelphia, an NFL city. It would be to the league's advantage if Bednarik was the bonus choice and got picked by the Eagles. Schubach remembers that two days before the draft the attitude in the Eagles' office, where he worked after school clipping stories on prospects from newspapers and magazines, turned to one of complete confidence. Yes, Bednarik was going to be an Eagle. Maybe the slip with the Eagles' name on it had a different kind of a "feel" than all the others and it was merely a question of searching for the right one before pulling it out of the hat. It's an interesting premise.

If this actually happened with the Eagles, could the same thing have transpired six years later to benefit the Colts, a team that was struggling to get to the top? Rosenbloom thoroughly enjoyed beating the system and its rules. What couldn't be denied was that the Colts had Shaw and Ameche. Both became immediate standouts, Ameche leading in ground gaining and Shaw finishing as runner-up to his teammate in "rookie of the year" voting. The 49ers offered ten players for Shaw; the Lions would have given six proven veterans for Ameche but the Colts weren't even tempted. The draft, down the line, was a bonanza for Baltimore. Coming in the same year of selection were halfback L. G. "Long Gone" Dupre of Baylor, center Dick Szymanski of Notre Dame, and tackles George Preas of VPI and Jack Patera of Oregon. It was rather unbelievable, but twelve rookies from the draft made the 1955 team, an assemblage of young talent that would carry the Colts to high places.

Baltimore got lucky in 1956 when it claimed Eugene "Big Daddy" Lipscomb. Again, there might have been an assist from Bell in the league office. The Rams put Lipscomb on waivers over the Labor Day weekend. He could be had for the $100 fee. The 49ers, with the poorest record from the previous season, had first claim on any player on waivers. Baltimore was second in line behind the 49ers. In making known their desire to have Lipscomb, the 49ers, as usual, sent a telegram to the league office. Because of the holiday the wire wasn't delivered until two days later. The Colts, meanwhile, had telephoned Bell to register a similar claim. Bell ruled Lipscomb belonged to Baltimore because he got its notification before word from the 49ers had arrived.

The 49ers complained and then let the matter drop. They weren't about to argue over a waiver claim, even if the player in question was the massive Lipscomb, who at 6-foot-6, 282 pounds, with foot speed, had extraordinary potential, even though he never had an opportunity to attend college. Lipscomb, actually, was signed by Pete Rozelle, when he was working for the Rams as a publicity director in 1953. Rozelle always spent part of the off-season visiting military bases looking for free agents. He came up with a winner in "Big Daddy."

In Baltimore, under Kellett, the Colts were busy shaping their image. They rarely made a mistake in the public relations area. When problems arose, they would ask themselves what was the best way to handle it to minimize criticism. Rosenbloom, however, blundered in 1958. After a lavish off-season press party at the Belvedere Hotel, he decided to announce that he was going to ignore the Naval Academy's long-held agreement with the Park Board that prohibited a team from playing five days before a Navy game or one day after. It was Navy's way of assuring that nothing could detract from its event. Navy's practice of playing in Baltimore preceded the arrival of the Colts by almost twenty-five years. But Rosenbloom announced his home schedule and, for the first time, there was a conflict with the Navy agreement.

Paul Menton of the *Evening Sun* wrote that what Rosenbloom had done was in bad taste. He had made the announcement while members of the Park Board, including its esteemed president, James Anderson, were enjoying the Colts' hospitality at the party. It was something they didn't expect. They had been lulled into an evening of enjoyment and then, boom, Rosenbloom hit them between the eyes with his message. The next day, Menton, who had strong ties to college football, described what happened and was mildly critical of Rosenbloom. That afternoon, with the evening papers on the street, I visited Carroll's suite at the Belvedere. He was visibly upset that Menton had ridiculed him.

Later Rosenbloom and Menton had a meeting, became good friends, and agreed upon a regular payoff of money that would go to Menton and Linthicum. They would be paid to keep their criticisms, if they had any, to themselves. The public had no idea what was going on. Neither did many of the rival newspapermen and other reporters who worked at *The Sun*. Rosenbloom had defused any potential knocks from two of the city's sports editors by getting Menton and Linthicum to sell themselves for a price. In that era, it was not unusual for sports editors to be "on the take," an earlier version of the practice disc jockeys had of accepting money to play certain records. Then it was called payola. The practice among Baltimore sports writers went out with the changing of the guard when Bill Tanton replaced Menton and Bob Maisel succeeded Linthicum.

Pippen wasn't included in the payoff, which was surprising, but, when he retired two years later, Rosenbloom asked me what the Colts could do for him. I said I thought any kind of a gift, be it golf clubs or whatever, would be appreciated by a veteran of more than fifty years of writing sports in Baltimore. A way to show him gratitude for past favors. I accompanied Rosenbloom to Pippen's house on Winterbourne Road, one Saturday afternoon, and Rosenbloom gave Pippin a check for $2,500 or $3,000, I'm not sure which.

I told myself that paying Pippen was different than what was going on with the other two sports editors since he was entering retirement. I was to follow Pippen, certainly not succeed him, as the new sports editor of the paper Pippen was leaving, the *News-Post* and *Sunday American*.

Rosenbloom was recovering from the flu and resting at his residence on Slade Avenue in Pikesville, when I went to tell him I was returning to the newspaper. He was gracious. "Are you sure this is what you want to do?" he asked. "Absolutely," was the answer I gave him. "Johnny, I just want you to do me one favor." "Yes, Carroll, what's that?" "Don't ever lose your individuality." At the time, I didn't know what he meant. He was also kind enough to say if I became disillusioned after going back to the paper that I could rejoin the Colts at any time. But I couldn't get it out of my mind that paying Menton and Linthicum was wrong, unethical, and something the Orioles would never have done. Rosenbloom had previously convinced me I should stay with the Colts when McCormick & Company called to offer the position of public relations director. This time, with the newspaper beckoning, he knew there was no way I was going to change my mind. I'd be going back to work with Frank Cashen, the man who had gotten me there when I came out of high school; Art Janney, Charlie Lamb, Don Frederick, Neal Eskridge, John Hall, Harry Feldner, Walter Penkilo, George Taylor, Hugh Trader the "Swami," and others.

Working on a newspaper had an appeal all its own and I signed a contract with the publisher, Fred I. Archibald, without even looking at the financial terms. I told him, "Pay me what you want." I was going from the Colts but would still be in the press box watching them play. Friends were surprised I made such a move. What they didn't know was that when you work for a team, at least one owned by Rosenbloom, too often you were expected to compromise yourself. It wasn't quite the fun and games the public believed it to be.

CHAPTER 10

# ECSTASY

There's a belief in sports, maybe a truism, that a team doesn't win a championship the first time it's in position to make the breakthrough. A close miss often portends success for the future, maybe even as imminent as the upcoming season. The Colts followed such a formula.

In 1957, they went to the last week of the schedule before they were eliminated. It was in San Francisco, with two games to play, that the 49ers tripped the Colts, 17–13, and all but took them out of the race.

The Colts contended a questionable offensive pass interference ruling that wasn't called against the 49ers decided the outcome. The result was painful to accept. Ewbank insisted Hugh McElhenny, after running his pass route, pushed off on Milt Davis, which allowed him to come open. John Brodie, a rookie coming in cold to take over for an injured Y. A. Tittle, threw to McElhenny in the end zone. Touchdown San Francisco. Victory San Francisco. A bitter loss for the Colts amid a sellout crowd in Kezar Stadium that was so exuberant that mounted police had to be summoned before the game to prevent a riot.

Fans responded in near-record numbers (59,696) and some of them were even shaking the ticket booths outside the stadium . . . with the ticket sellers bouncing around inside. Late in the game, with Baltimore protecting a three-point lead, Brodie reacted to the emergency at quarterback and, under heated pressure from the Colts' defensive line, threw to McElhenny. As he went down, Donovan is supposed to have told him in something more than a whisper, "You SOB, you just picked my pocket," meaning the chance to go to the championship game and earn extra money.

Years later, at a Super Bowl golf tournament in Pasadena, within sight of the Rose Bowl, while I was playing in the same foursome with McElhenny, he insisted Davis bumped him rather than the way the Colts said it happened. Films were inconclusive. What McElhenny related on the golf course is something I had never heard before. When the jubilant 49ers reached their locker room, the players voted both Brodie and McElhenny the "game ball." Usually, in such situations, a ball is given to each player to carry home but the team equipment manager, on that special occasion, gave the ritual an entirely different treatment. He took the game-winning football, sliced it in half and mounted equal portions for both on a plaque—the passer, Brodie, and the receiver, McElhenny.

The Colts, after the disappointment of San Francisco, still had a slight chance in the season finale to force a divisional tie but collapsed under the charge of the Los Angeles Rams and the passing of Norm Van Brocklin, who threw for four touchdowns. The Colts didn't play well. The season was over. And it was a long ride home from Los Angeles. The processing of tickets by Herb Wright and Ray Gilland for a possible playoff in Baltimore ended when the final result, 37–21, was posted.

Unitas, after throwing twenty-five scoring passes in his first full season, was voted the Jim Thorpe Memorial Trophy as the best player in the league. Kellett said to me, "I think you ought to go to New York with him. It's an important award. John might not be able to find his way around Manhattan. Make sure he knows where the TV studio is; it's not easy to find."

On the train trip (up and back in one day) Unitas said he remembered the first time he visited New York. Then he was a young stranger in town walking along Broadway looking at the tall buildings. Now, so suddenly, he was an exciting new name on the sports stage. His only previous trip to New York had been when the University of Louisville, his old school, was playing in the National Invitational Basketball Tournament at Madison Square Garden in 1954, and he rode in a friend's car to New York with only small change in his pocket, and slept on the floor of a hotel room that another Louisville student had rented. In 1957 Unitas had made a spectacular impression in his first full season as a regular quarterback. Management fondly contemplated his future and theirs, too.

In 1958, they would have the chance to make another run for a championship. Unitas was no longer an unknown. This time they wouldn't miss and, in the process, would write an unprecedented chapter in the annals of NFL history.

For the Colts, it was a hard road to get there—to Yankee Stadium on December 28, 1958—for the title showdown with the Giants, epic moments that have lived on in football history and will continue to do so because of their momentous impact. The Colts had beaten the Giants with ease in two preseason games, or exhibitions, and lost by a dropped touchdown pass during the regular season, 24–21. The loss, in New

York, came with Unitas watching on television in Baltimore's Union Memorial Hospital, where he was recovering from a punctured lung and three broken ribs suffered against Green Bay the week before. Unitas had been on the ground, the play virtually over, when defensive back John Symank of the Packers hit him, in kind of a "raking" action.

The game itself was a runaway, Baltimore winning, 56–0, against a totally inept Packer team. But now the Colts were confronted with the loss of their regular quarterback in the middle of the season. The injury to Unitas gave Shaw an opportunity to work the entire second half against the Packers, a chance to come back and play. With two road games ahead, Shaw provided what all teams need from a backup quarterback. In Chicago, where he had suffered a serious knee injury that opened the door of opportunity for Unitas to play in 1956, Shaw produced a creditable performance. He was returning to the same field, where his career almost ended only two years before on a clean-hit tackle by Fred Williams of the Bears. This time the Colts and Shaw put together a well-executed 17–0 win, the first time the Bears had been shut out at Wrigley Field in 149 consecutive games, going back to 1946.

The New York effort, the week before, following the Packer rout, could have been a victory, too. Shaw, starting for the first time since he had been knocked out of the lineup, passed for all three Baltimore scores and had another near-certain TD toss dropped in the end zone by Lenny Lyles. The scoreboard conveyed even more anguish, Giants, 24; Colts, 21.

Returning to Baltimore by train, Shaw sat all alone, disconsolate. "The last couple years sitting on the bench haven't been easy," he said. "You watch the rest of the players wanting so much to win. You sit there and hope when your chance does come that you will be able to make a contribution. We are close to a championship now, the first one for most of the veterans. If my efforts could have helped us win today and get closer to the title I would have been happy. That's all I wanted—just to make a contribution to a victory." But Unitas was to say there was no reason for Shaw to be so self-critical. The close defeat in New York, however, provided the Colts a rallying call when they met the same team for the NFL championship six weeks later.

Quarterback Charley Conerly, lending his name to a ghost-written column in the New York *Journal American*, with Dave Eisenberg as his collaborator, said the Giants had "out-gutted" the Colts. It wasn't intended to arouse the Colts but this was the reaction it created. The Colts vowed to get even and make Conerly regret the comment. But before that could transpire they first had to qualify for the championship by putting away the western division and then gaining a possible return shot at the Giants.

Such a possibility moved closer to realization after a Baltimore game against the 49ers. It was a cold, sunless afternoon. Temperatures, ranging from 16 degrees to a high of 27, were penetrating. Spectators still remember the raw weather and, of course, much more. The 49ers built a 27–7 half-time lead. The only positive for the Colts was Ordell Braase breaking through to block a Gordy Soltau extra-point attempt. Instead of 28–7 it was 27–7. A commanding lead. I encountered the 49ers' owner, Vic Morabito, at half-time. I walked past him and said, "Well, Vic, things look good for you now. What happened last year against Detroit [when the 49ers led a divisional playoff by the same score and lost] won't happen again." He pounded his fist on the tabletop and said, "Don't even mention it. Don't say we're home because we aren't."

In the dressing room, Ewbank, in front of his then-trailing team, chalked "4 TDs" on the blackboard—what was going to be needed—and told the defense it had to keep the 49ers off the scoreboard in the last two periods. The team fulfilled both requests, shutting down the 49ers without another point and scoring 28 in a second-half surge that stamped the proceedings, at least to most observers, as the "greatest game" the Colts ever played. Announcers Chuck Thompson and Vince Bagli are in agreement. Lenny Moore capped the comeback with perhaps the most electrifying run of his Hall of Fame career.

What started out as a simple end run, with Berry and Spinney helping to clear the way, accounted for 73 yards and the tying touchdown. Steve Myhra then tacked on the point to put the Colts on top, 28–27, as the first half conversion block by Braase loomed far more important. On the masterpiece run, Moore came down the east sidelines, headed toward the south end of the field. He was under control, with something in reserve, waiting for the most propitious instant to accelerate. He made the 49ers miss, feinting with his head and shoulders as Jim Ridlon and Jerry Mertens took their shots and failed. He looked for an open path, broke free, and then exploded for the goal line as he picked up Preas as an escort. Exciting moves and brilliant runs were a Moore characteristic. "Something just told me to 'run Lenny, run,' and that's what I was trying to do," he said later, making it sound all so simplistic.

Before the astonishing Baltimore comeback was completed, with part of the ecstatic crowd so carried away it left its seats and invaded the sidelines, word flashed to the press box, via Western Union, that in Pittsburgh, where the game started an hour earlier, the Steelers had upset the Bears, eliminating them from the chase. This meant the Colts were the outright Western Division winners and assured of going to the championship game. They would meet the survivor of an eventual playoff between the Browns and Giants. The Giants won by a 10–0 score in Yankee Stadium on Sunday, December 21. The Colts' schedule had been completed and they could either go hunting, fishing, watch television, or rest their tired bodies from the long season of football that had commenced in July with training camp in Westminster.

The Giants had come down the homestretch with momentum, winning four in a row—but all were tough games, the kind that take a lot out of a team—and then the tie-breaker with the Browns. Unlike the Colts, they were physically worn. They didn't have the Colts' luxury of clinching early, letting up, and then regrouping for the grand finale. As some compensation, they would have home field advantage in Yankee Stadium. But the Colts were well-prepared and quietly confident.

The week of the game, while the Giants were practicing, the Colts found a way to steal a secret look at them in a workout. A Colts assistant coach, Bob Shaw, who had prepared scouting reports all year long, was told to try to get inside the stadium in a covert manner to see if he could observe what the Giants were doing. Shaw, fearing he might be caught and dishonored in the coaching business, wasn't sure it could be done. He had earlier watched the Rams at practice in Washington at Georgetown University, prior to a Colts game, but that was easy. It was an open field. But Yankee Stadium? It was enclosed on all sides, fortresslike. If he got caught, Rosenbloom, who liked a dare, and encouraged Shaw to try it, guaranteed him a job for life if he was barred from getting another coaching position.

As Bob circled Yankee Stadium from the streets outside, he found all entrances locked and was forced to decide on another approach. Security was tight. What he would try, he told himself, was to attempt to get on the roof of one of the nearby apartment houses that towered over right centerfield in Yankee Stadium. Maybe he'd be able to "sneak a peek" from there as the Giants practiced and try to learn if they had any special plans for the Colts. Shaw entered the high-rise building, acting the part of a casual tenant, pressed the elevator button, and went all the way to the top floor. He got off, found a short flight of steps, went up and, presto, came out into the daylight of the Bronx. He was on the roof of the building. With binoculars, he looked down into the stadium and watched as the Giants conducted a signal drill, running their normal plays. It all seemed to be the standard stuff, what the Giants had been using all year. He relaxed at his secret vantage point, a so-called "spy in the sky," knowing the Giants were not readying any major surprises. This was important to know. What he didn't want to have happen was to be caught on the roof and be arrested for trespassing. There was one small change he picked up from watching the practice. The Giants were rehearsing a double-reverse, with Frank Gifford involved as the key component, with an option to pass or run. The Giants hadn't used that before. Shaw viewed the Giants for as long as he wanted, only interrupted by a young boy who happened to come up on the roof and meekly inquired as to what he was doing? Shaw didn't answer.

In a matter of minutes, after the Giants concluded practice, Bob left the roof of the building as inconspicuously as he entered and walked away. He caught the next train for Baltimore and related to Ewbank what he had observed. It was valuable to the Colts on the basis that they could then confidently concentrate on normal preparations without having to be worried that the Giants might utilize new defensive alignments and add a variety of moves on offense.

The Colts were in sound shape physically. The only casualty was center-linebacker Dick Szymanski, who had his knee operated on and was back home in Toledo watching the telecast. There was a newspaper strike in New York and the crowd was held down to 64,185, which was 6,000 less than the in-season game with the Giants on November 9. Pleasing to the Colts was the fact that 12,000 Baltimore fans made the trip by rail and bus excursions so it wasn't going to be an entirely hostile environment. Before the game Ewbank gave one of the most inspirational talks any coach had ever given to a team in any locker room. It might have fallen short of the gripping emotional message Knute Rockne delivered in that same stadium in 1928 in his famous "win one for the Gipper" speech that sent Notre Dame in quest of a victory over Army. Ewbank didn't harken back to such "ghosts" of the past but preferred to deal with his players in a personal running commentary. Fourteen of the Colts' thirty-five-man roster had been rejects from other teams, players deemed not capable of playing in the NFL. That's where Ewbank developed his story line; he related how Taseff, Rechichar, and Pellington were unwanted in Cleveland, how Unitas had been dropped by the Steelers and signed by the Colts from a sandlot team, how Nutter was released by the Redskins and even how he, Ewbank, had cut Donovan in Cleveland because he preferred to keep a two-way tackle, one John Sandusky, who would be more versatile.

Then Ewbank told the players as they sat in front of their lockers contemplating what was before them that he also realized he was a "second choice"; that the Colts owner, Rosenbloom, had made Blanton

Collier his preferred coach in 1954 but couldn't get him signed to a contract. The Colts had been reminding each other the entire week that it was pay-back time for Conerly's "we out-gutted them" newspaper comment. For the most part, the Colts were an all-veteran team, with the exception of rookies John Sample, Lenny Lyles, and Ray Brown, who was to play and punt superbly against the Giants. In addition to the twelve thousand partisans in the stands, mostly occupying the end zones, the Colts' Band was there. For the players and the spectators it was to be one of the most unforgettable games of their lives.

The Giants had an early chance to score on a pass but Alex Webster wasn't in position, although open, to make the catch. Pat Summerall, hero of the Giants late-season comebacks, drilled a 36-yard field goal for a 3–0 lead. Baltimore got a break when Ray Krouse, a pickup from the Lions who had earlier played for the Giants, and Lipscomb separated Gifford from the football at the 17 yard line. Moore and Ameche combined to move the Colts to the two, where "The Horse" barreled across behind Spinney and Parker. That made it 7–3, offering little indication of what was going to come later to turn this gray football afternoon into a glorious performance.

Jackie Simpson bobbled a punt at the 11 yard line and the Giants recovered. "Going back to the Colts bench to see Ewbank was the toughest walk I ever took," he said later. But quickly, Simpson was extracted from the predicament when Gifford took another hard shot, lost possession, and Joyce recovered. No harm. Simpson was off the hook. In the second period, the Colts, showing their superiority, orchestrated an 85-yard drive—a precursor of things to come—in 15 plays. From the Giants' 15, Unitas pitched to Berry for a touchdown, raising the count to 14–3. At halftime, Ewbank told his team that instead of being on top by 11 points they should consider themselves two touchdowns behind—another way of reminding the players to get ready for an all-out battle in the second half. This was for the championship, remember.

Once again, the Colts quickly and effectively moved the ball, covering 58 yards to the Giants' one yard line and a first down. Two tries by Ameche and a quarterback-sneak by Unitas didn't get it across. Now it was fourth down and Ewbank was going for the six, not the field goal. In the huddle, with the crowd screaming at the enclosed end, Ameche didn't hear the entire signal, only part of it. The intended play was "428," something they hadn't used all year. All Ameche heard were the last two numbers, "28." Actually, "428" was designated as a fullback pass to Jim Mutscheller. Ameche tried to go outside, was indecisive because the play didn't look right to him and, with Mutscheller all alone in the end zone, deliberated.

The Giants' Cliff Livingston came up fast after a quick read and dropped the tentative Ameche for a four-yard loss. The Giants' respected defense had escaped a score, turning back the Colts four straight times when they were only an arm's length away from the goal line. The Giants had avoided a touchdown that would have taken the Colts to a 20–3 or 21–3 lead and changed the entire aspect of the game. Under those conditions, the Giants would have had to gamble and the Colts, when they had the ball, could have dictated the tempo.

Then came another strange play. From their own 13, Conerly lofted a down-the-middle pass to Kyle Rote, an exceptional receiver, who stretched to make the catch at the Colts' 45. He traveled on to the 25, where he was tackled by Andy Nelson and fumbled. Almost as if it had been rehearsed, Webster was right there to gather in the bouncing ball and continue toward the goal line. Meanwhile, he was chased by Taseff, who got back in the play after missing a tackle up-field on Rote and getting up to overtake Webster, ran him down at the two yard line. Fullback Mel Triplett, though, pounded it across and the Giants were closing in at 14–10.

At the top of the fourth quarter, the Giants, outplayed but hardly outscored by a team that obviously had more skills, incredulously forged ahead. Bob Schnelker, another gifted receiver, put the Giants in position with two catches before Conerly reached Gifford for a score that made it 17–10. The Colts were astonished. Here was a better team, Baltimore, fighting for its "life" in a game it knew should have been going its way. But the numbers on the scoreboard provided ample evidence that the Giants might find a way to win.

In fact, it took another unusual play, one of the game's most talked-about, to bail out the Colts. From their own 40 and with the game clock moving, inside four minutes, the Giants were in a third and four situation. If they had gotten a first down, they conceivably could have held on to win, 17–14. Gifford, the man the Giants relied on, got the call and went off the right side. He got all he needed—with the exception of 12 inches. Marchetti was underneath, aided by Lipscomb, in a massive effort to stop the advance. Lipscomb inadvertently dropped part of his 282 pounds on Marchetti's leg. Under the pile, Marchetti was hollering, "my ankle . . . my ankle." It was broken in two places.

Referee Ron Gibbs and head linesman Charley Berry measured for the first down and signaled that the Giants had come up short. Gifford thought he had made the distance. "I was certain I had it," he said. "No doubt in my mind. Our team didn't argue about it too much. That's because there was more discipline then among the players.

Now, in today's football, they would be charging the officials and creating a scene."

On the sidelines, Jim Lee Howell had to make a call. Go for it or kick? He played by the book, electing to punt. Kicker Don Chandler got it off cleanly, with Taseff, back at the 14, calling for a fair catch. Only 1:56 remained. The Colts were 86 yards away from the goal line and trailing. Then Unitas went to work again. He missed with two passes to Mutscheller and Dupre. Time was running out. It was third down and 10. Unitas noticed Sam Huff, who called defensive signals for the Giants, making a deep drop. That's when, backed up in his own end of the field, he passed quickly to Moore, who squirmed 11 yards for the first down.

Unitas, at his best fighting the clock, knew precisely what he wanted to do. Three times he went to Berry, who was victimizing Karl Karilivacz in an embarrassing way. Berry had his number and Karilivacz was playing so far off he might just as well have taken a seat in the end zone. The Unitas-to-Berry combination was eating up yards, first for 25, then 15, and again for 22. Berry was running with a long, strong stride, fighting for every inch and making it difficult to tackle him. The Colts were moving. So was the clock. The last Berry catch took the ball to the 13 but time was fleeting away.

With less than 20 seconds remaining, Ewbank hollered for the kicking team. In went Myhra, who had also been playing linebacker after an injury to Leo Sanford. Holder George Shaw remembers, "The field was frozen and it was cold. We didn't have hand warmers or heaters to keep us warm. We just put our hands between our legs and tried to keep them from freezing. I've woken up since then in the middle of the night thinking, 'What if I dropped the ball?' I got the snap from center, spun the ball to put the laces in front and Steve kicked it through. When the ball reached my hands it felt like a heavy hunk of ice."

Only nine seconds remained and it was tied, 17–17. Myhra, who handled the pressure, was to say later, "I thought to myself that if I didn't make it good it was going to be an awfully lonesome winter for me in the wheat fields of the Dakotas."

Just minutes before, Marchetti had been hand-carried from the field of play. It took six men, including trainers and equipment handlers, to put him on a litter and transport him to the Colts' bench for further review by the doctors. He wanted to stay there to watch the outcome, to see what was going to happen. The crowd was chanting his name: "Gino . . . Gino . . . Gino." It was an appreciative recognition for the way he played. Still, Marchetti was intent on what was going on in the game he had just left. Dr. Erwin Mayer suggested he be immediately taken to the locker room, before the game ended and the crowd rushed out of the stands.

Trainer Bill Neill, Vince DePaula, who was a moving van operator and a professional wrestling referee, and his helper, Bill Naylor, carried the injured Marchetti on a stretcher down the sidelines. Every 10 yards, he would ask to be put on the ground so he could sit up and watch what was happening in the game he had just been forced to leave. Then the booming cheers would start again. "Gino . . . Gino . . . Gino." After the Colts' Myhra had tied the score, there were still seconds left to be played—time for a Bert Rechichar kickoff, a runback and then Conerly taking the snap from center and conceding a tie to the Longines clock on the stadium wall. So now football was going to have its first overtime in history.

The rule to institute continuation of a championship game, in the event of a tie, had been put in the books in 1947 by Curly Lambeau, Hall of Fame coach and general manager of the Packers. One reason for it was that the league didn't want to have co-champions because it would lead to myriad problems, especially since there'd be no way to determine which of the two teams would represent the league the following August in Chicago against the College All-Stars.

The "sudden death" arrangement had never been needed, so it wasn't clear to the coaches, players, and sportswriters what was going to happen. How would the game resume? And where? But the officials were aware of what had to be done and explained the procedures. Referee Ron Gibbs, Umpire Charles "Chuck" Sweeney, Head Linesman Charley Berry, Field Judge Lou Palazzi, and back judge Cleo Diehl instructed the coaches. There would be a three-minute waiting period and then a flip of the coin between the captains. Marchetti wasn't able to take part in the toss so Unitas went to the center of the field as the stand-in captain. The Giants were represented by cocaptains Bill Svoboda and Rote.

The silver dollar tossed by Gibbs went spinning in the air and while it was airborne, Unitas hollered "tails," the only wrong call he made all day. It came down "heads," which meant the Giants would receive. If they scored, it would all be over and the Colts wouldn't even have the chance to touch the ball. That's why it was called "sudden death." The Giants took three cracks and came up short, once again by a foot, as Conerly, on third down, finding all receivers covered, tried to run for the first down. Chandler lifted another spiraling punt to Taseff, this time to the 21.

The Giants were continuing to alter their defensive alignment and Unitas was countering their every move. It was an intriguing guessing game and Unitas, as masterful as any quarterback has ever been, was continually beating them.

"You know," said Huff years later, "I thought something had to be wrong. Either Unitas was a mind reader or we were tipping our defenses. Everything I called, he beat with a play or a check-off. It was uncanny. The performance he gave that day was so typical of what he could do. I saw and played against him many times and left football realizing how much respect I held for him."

By the time the Colts got their hands on the ball in overtime, Marchetti had disappeared through the first base dugout, into the tunnel and on to the dressing room. Dr. Edmund McDonnell, Marchetti, Neill, DePaula, and Naylor weren't aware of what was going on in the game, so they tried to interpret the noise of the crowd. They'd listen to the roar—then make a judgment. Were the Giants on the move or was it the Colts? They didn't know as they gathered around Marchetti in the catacombs of Yankee Stadium. There was no locker room television or radio, so all they could hear were the sounds of the fans as they reacted, one way or the other, to the movement of the ball.

The game, still not over, was all-out physical combat. A championship was on the line and only one team could win it. Would it be Baltimore? Or New York? Now it was Unitas's turn to take command. As Raymond Berry said, "Looking at the goal posts at the opposite end of the field made it look like we had to go all the way to Baltimore. It might have been 79 yards but, at a time like that, it seemed it was 79 miles. But Unitas could do astonishing things. The highlight of my career was having the opportunity to play with him."

On the Colts' first play of the extra period, Dupre, good under pressure, ran off-tackle for 10 yards. Then Unitas went for the jugular. He tried to reach Moore deep down the sidelines but Lindon Crow broke up the pass at the 25 yard line. It was back to Dupre, who got three yards on a cut-back. Next a flat pass to Ameche, who gained the first down but just barely. Harland Svare made the tackle but, when it was measured, the Colts had succeeded by two inches. Dupre got four yards but was dropped by Huff (who led all tacklers that afternoon with fourteen stops), Jim Katcavage, and Emlen Tunnell.

Now it was a passing down but Unitas never got the ball away. He was instantly overwhelmed by the onrushing Dick Modzelewski, who broke free and dropped him for an eight-yard loss. But Unitas was to remember and, after one more play, took advantage of the aggressive Modzelewski. On third down and six, Unitas intended to go to Moore. He looked toward him but he was covered. Then he began to run, faked a pass, kept searching downfield for a place to throw and finally picked up a receiver. It was Berry, who came open and Unitas fired. Completion. First down. The Colts were at the Giants' 44.

Unitas came to the line of scrimmage with a pass in mind. But he saw Huff had moved from the middle in some type of compensation. He quickly went to a check-off call. The Giants were anticipating a pass, so he canceled out and went to a fullback trap. Here comes Modzelewski again. Actually, he was invited to do just that. Sandusky played it soft and Modzelewski fired across the scrimmage line, intent on getting to Unitas again. He had taken the bait and John was preparing to deceive him. He slipped the ball to Ameche. Meanwhile, Spinney took one step back, paused half-a-count, and knocked the legs out from under Modzelewski. Perfect execution. Sandusky invited him to charge but Spinney, in waiting, was ready to spring the trap and deliver a devastating block. Preas cut off Huff and "The Horse" Ameche went rolling for 23 yards until Jim Patton and Karilivacz rode him to the ground.

The Giants had the utmost respect for Moore and were trying not to let him be the one to beat them. Tom Landry, then a Giants' assistant coach, always said, "Any time you play Baltimore, you concede a 7-point lead because of Moore"—the epitome of professional respect. Unitas knew they had Moore in double coverage so they'd be limited in what the two of them could do passing. He gave to Dupre again. This time there was no gain; Livingston and Huff took him down. Now Unitas picked up the tempo. He quickly hit Berry on a slant. Berry was running with determination, extracting all he could get, almost a receiver-possessed after he caught the ball. Raymond had gotten the first down and more. He was at the ten when Patton hit him but he carried the Giant defender to the six yard line. The officials put it back to the eight, which seemed more of an adjustment than was necessary.

Pressure was intense. Collars tightened. I figured the excitement might lead to a heart attack and I actually said a prayer to the Lord, right there in the overhanging press box at Yankee Stadium. Before Unitas could give the ball to Ameche once more, there was a pause in the action. A man had slipped out of the stands, made his way to the field and was racing up the middle of Yankee Stadium for 80 yards, the longest run of the day, with police in pursuit. Automatic time-out. Meanwhile, with other fans streaming down out of their seats to crowd the sidelines (something that never happens today because of increased security), a power cable was kicked loose that led to the NBC television trailer. The picture left the screen for two and a half minutes; the sound for two minutes.

Radio, especially in Baltimore, was making an instant comeback as viewers tried to find the game on their sets. Order in Yankee Stadium was quietly restored with removal of the interloping fan, and power came back to NBC. The picture and audio, with Chris Schenkel and Chuck Thompson announcing, resumed. Thompson was to joke later that if he heard the man running up the field was an NBC vice president he wouldn't have been surprised.

But what Unitas tried and accomplished shortly thereafter was typical of this quarterback of superb competence and confidence. First he gave to Ameche for two yards. It was now second and six. Unitas called a pass to Mutscheller in the right flat. If it had been tipped or intercepted, the ball could have been returned for a touchdown—94 yards the other way. There was also the chance for a chip-shot field goal, right there in front of the uprights, the same posts where Myhra had kicked the tying 19-yard field goal only minutes before to set up this classic struggle. But the Colts—rather Unitas—had something else in mind. He put the ball up in a pass to Mutscheller between the receiver and the sideline. The reliable Mutscheller caught the ball, stretching to grab it and, with icy ground under foot in that corner of the field, wasn't able to keep his feet when he tried to cut and fell out of bounds. The ball was at the one.

Now play number 13 of the sudden death, which had brought the Colts 78 yards, was coming up. Unitas called for "16 power," a handoff to Ameche over the right side. He charged with head down, expecting resistance, but didn't find any, almost stumbling into the end zone. Touchdown. Baltimore had won. There was a new champion, a team that only six years before had been abandoned in Dallas and was taken over as a ward of the league. The result, for the record books, was 23–17. Magic numbers. On the Ameche scoring thrust, Mutscheller blocked Livingston, Moore cut down Tunnell, and Preas eliminated Katcavage.

After Ameche hit the ground, a fan who jumped on the pile tore the football out of Ameche's arms, but Nutter reacted and got it back. Baltimore partisans, celebrating as never before, took over Yankee Stadium. Grown men were little boys again. They were on the field, running to touch the players as they fought to clear themselves of the crowd in a hurried dash for the dressing room. The Colts' Band was playing. Both goalposts were down.

Eight minutes and 15 seconds into the first "sudden death" ever played, and the Colts were kings of professional football. A game never to be forgotten, not because the Colts had won and the Giants had lost, but more so for all the elements, historical and otherwise, that had come into play. "Sudden death," the distinguishing characteristic that set it apart from all other games, had made it so. *Sports Illustrated* was to describe it in headline form as "the best football game ever played," but that was soon altered in ordinary conversation to become "the greatest football game ever played."

Whole books have since been written about events of that day. When the elated Colts bounded into the locker room, they were chanting, "We out-gutted them," referring to Conerly's slur. They found Marchetti on a table in the training room with Dr. McDonnell, the highly respected surgeon from Johns Hopkins, and the trainers. Marchetti, Neill, DePaula, and Naylor knew by what they were hearing how the game had turned out. Fans were on their hands and knees, all over the field, picking what little grass was left to carry home for souvenirs.

"I got a piece of the goalpost, picked up some dirt to put in my pocket, and made a little trellis out of it," says Romeo Valenti, of Westminster. "I gave it to my good friend Alan Ameche."

On the way from the press box to the locker room, I realized, for the only time in a sportswriting life, I had actually predicted the exact outcome, the Colts winners at 23–17, and published it in the *Sunday American* only hours before the kickoff. On another turn of luck, I encountered Commissioner Bert Bell, who was with two of his children, and friend Art Rooney, owner of the Steelers. They were walking with the crowd that was leaving the stadium. Bell said it was "the greatest game he had ever seen" and then added, so cryptically, something I will always remember: "I never thought I would live to see sudden-death."

Bell said Unitas was the game's greatest advertisement; Emlen Tunnell, of the Giants, speaking of Unitas, added, "Everything we expected him to do, and what you absolutely believed he would do, he didn't do. He did exactly the opposite. . . .Those of us who have been around knew we had been beaten by a better team."

In the bedlam of the locker room, Spinney was hollering, "Who out-gutted who?" and Taseff joined in, "I guess we had a few guts ourselves."

Baltimore, the city and its people, were carried away with the joy of victory. When the team returned by chartered plane to Friendship Airport, now Baltimore-Washington International, the largest crowd to ever assemble in anticipation of greeting a Baltimore champion was on hand. Police estimated the gathering at 30,000. Many of those present got caught up in the ecstasy of the moment, and it soon got out of hand. Barriers and restraining ropes were of little use. The crowd broke loose and was outside the terminal building, standing along the sides of runways.

Police captain Carl Kunaniec said the fans began to arrive at five o'clock and had inundated the entire airport property. All 6,000 parking spaces were taken. Adjacent roads were lined bumper to bumper. Some drivers abandoned cars on the sides of highways and walked to the airport. Travelers, coming and going, with little regard for football, were trapped in the vast turnout of spectators. Those hoping to leave on evening flights never had a chance. If they were fortunate enough to inch through the congestion, there was then no place to put their cars. The airport was paralyzed, under siege.

The men, women and children in the welcoming party were caught up in a hysteria I have never seen before or since. It was such an uncontrollable scene that airport authorities, from that time on, discouraged anything similar from taking place. There was worry that some fans, in this rush of enthusiasm, might spill out onto the runways and put themselves in danger of being killed or injured. Also, if they started to throw firecrackers near the airplanes it might ignite fumes from the fuel and cause an explosion.

The Colts' plane landed at a remote and dark end of the airport and slowly made its way back towards the terminal. It was decided that the two buses waiting to transport the coaches and players to downtown Baltimore would come out to get them, rather than having the players leave the plane within view of the crowd. As the buses slowly made their way toward the airport exit, the crowd engulfed them.

Men and boys climbed on the roof of one of the buses. I was inside with half the team. Looking out the window, I saw a crushed police cruiser that resembled a stepped-on tin can. The roof had collapsed from the weight of too many pedestrians standing on top, hoping to gain a better view of the team's arrival. Police were trying to regain some semblance of order. One minute, a huge part of the crowd would run in one direction—a tidal wave out of control. Just as quickly, they'd reverse themselves and run back to where they were before. The Colts, meanwhile, were peering from the bus windows at what was going on around them.

They were physically marooned, caught in this screaming sea of humanity. John Bridgers, an assistant coach, hollered through the window and asked the people to control themselves. He had no chance of getting them to listen. Kellett and Ewbank agreed that none of the Colt traveling party should attempt to get off the bus or even open the door. "They'll tear us to pieces," Ewbank said. Leo Sanford, who had played in his last professional game because of a knee injury, asked to no one in particular, "Do you think we'll get out of here alive?"

After almost an hour of being isolated, with the screaming crowd surrounding the buses, the police gave the drivers an escape plan. They would provide a vehicle escort, but instead of proceeding directly toward Baltimore they would leave the airport at the south exit, head toward the Fort Meade Army base, make a westerly turn over secondary roads, and then pick up the Baltimore-Washington Parkway. They'd make stops at the Lord Baltimore Hotel for those who wanted to get off downtown and then go to Memorial Stadium, where many of the players had parked their cars on Saturday morning. At one time, over a hundred men and boys were on top of the bus I was in and others were clutching the luggage carriers on the back. So many were standing on the front bumper that the driver couldn't see out the window.

Slowly the bus made its way. Some on-the-roof riders slid off but others were holding on with their fingertips. Once the buses got off the airport grounds, with the coaches and players feeling a bit more relieved, they began to pick up speed to keep pace with the police cars in front of them. Some kids were still going along for the ride. Police behind the buses recognized the danger and finally drew abreast of one bus and told it to turn into a dark churchyard. The police were right with them, jumping from their cruisers, plucking the boys off the top, like pulling cherries from a tree, and putting some of them in their squad cars.

The police had their patience stretched to the limit at the airport. Now they were angry, realizing the danger the kids had caused for themselves. Fourteen were on top of one bus. Half of them raced for a nearby thicket but the police had seven of them in the backseats of their squad cars as they hunted for the others.

I got off the bus and talked with the boys. They were scared, wondering what was going to happen. One kid said, "Mister, I want to meet some Colts." When I got back on the bus, I mentioned to Unitas and Sanford what one of the boys being held by the police had said. With that, Unitas and Sanford got off and went over to shake their hands. A kid with a smile on his face expressed the elation of all when he said, "I don't care if they do lock me up. I just met some Colts." No charges were filed, but from what the police told them they knew better than to ever again attempt to ride on top of a bus that was moving down a highway.

Baltimore celebrated long into the night. Men and women still remember where they were when Ameche scored and recall Unitas and Berry having two of the greatest days any players ever had in a championship game. Meanwhile, on a farm in Gettysburg, Pennsylvania, the thirty-fourth president of the United States, Dwight D. Eisenhower, who had once been a coach but a much better general, was explaining the fine points of football to his grandson David, age ten, after they had watched the telecast.

In the aftermath of the thriller in Yankee Stadium, some critics wondered why Unitas took a chance with that last pass to Mutscheller instead of letting Myhra kick a field goal. For one thing, it was only second down when he tossed to Mutscheller and it would have been premature to go for a field goal when he still had two more chances.

Unitas was calling the game but, of course, if Ewbank had sent in the field goal unit he would have had to obey the order. Ewbank made no such move. He could see how the Colts were driving the Giants off the ball and figured there was no reason to kick for three points when a touchdown, to him, seemed imminent. Then another subject was introduced, one that had ominous implications. Had Unitas, on instructions from Rosenbloom, tried to beat the point spread of three and a half by going for the touchdown? Rosenbloom had a reputation—but no hard proof was available—of being a bettor and was often in the company of known gamblers. But suggestions, mere gossip, that the owner had tried to somehow influence the outcome were exceedingly unfair to the team and completely unfounded.

Unitas answered questions about the toss to Mutscheller by explaining how easy it was to complete. He said the Giants were stacking their defense and he decided a pass was the safe way to proceed. "There was one man out there and he was in no position to intercept it," he explained. "As it was, I played it safe by over-throwing Jim a little on the out-of-bounds side. The pass wasn't meant just to get us close to the goal line. It was meant to be a touchdown. Jim made a good catch of the ball and fell outside. If I hadn't thrown it so far out, he would have fallen straight back and we'd have had the touchdown right there. It was my fault we didn't."

To a sportswriter who suggested that a Giant defender could have intercepted and been off for a touchdown in an open field, Unitas, without a trace of a brag, said most emphatically, "When you know what you're doing, they are not intercepted."

As for the championship spoils, the Colts cashed in with each player receiving a winning check for $4,718.77, an NFL record up until that time and more than Art Donovan had made his entire season of 1950 as a Colts rookie. There were two other checks that arrived in the mail, one from an announced and creditable source, the other more mysterious. The National Brewing Co., as part of its broadcast contract, was to pay $25,000 extra to the Colts organization if it won a championship, the rationale being that more people were watching and, thus, increasing the game's value to the sponsor from a listening and viewing standpoint. The players and coaches divided that money, plus another check that came from an unknown benefactor.

Speculation had it that the second $25,000 came from a "friend of the team," thought to be Lou Chesler, a major developer and for a time a chum of Rosenbloom. Whether it was money he drew from the bank, or won on a wager, was never confirmed. And there was no way to tell for certain if Chesler was the donor. One thing for sure—the Colts players weren't about to turn it down.

Rosenbloom took good care of the winning coach, Ewbank. He rewarded him with a $25,000 bonus, an improved contract at $30,000 annually, and a perpetuity clause that brought him an automatic renewal that added another three coaching seasons at the end of each year.

But the "greatest game ever played," even if it wasn't, is more than talking about something that happened in the dim past. It is a keepsake for the ages, a memorable event that left a lasting impression on those fortunate enough to have been there. For Baltimore, it was a historical highlight that set the city apart and provided a sports identity no other could claim. It had the first team to survive "sudden death."

CHAPTER 11

# ANOTHER TITLE . . . THEN A SLUMP

It stands as the only championship the Colts ever won before the home audience, right there in Memorial Stadium, a frantic place that was once referred to as "the world's largest outdoor insane asylum" by Cooper Rollow, a sportswriter with the *Chicago Tribune.*

The 1959 matchup was identical to the previous year: the Colts and New York Giants again lining up to contend for the title. Basically, in the general complement of personnel, they were much the same two teams but there was no way the proceedings, regardless of how spectacular they might be, could even remotely rival the impact of the previous "sudden death" collision in Yankee Stadium and all the pulsating subplots that unfolded. The '58 game simply had it all.

In the rematch, the Giants didn't record a touchdown until only thirty-two seconds remained to be played. Their earlier "offensive" production came from Pat Summerall, who kicked a field goal in each of the first three quarters. Meanwhile, the Colts were storming their way to a 28–9 lead and assuming total control. Charley Conerly finally dented the defense with a scoring shot to Bob Schnelker that allowed the Giants to at least realize what it was like to reach the end zone, if there was any solace in that.

For John Unitas it was another banner day; he completed eighteen of twenty-nine passes and touchdown tosses to Lenny Moore and Jerry Richardson. Defensively, John Sample, with deft fingertips, pulled down two of Conerly's passes for interceptions, returning one for a striking 42-yard touchdown. The Colts' entire defense, especially Gene "Big Daddy" Lipscomb, Dick Szymanski, and Andy Nelson, dominated the Giants on an unseasonably warm day in late December. Center Buzz Nutter silenced Sam Huff in such a commanding way that the Giants' proficient and loquacious linebacker rarely got a call. Beating the Giants, once they kicked off, wasn't the problem it was expected to be. The Colts had things all their own way.

In fact, they had a more difficult time qualifying to get there and defend the championship. They made it extremely difficult by losing three of their first seven games and, much later, had to go to the West Coast facing the pressure of needing to win in successive weeks against the 49ers and Rams. Beating the 49ers was relatively easy, if such can be said about any football game. As coaches say, there's no such thing as a walk-over. Unitas threw twice to Berry and once to Moore for touchdowns in a 34–14 breeze. The Colts defense made an enormous effort, intercepting six 49er passes. It was then on to Los Angeles where things became much tougher.

As they headed into the last period, the Rams were holding a 26–24 lead. The Colts, with the game on the line, asserted themselves in no small way, scoring twenty-one points in a span of four minutes and forty seconds. Unitas passed to Richardson, Szymanski rambled in with an interception, and Taseff retrieved a missed field goal and ran it back, 99 yards in all. The Rams were never heard from again, losing 45–26 to the stampeding Colts.

So Baltimore, assessing the performance chart, had won two titles in a row. Impressive. They tried to make it a third title in 1960 but finished the year losing their last four games. Instrumental in the late season demise of the Colts, oddly enough, was the final game they won—certainly one of their most thrilling finishes ever. It came in Chicago against the Bears, undoubtedly the most all-out physical encounter in the history of the franchise.

Baltimore and Chicago, with the offensive and defensive lines battering each other to a near standstill, met in Wrigley Field. The Colts trailed by three points and with only nineteen seconds left, Unitas went down after "being run over by a truck," meaning the Bears had put it to him with a hard but clean shot. He was bleeding from a cut above the eye, his nose torn and swollen. It took almost five minutes, during an emergency time-out called by the officials, for trainers and the team doctor to make repairs. The Bears, looking on as the battered Unitas was patched, anticipated victory as they waited at the scrimmage line for play to resume.

The shape of the injured Unitas didn't lend itself to believing he had any chance to beat them. But any time Unitas could stand up he was a threat to turn a game around. Courage was something he brought with him, and getting hit, or the thought of it, never led to even a hint of intimidation. A field goal at that point wouldn't do the Colts any good. They had to go for the "bundle," a touchdown, if they were to pull it out. From the Bears' 39 yard line, the bruised and bleeding quarterback took the snap, faded back to throw, set-up and waited patiently for the elusive, speedy Moore, an artist, to make his cut. It was "on the money," a bull's-eye pass. Moore, with sure hands, pulled it in for the reception. Touchdown. Just like that it was all over. The Bears were stunned, the crowd in awe. Final score, Colts, 24; Bears, 20.

Halas said it was one of his toughest defeats (and he had helped start the league in 1920), but was generous in praising Unitas for the way he reacted when he had only one shot left in the gun and made it count for a score that decided the outcome. I left the locker room with Unitas a full hour after it was over and walked to the team bus with John and his brother, Leonard, who had been there to watch what had been an extraordinary afternoon of football. It was a different kind of a scene, rarely witnessed.

A multitude of fans had remained, maybe as many as 3,000, for no other reason than to try to get a close-up look at Unitas, this quarterback, who even though under duress, seemed to have almost supernatural powers to turn a game around with one move of his passing arm. As we headed for one of the two buses that would take the team to the airport, the fans, in deep respect, crowded in to see him, to say hello, and try to shake his hand.

One man confronted Unitas and he trailed behind to talk with him for what was a brief dialogue. Of all things, he said he was John's father. Unitas was stumped, mystified, but didn't place any belief in what he was hearing. John's father had died in Pittsburgh when he was a mere child. John figured this man to be emotionally disturbed or someone who was certainly in need of help. John and Leonard talked briefly about it, but knew it was pure fiction.

At Christmastime, the same fan sent Unitas a parlor football game, the kind children enjoy and, usually, in a matter of hours, get tired of playing. Following numerous letters from the fan, the Colts' attorney, William D. Macmillan, Sr., wrote the man telling him if he didn't cease bothering Unitas legal action would be taken. Unitas never heard from him again.

As he boarded the waiting bus, parked outside Wrigley Field, and took a seat, a kid hammered on the window to get Unitas's attention. He could have easily shook his head or ignored the request but, as tired as he was, he pulled back the glass, took the program from the boy, signed his name, and handed it back. Unitas was entirely spent, exhausted after the beating he had taken, and looked forward to the flight home. Other players felt the same way but realized they had witnessed another remarkable show of ability and determination put on by Unitas. It seemed that Marchetti, Donovan, Unitas, and Spinney spoke for all the rest of their teammates when they said it was the most brutal football game, from a punishment standpoint, they had ever played.

The hitting was, in a word, violent. Marchetti even likened it to World War II combat, which he knew something about since he had been in the Battle of the Bulge as an eighteen-year-old infantryman. In this hand-to-hand fighting in Chicago, they weren't using guns, grenades, or bayonets. The Colts and Bears, after this all-out assault on each other, never won another game the rest of the way and, consequently, had eliminated each other from the divisional race. They had given so much to one afternoon of football that neither team had anything left. It was comparable to two fighters going at each other with such maximum exertion they had nothing more to give. Their tanks were empty.

"Do you realize we could just as easily have won four titles in a row," remarked Donovan ten years later. "If we had won in 1960 that would have made it three straight. But go back to 1957, when we just missed. I still believe that team, in '57, was the best we ever had, even if we didn't win. We were young, hungry and in our prime. Oh, well, like knocking over a cold beer, you can't cry about it after it's been spilled on the barroom floor. Those four years with the Colts were special times in Baltimore. A lot of other outstanding teams we played never even got to play in a championship game. We were able to do it for two in a row. The Giants were good. They had to be to get to the championship but we were just so much better, in every way, that it wasn't something you'd even want to argue about."

The 1960 disappointment, considering the hard-earned win over the Bears, and then falling to a so-so 6–6 record, was difficult to accept. The Colts never got it back after that. It seems so simplistic to try to explain it that way but that's what happened. In 1961, both Berry and Mutscheller were injured, so the passing game regressed. In the finale against the Rams, a 10–3 loss, Unitas failed to complete a touchdown pass, ending his remarkable string of throwing scoring passes in forty-seven straight games. It's a mark that has had a long life in the record book and so far, in over three decades, hasn't been even remotely challenged by any other quarterback.

In 1961, the Colts got back up to eight and six but fell back to six and six again in 1962, a year that saw Lenny Moore fracture his kneecap by landing on hard ground in the final exhibition against the Pittsburgh Steelers at Forbes Field. It was as if all the breaks were now going against them. Or maybe it was just the cyclical nature of sports, where the wheel continues to turn and different numbers keep coming up.

Sustaining success in any pursuit is the most demanding of all challenges. And there are occasions when the best team doesn't win. As a for-instance take a game against the Packers in 1962. The Colts outgained coach Vince Lombardi's team, 380 yards to 116, recorded 19 first downs to 8 and had the ball for 30 more plays, 79 to 49. Checking the scoreboard seemed a mirage. It read Packers, 17; Colts 13.

That also was the year Donovan went to training camp and retired, gracefully but reluctantly. Ewbank wanted Donovan to make way for a new tackle and was constantly telling the sportswriters that in John Diehl of Virginia he had a solid replacement. It was as if he had talked himself into believing just that. Once on a fishing trip, hosted by Orioles owner Joe Iglehart in Florida, I listened but didn't agree with Ewbank, who believed he had to make way for younger talent and specifically mentioned a plan to move Donovan aside.

Still, Art went to camp in 1962 and the writing was on the wall. Athletes have a way of reading situations, knowing almost instinctively whether they are part of the coach's plans. General Manager Kellett asked Donovan to meet him on a Saturday afternoon at his house in Hampton, a suburb of north Baltimore, so they could discuss the matter in detail away from training camp. Quitting football was the last thing Art wanted to do. He loved everything about it, even tolerating the heat, the workouts, and the hitting. The camaraderie meant so much to him. When Kellett, ever the suave diplomat, broke the retirement news to Donovan, he softened the blow as best he could. Kellett had a way with words, was as honest as a general manager could be, and had the confidence of the players.

Donovan accepted what Kellett was saying, even if he disagreed. Then Artie interjected, "Before we do anything else, I have to make a telephone call." Kellett asked who it was he was interested in talking to at a time like that? "I want to tell the best friend I have in this town," he answered. Surprisingly, as it turned out, I was the one Donovan felt compelled to call. I listened and told him what a fulfilling career he had had; that he had come a long way from being a raw rookie with the Colts in 1950, when he was paid $4,500 for a twelve-game regular season, plus seven exhibitions. Art finally couldn't talk anymore. He broke down and, with the words so difficult to dislodge, simply added, "I'll see you later." His passion for the game was something more important than a vehicle to make money. At age thirty-seven—or was it thirty-eight (Donovan was reluctant to reveal his true age)—football left him but he never left football.

Before the opening game, against the Rams, a day was set aside to honor Donovan in front of a crowd of 54,749. A thirty-five-man arrangements committee was formed that included Bob Robertson, who originated the idea; Lou Grasmick; Jim Lindsay; Joe Clifford; and another retiring teammate and close friend, Mutscheller. It was Donovan's desire to show up in a sport coat for the prekickoff ceremony at the stadium but Grasmick, in charge of the staging, insisted he wear a full uniform. Then Donovan balked again. He didn't want to put on shoulder pads. Cumbersome. Just too much trouble. Again, Grasmick told him it would be more appropriate if he would wear them.

Finally, in the first base dugout, waiting to be introduced, he said, "Where's my old man?" His father, Arthur Sr., the famed boxing instructor and referee, had come down from New York and being the gregarious type, had wandered off to mingle with fans and exchange pleasantries. In 1950, when Arthur came to camp almost a week late, it was because his father warned his wife, Mary, not to let their son play any more football. "If he goes to that training camp those big guys will kill him," is what he told her.

But Art, as it turned out, was quite capable of taking care of himself. Witness to this: a twelve-year pro career, four times an all-pro selection, and playing in five Pro Bowls. As the stadium ceremony approached, his father reappeared and Art was satisfied to know where he was. Then Donovan made the long journey to midfield to overwhelming applause. Gifts were presented. A new Cadillac automobile; a set of golf clubs from Johnny Bass, the Pine Ridge professional; and numerous other mementos and proclamations to mark the occasion.

At the microphone, Art said how pleased he was to have played for the Colts and what it meant to him. His voice began to break. He was choked emotionally. Finally, the sentimental moment turned into a deluge, for both Donovan and the fans. It was a moving tableau of avowed love. Then he tore himself apart, and his listeners, too, by saying, "Up in heaven there is a lady who is happy the City of Baltimore was so good to her son—a kid from the Bronx."

He turned away, trotted off the field, under the goalposts and turned toward the locker room. I was standing there in the dugout and witnessed another outpouring of emotion. Art, out of view of the crowd, leaned forward, with his hands bracing the full weight of his upper body against a concrete block wall and cried as hard as any grown man ever has. The packed stands he had left, many of the spectators with tears welling their eyes, was still applauding his exit. They didn't realize how overwhelming it had been for him. There have been farewells to numerous Baltimore athletes, all of them significant and well-earned, but the Donovan departure leads the list.

Not only was he retiring but the number he wore, 70, also was being taken out of circulation. It would never be issued again. Yes, Arthur Donovan loved football and got his just recognition when in 1968 the Pro Football Hall of Fame notified him he was to be enshrined, the first Colts player to qualify for the highest honor the game bestows.

As a contender in 1962, the Colts were still there making their presence felt. But, overall, they had slipped. They were still a formidable team, but not quite what they were. Ewbank, despite what he had achieved in taking over the league's worst team and making it the best, was taking hits from the critics. It had happened to all of them: Curly Lambeau, Steve Owen, Buck Shaw, and even Paul Brown. The only coach immune from the "firing squad" was George Halas, and his security vest came from the fact that he owned the team. Rosenbloom provided well for the Colts' coaches but he once told me, quite succinctly, "I'm a result man."

He was interested in making a change, and the news greeted Ewbank upon his return from scouting the Senior Bowl in Mobile—the same place where Kellett had opened talks with him in 1954. Ewbank left with a commendable record of fifty-nine wins, fifty-two defeats, one tie. He also had two world championships dangling from his belt, those back-to-back victories over the Giants. In a twist of irony, Ewbank was fired by Rosenbloom during the same off-season that his mentor, Brown, who had brought him to pro football, was dumped in Cleveland by Modell. Temporarily, Ewbank entered the oil business, buying a Phillips 66 Service Station as an investment but, of course, not having to pump the gas. Weeb was just marking time and within three months was available to be hired when Sonny Werblin bought the New York Titans of the American Football League, renaming them the Jets, and began searching for a coach.

Rosenbloom recommended him and Ewbank was hired in New York. Ewbank was to facilitate the same kind of transition in New York as he had in Baltimore and, ultimately, experience his most satisfying moment when the Jets jolted the Colts and his successor, Don Shula, in Super Bowl III. The naming of Shula to follow Ewbank was close to automatic. After being put on waivers by Ewbank in 1957 and finishing out the year with the Redskins, he hired on as an assistant coach at the University of Virginia, then went to Kentucky and on to the Detroit Lions. As a Colts' cornerback, Shula virtually coached the coaches while still a player and called defensive signals, a role that usually went to an interior lineman or a linebacker.

Shula was respected for his knowledge of the game. His hiring by Rosenbloom was promoted by two of his friends and former teammates, Marchetti and Pellington. Little did they, or anyone else, realize that Shula, beginning in Baltimore and then going on to Miami, would put up the greatest coaching record in the history of the National Football League, surpassing Halas in total number of games won in a thirty-three-year head-coaching career that logged 347 victories.

Only two men witnessed both the first game Shula won in 1960, over the 49ers in San Francisco, and his record-setting win that sent him past Halas in the 1993 season, twenty-four years later, against the Eagles in Philadelphia. One was John Sandusky, his long-time assistant coach; the other also had J.S. initials. Guess. During his Baltimore stand, lasting seven years, before Rosenbloom became disenchanted, Shula won seventy-four, lost twenty-two, tied four but wasn't able to win a championship. Shula's rookie season, when he was the youngest coach in the NFL at age thirty-three, was an encouraging indication of what was to follow.

The team went eight and six despite the fact Raymond Berry had a shoulder injury and Lenny Moore wasn't himself, complaining of a strange "buzzing" in his head. Tom Matte, then in his third year with the Colts, proved he could play. Ewbank named him as a first-round draft choice from Ohio State and visualized him as "another Paul Hornung." It was Ewbank's idea that he'd be able to give the team a surprising two-way threat—a running halfback, who could get outside, pull up, set himself, and pass for yardage at propitious moments, keeping the defense honest.

However, Matte saw little service as a rookie and Brown, realizing he was technically a free agent, tried to sign him for Cleveland, which was his hometown. Matte had nothing holding him to Baltimore and, contractually, was eligible to go anywhere. But he opted to remain. No doubt the "spell" of Kellett had worked again. This was an enormous break for the Colts. Had Matte signed with the Browns, or any other team, the Colts wouldn't even have collected a draft choice since he was a free agent.

Shula's second coaching year was a revelation. He showed what the future held for his teams when, at one point, the Colts won eleven straight. In clinching the Western Division against the Los Angeles Rams, the defense sacked quarterbacks Roman Gabriel and Bill Munson eleven times. It was often said that Marchetti collected that many in an afternoon by himself. Perhaps an overstatement but, in a way, a compliment to the greatest defensive end the league has ever seen. Marchetti and Pellington had a "co-day" held in their honor when they retired so more changes were coming about—veterans moving out; new faces arriving.

It hadn't taken Shula long to put things in order. Following the Western Division win, Shula was going back home to face the Browns in the city where he had played college football at John Carroll University, and also against the team that had originally drafted him, before dealing him to Baltimore in 1953. Nearby Painsville was where he was born, so all was in readiness for a victorious homecoming. It never happened.

The day before the game in Cleveland there was an undercurrent of sorts. An unconfirmed report circulated that the FBI was monitoring some aspects of a betting angle. This was never entirely documented. It could have been nothing more than talk. But it was being heard, substantiated or not.

The Colts, a heavy favorite, weren't able to score a single point. Frank Ryan, the Browns' quarterback, threw scoring passes of 18, 42, and 51 yards to the same receiver, Gary Collins, to help record a 27–0 shutout. In the days before the game, the Colts Band was stunned to silence when it was told it wasn't going to be able to accompany the team or attend the championship.

Rosenbloom, at one point, said since Modell didn't have a band he didn't want to embarrass him by having the Colts parading all over Cleveland Municipal Stadium. What a reason. The league, though, was running the championship and had engaged Florida A.&M., a flamboyant college unit, so there was no need for the Colts Band, except it was anticipated they'd be there since the team the band represented happened to be playing. Excuses were made for why they had to stay home, but none of the reasons were valid. The dispute wouldn't die.

Finally, with pressure applied, the Colts Band was allowed to travel to Cleveland, to enter the stadium to watch but not to play a note or even to sound a toot or tap their drums. They circled the field and then were seated in the end zone, temporarily estranged, totally muted. The musical instruments, according to instructions, were to be placed in their carrying cases, piled on the ground, and guarded by the police so they couldn't be used. Obviously, the league wasn't interested in catering to the musical interests of one of the competing teams. And Rosenbloom was just as happy they weren't going to be playing.

There had been an earlier crisis that had nothing to do with the Colts Band. It concerned the barring of the Baltimore Bugle Boys from Memorial Stadium. They were a group of fans from East Baltimore who enjoyed making noise at the Colts games by blowing bugles. There was a time when the Colts were hard put to sell tickets, and they would have been elated for the Baltimore Bugle Boys to be there. But now there was opposition from management. They considered them annoyances.

It made for a week-long controversy that gained so much attention that a visiting publicity director, Art Johnson of the 49ers, went to a hockshop on Baltimore Street and bought a World War II army bugle that he presented to me. A photographer took a picture to document the occasion. I took to playing it—not blowing it—at appropriate moments in the press box. It was a show of support for the Baltimore Bugle Boys. A reward was forthcoming; they made me an honorary member. And what happened to the bugle? It was given a "burial at sea." I dropped it off the stern of a fishing boat underneath the Chesapeake Bay Bridge while in the company of Chuck Thompson, Norman Almony, Herb Cahan, and others serving as "pallbearers." A eulogy to a bugle was delivered, and cold cans of National Bohemian were passed around. The burial of the bugle, although a private service, was no doubt a joyous occasion for those whose press box sanctity had been disturbed by the sour sounds emanating from the battered brass horn. Although it wasn't intended to be a cause célèbre, the bugle had created consternation and attention. Friends around the country, when they heard I was carrying a bugle to the press box, along with a portable typewriter and binoculars, couldn't believe it. This seemed like a grown man who had taken leave of his limited senses, but it was intended as a protest, to stand up for the rights of fans.

Furthermore, when they listened to what was supposed to be a bugle call, they held their ears in anguish. In San Francisco, at the Jack Tarr Hotel, I gave in to temptation, threw open the room window, and sounded off. When Prescott Sullivan, the whimsical columnist of the *San Francisco Examiner* heard what happened, he wrote an entire column about his visiting friend from "back east" defending the cause of the buglers, concluding that the campaign I had waged in Baltimore was another occasion of a man with good intentions fighting and winning for the wrong side.

In Los Angeles, at a season-ending party, I played it on the streets of Hollywood. Why not? Claude "Buddy" Young, a team executive but before that a player and the first Colt to have his uniform jersey retired, laughed so hard he went out of control and slipped on the sidewalk, hitting his head and rendering himself unconscious. I ran to his side and was actually praying he'd awaken but decided it wouldn't be appropriate to blow the bugle. He might, I thought, somehow confuse it with Gabriel blowing his horn and think that he was checking in at the Pearly Gates.

After Buddy was up and about, complaining only of a slight headache, I told the story to Chuck Thompson, Bob Robertson, and Don Kellett. They were beside themselves with laughter. Thompson put it in proper perspective by saying, "No, John, you couldn't be confused with Gabriel. Not the way you blow the bugle."

The bugle, still later, was the source of another controversy. Before the playoff in Cleveland, on the bus from the airport to the hotel, the bugle vanished. It had all the suspicions of being an "inside job." Kellett, highly superstitious, passed the word, "I want the bugle back." He regarded it as a good luck symbol, which was really stretching the point.

The bugle turned up outside my hotel room. There was only one suspect, the mischievous Bert Bell, Jr., the team business manager. However, because of the devastating way the Browns handled the Colts, there was no reason to blow the bugle, unless it was to signal lights out. The score again, 27–0. The season, the one that held so much hope, was over.

What happened in Cleveland—to get so close but yet, in the end, be so far away—almost became a chronic condition for Shula and the Colts. Bad luck bedeviled them. And through no fault of their own. Take what occurred the next year when the situation was similar—a team that deserved to win found a new way to be beaten. It was an official's call that should have gone Baltimore's way that forced them into defeat and eliminated them from championship consideration. But before that, there were other problems. John Unitas injured his knee severely, necessitating a heavy cast and the use of crutches for the rest of the season. This brought in a replacement, Gary Cuozzo, who, in turn, separated his shoulder in a 45–27 loss to the Packers, the same afternoon Paul Hornung scored five touchdowns against them.

Both quarterbacks were gone. Shula, ever the improviser, turned to Tom Matte, who had been a split-T quarterback at Ohio State but had never quarterbacked a single play as a professional. Shula limited the offense to mostly basic running plays and equipped Matte with a wristband that he wore in the game as a prompter to help him call signals. It was shielded by a see-through plastic cover that allowed him to read the list of plays and their numbers by merely glancing at it.

In a game they had to win in Los Angeles, the high-strung Matte, who had problems with stomach ulcers, wearing the portable "cue-card," reacted impressively to the challenge. He ran the ball 16 times from the quarterback slot and gained 99 yards. It was a different kind of look, the Colts using so many basic plays from a modified split-T formation they had never used before. Necessity, once again, had mothered the invention. The Colts didn't annihilate the Rams. Far from it. It took a field goal by Lou Michaels from 50 yards out for them to win, 20–17.

This meant the Colts and Packers finished with a season record of ten wins, three losses, and a tie. There would be a playoff, in Green Bay, with Matte again the hope at quarterback. On the first Packer series, Bart Starr, their methodical, almost mechanical quarterback, was hit hard, injured, and needed help to leave the field. Zeke Bratkowski took over. The Colts' only score occurred early when Don Shinnick picked up a fumble and ran it in for a touchdown. But with the second-string Bratkowski at quarterback and the "no-string" Matte, a converted halfback, working for the Colts, it became a defensive argument, like watching two counterpunchers in a boxing match.

Both teams were almost compelled to play conservatively, hoping to hold on and not commit the mistake that might open the floodgates. The Colts were still ahead in this all-important showdown, clinging to a 10–7 lead, with only 1:58 left to play. If they were able to pull it off, a win would qualify as some kind of a history-making event, beating the Packers on their home field minus a regular quarterback. From the 27 yard line, the ball was spotted for a game-tying field goal attempt. Don Chandler, who had been in two losing title games for the Giants against the Colts, was the specialist for the Packers. Now he was trying to tie the game with a field goal from short range. He kicked the ball with a fluid leg motion but it traveled precariously close to the right upright and was slicing. The flying football was going to make for a close call—but the wrong one.

The ball, amazingly, flew inches outside the ten-foot-high post, but official Jim Tunney raised his arms, signaling it was good. Chandler, unknown to Tunney, had turned his head away in despair, much the way a golfer often reacts when he misses what he thought was an easy putt. Shinnick, Michaels, and Fred Miller were outraged. They screamed at the officials, insisting the ball was wide of the post. Others did, too. Instead of winning, 10–7, and going home to prepare for the NFL championship, the game was tied, thanks to the debated field goal call. The Packers, furthermore, would cash in later with a legitimate Chandler field goal to win in overtime. Baltimore cried foul.

Commissioner Pete Rozelle, in attendance, was aware of the Colts' protests. Before he boarded a plane at the Green Bay airport, he got a telephone call from New York that told him the field goal, viewed on in-house television replays, looked wide of the mark. The Packers, getting a bonus with the field goal, forced the sudden death. This, too, the tie-breaker, came via a field goal. Chandler connected from the 25 yard line with a placement that wasn't to be questioned, making the final score 13–10. Baltimore had been victimized again.

In the locker room, Miller, a strong, mobile tackle and never one to pollute the atmosphere with unnecessary verbiage, said with strong conviction, "If that kick was good I'm ready to start eating the football." Weeks later, mailed from a Green Bay service club, came a gift box for Miller. It contained a football. A message enclosed simply read: "Start eating." But there was much more to the decision and what was to come in the aftermath. This was something far different than the usual postgame furor. I was able to get a clip of the film from an out-of-town source that I wouldn't identify. Had it been known where it came from, his position could have been jeopardized.

The NFL office, as policy, doesn't go around supplying film clips that make the officials look bad. This time, which was no surprise, it wanted to know how I had gained access to the tell-all sequence, which confirmed beyond any semblance of doubt that the call was in error. I got the film as a result of an earlier favor extended to a friend in Philadelphia, but that's all I've ever said. This was an authentic version of the Chandler kick that wasn't included in the regular team films. It was a close and difficult decision but when the film was slowed for clarification, the proof was there. The kick was bad. But I wanted a technical opinion to support what I believed I saw. It would add more substance to the story if an experienced cameraman and producer could view it in a studio. I visited Pete Greer, Sr., at WBAL-TV, a man who had worked with movies all his life. He slipped the reel on the projector and watched. "No way that kick is any good," he said. "I agree," I said, "but can you be 100 percent sure?" With that Greer put it in slow motion and then, after going to a precise frame-by-frame study, was even more certain the official's call was wrong.

Other photographers, asked to review the segment, agreed. A similar opinion, without the aid of film, came from the city editor of the *Green Bay Press-Gazette*, who was seated in the end zone and said he was shocked, as were other fans near him, to see the kick signaled good. There was no way the score could be changed or the game replayed. The Colts had to live with the misery. If there was any dispute about what happened, remedial steps taken by the league for the next season removed all doubt.

In an unprecedented move, the league decided that not just one game official, but two, should be stationed under the goalposts on all field goal tries. One official for each upright. And, oh yes, the posts were raised ten feet higher, which is where they are today, causing some people in the league to refer to them as the "Baltimore Extensions." Another postscript: The Packers, coming off the disputed outcome, faced the Cleveland Browns for the NFL crown and won, 23–12, on their way to becoming the dominant team of the 1960s.

As for Matte's wristband, he dropped it on the floor of his locker in Green Bay. It was about to be swept away by the cleanup crew, along with discarded adhesive tape and other trash. I asked Tom if he wanted it and he shook his head. He picked it up, handed it over, and I told him it was going to the Hall of Fame as an exhibit. It's still on display there and draws continuing attention from visitors. Matte has been forever grateful to me for rescuing it but, in truth, I was motivated by nothing more than a sense of history. As another postscript to what has always been referred to as "The Kick," it happened that thirty-one years later, in 1996: Chandler admitted that he believed the field goal that caused so much consternation was a bad call. So much for setting the record straight.

The next season, 1966, brought more dejection. Off to a seven and two start and tied with the Packers for first place, the Colts felt more pain when Unitas injured his throwing arm against the Atlanta Falcons. He continued to play; however, a quarterback, the same as a pitcher in baseball, can't properly throw with an arm that won't function in a smooth, rhythmic delivery. It meant that backup Gary Cuozzo got more playing time. The previous season, in a 1965 game in Minnesota against the Vikings, Cuozzo threw five touchdown passes, two short of the NFL record—something Unitas, with all his extraordinary deeds, had approached but never equaled.

On the morning of that Minnesota game, I walked to early mass with John in downtown Minneapolis. When other churchgoers recognized Unitas, they surrounded him on the sidewalk outside the church. He signed autographs, answered questions, and was delayed in returning to the hotel for the pregame meal. Meanwhile, Cuozzo, in church at the same time with other players, wasn't given any attention and walked away like just another face in the crowd. But that afternoon, Unitas, recovering from the injury, didn't play. Cuozzo was the story. Now for the contrast that makes sports so much like life itself.

At game's end, Unitas left the locker room without a single reporter asking him a question and Cuozzo, the replacement, was so besieged with interview requests that the bus for the airport had to be held for him. How quickly they forget. Unitas only laughed when the strange set of circumstances was pointed out to him. But the Colts came home with another second-place finish. The Packers of 1966 were playoff bound, not the Colts, and went on to win the first Super Bowl ever played, a 35–10 conquest of the Kansas City Chiefs.

In 1967, the Colts told themselves things would be better. They were, but in the final analysis, there was still a new way found to sidetrack their aspirations, one that the league created by way of establishing a tie-breaking rule in the event two teams wound up in a deadlock. Offensively, that year, the Colts amassed 5,008 yards, the best in football, and established a club record for fewest points allowed by the defense. You can't get any better than that.

They concluded the year with an 11–1–2 mark, the same as the Rams. Because the Super Bowl date was "set in stone," there wasn't room on the calendar for another open and available Sunday to play the Rams again in a deciding game, or a preplayoff. The league had determined before the season, with membership approving, that in cases of ties the team scoring the most points when playing against each other would be declared the champion. The Rams and Colts played to a 24–24 standoff in Baltimore. This was seven years before sudden death was introduced to regular season games. The Rams' Bruce Gossett hit with a field goal from the 47 yard line that scraped the goal post. Out or in? It caromed inside, a favorable and point-scoring break for the Rams. They were able to get the tie. Had Gossett's kick gone the other way, out instead of in, by the mere luck of a bounce the Colts would have won.

This would have decided the entire issue and the subsequent 34–10 victory by the Rams in the second game, played in Los Angeles, would not have carried divisional connotations. It would merely have been the season-closer for both teams. The Colts made the long haul by charter back from the West Coast in the dark skies of night and early morning. They drank some beer and either slept or commiserated, wondering why titles couldn't be decided on the field and not by such a contrived process as counting points scored.

Shula was never one to engage in sympathy for himself or the team he coached. That was one of his strengths, the way he approached the game. Yet he began to wonder what had to be done to get what he felt the Colts rightly deserved. Kellett had gone into retirement at the close of the 1966 season and his successor was Joe Campanella, who had played middle guard for the Colts and had demonstrated exceptional ability as a businessman. He helped put together the enormously successful chain of drive-in restaurants known as Ameche-Gino, Inc., along with the man who gave them the idea, Louis Fischer, who had been a Campanella teammate at Ohio State. But after only one season, Campanella was gone, struck down tragically by a heart attack at age thirty-six while playing handball with Shula at a court in downtown Baltimore.

It was Rosenbloom's decision, and a popular one, to elevate Harry Hulmes, who had joined the Colts when I left in early 1958 to accept the position as sports editor of the *Baltimore News-Post*, later to be called the *Baltimore News American*. Hulmes was smart, honorable, and dedicated. If any man never had an enemy, it was Harry. He had graduated from the University of Pennsylvania, as had Rosenbloom and Kellett, and everything about him was first rate, including a vast knowledge of all sports, a meticulous approach to his job, a sense of fairness, and complete integrity. He was almost too good for his own good.

The 1968 season was highly successful. The Colts were such a force they were being described as one of the greatest teams the league had ever known—almost as if they should be shipped en masse to the Hall of Fame. For one month, four games, they never allowed a touchdown. This was unheard of since the advent of the T-formation and the Bears'

73–0 annihilation of the Redskins in 1940. In the old ponderous single and double-wing football, perhaps, but not in the so-called modern day where points often came in bunches. Actually, it was necessary to research all the way back to the Giants of 1937 to find such a similar demonstration of defensive strength.

The Colts simply dominated the league. They were an impressive group, even without Unitas, who had torn the ligaments inside his right elbow in the final exhibition against Dallas and was lost for virtually the entire season. Unitas was going down under a pass rush when his arm was almost separated from the rest of him, but Earl Morrall, secured in a trade only two weeks before with the Giants for substitute tight-end Butch Wilson, filled the void. He had what evolved into a career season. Morall opened against the 49ers, the team that had originally drafted him as a number one in 1956, and beat them. He later directed the Colts to a win over the Giants, the club that sent him to Baltimore, in a 26–0 romp. So Earl was getting even in a hurry.

Morall had been shunted off to other places, too, subsequently being dealt by the 49ers to the Steelers, then to the Lions, and on to the Giants before making the quarterback scene in Baltimore. He realized he was coming in as a backup to Unitas with little to do—except if there was an emergency, which almost coincided with his arrival.

As it turned out, Morrall was to become the most important insurance policy the Colts ever bought. Shula had known him from his brief time as an assistant in Detroit, where Morrall impressed him with both his ability and personality. He had a good arm, not a great one, mixed plays well, relied heavily on play-action passes, and was an outstanding leader in a jovial, friendly sort of way. The Colts, with Morrall at the wheel, put up a thirteen and one season, the best in team history. Earl was voted "Player of the Year" in the NFL, an honor that had gone to Unitas only the season before. As a team, the Colts continued to be described as one of the strongest ever assembled. Maybe even of all time, but this was far from factual.

The media too often acts in haste, jumping quickly to confer greatness, and this qualified as a classic example of premature canonization. The Colts were good but, in my estimation, didn't compare to the Cleveland Browns of 1950, the best I ever saw. Morrall, though, was a steadying influence, the same as Unitas had been. It wasn't until late in the season that John fully regained the use of his passing arm. It was not quite 100 percent, but close. He slowly worked back into the offense. Since Morrall was doing everything right, this presented Shula with another kind of a problem. He was reluctant to make a change, but Unitas pronounced himself ready to go. The team polished off the Minnesota Vikings in the playoff, 24–14, and moved on to Cleveland, where, with a crowd of 80,628 in the seats, they delivered another impressive performance.

Matte averaged over 5 yards per carry and scored three touchdowns. The Colts minimized Leroy Kelly, the league rushing leader with 1,239 yards, now that Jim Brown had retired; Kelly could do no better than a total gain of 27 yards. The thrashing was complete. The Colts won 34–0, easily reversing what happened to them when they lost 27–0 in the same stadium four years before. Some football writers continued to hail them as virtually unbeatable. All they had to do was play one more game, which would be a step down in competition, or so they imagined. It was to be against some still-obscure team from New York in this newfangled postseason event that for the first time was being called the Super Bowl. A massive shock awaited.

CHAPTER 12

# SUPER BOWL MADNESS

For the first two years, following the activation of the merger agreement between the American Football League and the National Football League, the game between the two best teams representing each side was simply called the AFL-NFL World Championship. In the third meeting, it was to become officially known as the Super Bowl; it was an effort to add pizazz. The Colts were there to play the New York Jets, not the Giants.

The AFL, an upstart organization that wouldn't quit, had struggled to get where it was and was willing to slug it out with the NFL in checkbook warfare and forge onward despite demeaning comments about its quality of play. The leagues were head-to-head rivals for six years and both would have drowned in the waters of bankruptcy except for the monies derived from network television contracts: the NFL affiliated with CBS and the AFL tied to NBC.

A peace agreement was eventually signed and out of it the Super Bowl was born. Commissioner Rozelle, being a Californian, foresaw it as pro football's answer to the Rose Bowl. He wanted it located in a warm-weather city, where the teams would have a frost-free field to play on and the spectators would be assured of reasonably comfortable weather.

Super Bowl, which sounded so hokey when it was first mentioned, originated with Lamar Hunt, owner of the Kansas City Chiefs, who watched one of his children playing with what was known as a Super Ball. So the league, in quest of another name, was desperate enough to go for Super Bowl, per Hunt's suggestion. The truth of the matter is they had asked for recommendations and got few proposals. Hunt's was the best of a weak list but the league hoped it could do better. Now, presto, it's a part of the everyday language—an American original, the Super Bowl.

That's where the Colts found themselves on January 12, 1969, in Miami's Orange Bowl, before a capacity crowd of 75,389. They were to meet the New York Jets, led by Weeb Ewbank, the coach they had fired after he won two championships in Baltimore. And the man picked to replace him, Don Shula, had been released by Ewbank as a player in 1957. He got into his "life's work," as Ewbank used to say, in the same business, coaching football. It was a storied matchup. A former player going against his onetime coach. And, then, too, Ewbank had been signed by the Jets after Rosenbloom offered his name to Sonny Werblin, the club owner.

Ewbank had been away from football for only two months, but never missed a beat and threw himself into the Jets position, as bleak as it appeared, with the same enthusiasm and intensity he showed when he came to the lowly Colts in 1954. Baltimore was a power-in-waiting compared to the woeful Jets. There was no semblance of a foundation in the organization. With the Colts, a certain structure was in place, with far better personnel at Ewbank's disposal. The Jets had little more than a football and an assortment of warm bodies.

But Ewbank went about improving them, signing free agents, gathering rejects from the NFL, including three ex-Colts (John Sample and Sherman "Big Boy" Plunkett, members of the 1959 title squad; and a swift wide receiver, Bake Turner). The Jets, of course, were being led by Joe Namath, the celebrated "Broadway Joe," a nickname given to him by Plunkett when he was a dashing lothario amid the sparkling lights of Manhattan. The Jets were being lampooned as they prepared to play the Colts. Members of the press corps, with few exceptions, gave them little chance to win.

Tex Maule in *Sports Illustrated*, an avowed knocker of the AFL, said the Jets would lose 55 to 0. Gamblers installed them as 16½-point underdogs. Rosenbloom had a party planned after the game at his nearby Golden Beach residence. It was intended as a victory celebration. Hours before the kickoff, when he met Ewbank on the field, he invited him and his wife, Lucy, to stop by if they had a chance. A nice thought but, win or lose, Ewbank wasn't interested in going to a reception in the camp of the enemy.

On the previous Sunday night, after the Colts arrived in Fort Lauderdale and checked into the Galt Ocean Mile Hotel, prior to a week of practice, the players were free to relax with no curfew involved. Lou Michaels and Danny Sullivan went to a nearby restaurant and seated at the bar was the man himself, Namath. Michaels entered into a discussion, and it became animated. Being opinionated, Lou told Namath what Morrall was going to do to the Jets. And, if Morrall couldn't get the job done, then "We'll bring in the master (meaning Unitas)." Namath responded with a bit of sarcasm and Michaels, in short order, invited him to step outside to go one-on-one. Right there, Namath made one of the great no-calls of his career. He remained on the bar stool.

To fight the strong, bearlike Michaels would have been no contest. Namath had better sense than to try to accommodate that kind of trouble. The boys eventually cooled down and Namath bought a round of drinks. The story of the confrontation was being quietly talked about among some of the Colts the next day, which led to my interview with Michaels in his hotel room. The *News American* was able to reveal details the next day, which didn't make the Sunpapers any too happy. After the paper was on the street, I gave a duplicate to Milton Richman, sports editor of United Press International and one of my most revered friends. Richman then mentioned what he had to Norman Miller, of the *New York Daily News*, and Miller wanted to know if he could share the same report. It is regarded, even now, when those things come up, as one of the most talked-about stories of the entire Super Bowl series. Later in the week, Namath made news again, in a more spectacular way.

While appearing at a football dinner at the Miami Springs Villas, near the airport, Joe predicted, after a challenge from a heckler, that the Jets would win. No question about it. Then he said, "I guarantee it." Namath was to say later that when he viewed films of the Colts, he couldn't believe how vulnerable they appeared. He went public in criticizing Morrall and said there were four quarterbacks, including himself, in the AFL who were much better. If this was a true assessment, what did that say for the so-called superiority of the NFL? Here was Morrall, quiet and reserved, already hailed as the "player of the year" in the NFL, being subjected to what was considered cheap-shot ridicule by a rival who was not showing even the slightest regard for another professional. Namath was taking a chance.

Was it contrived? No. It just flowed from Joe, free and easy like, and probably reflected exactly what he believed. His coach, Ewbank, liked his players to keep a low profile and never say anything that might provoke the emotions of an opponent. When he talked to Namath about his public statements, Joe told him he was only telling the truth and not to worry. The Jets would take care of the Colts. And they did.

What Namath had succeeded in doing was to knock, or at least tilt, the Colts off balance. They had never encountered such braggadocio. Namath had nothing to lose with his bold declaration. Since the Colts were so heavily favored, a wild prediction could do no harm from the Jets' standpoint. They were already confined to the loser's bracket.

Here were the Colts riding along as prohibitive choices and feeling supremely confident. Ewbank, when he was coaching the same team, would warn about "getting all puffed-up like a big toad." In a way, the

Colts were perceived as having to drop down to meet a foe from a lesser league, one perceived as grossly inferior. Namath's talk had gotten the attention of the Colts but the players dismissed it, even though they were astonished at some of the things he was saying. In truth, they didn't have much respect for Namath, figuring he had fair ability and was merely a noise factor, covering up for a team that didn't belong on the same field with the Colts.

At game time, they thought, they'd surely take care of him, the implication being that he'd regret all this extraneous ranting and raving. Ticket sales didn't need to be hyped, a sellout was already assured, but people were discussing the Super Bowl in a way they never had before, as when the Packers, ho-hum, were playing and beating the Chiefs and Raiders in the two earlier games. The Colts were accepted as one of the NFL's all-time best and Namath was regarded as this impudent, filled-up-with-himself, overbearing bore. Actually, he was a gentleman, bright, entertaining, and accommodating. He also knew how to create a story.

During the week leading up to the Super Bowl, the Colts' management invited the wives, children, and other family members to join the team at their beachfront hotel. It was a chance to get out of the mid-January weather in Maryland. Maybe this was a distraction but, again, that's second-guessing. Had the Colts won, other teams would have been wondering if that wasn't "the way to go," to create a family atmosphere, only, admittedly, this was a vacation setting. One unusual visitor to the hotel was Frank "Red" Cumiskey, a former Ewbank assistant in his early Baltimore years. It was strange that he showed up. Obviously, he was there to do more than renew old acquaintances; he just might have been searching for scraps of information. More than likely, he was reporting back to Ewbank. This was typical of Weeb, something he had learned from his years with Paul Brown in Cleveland.

I arrived at the Orange Bowl on the day of the game with Claude "Buddy" Young, who was working for the league office as a special assistant to the commissioner. He had a parking pass and put his car in a preferred location. As we pulled in, another car drew alongside. Out stepped Lou Chesler, a one-time friend and associate of Rosenbloom. It was Chesler who was suspected of being the donor of extra money for the Colts players to share after the 1958 win over the Giants. I recognized Chesler. Young introduced us. "Yeah, I remember you," he said when we shook hands. "Rosenbloom always told me he was going to fire Kellett and make you the general manager. By the way, how is that dirty son-of-a-bitch?" What Chesler didn't know was that one important reason I pulled away from the Colts and Rosenbloom was because I didn't want to be placed in just such a cross-fire position.

The general opinion inside the Orange Bowl, especially in the press box, where genius abounds, was that what we had gathered for wouldn't be much of a contest. There was no way to foretell that when the Colts showed up they would be there in body but had left their minds somewhere else. In short, they weren't ready to play. For them, the afternoon was replete with missed opportunities, again a sure symptom of a team that wasn't keyed mentally or emotionally to make anything close to a maximum effort. The Jets went 80 yards for the only touchdown of the first half, as Matt Snell drove over from the four, and at intermission it was 7–0. The exalted Colts hadn't exactly blown the Jets away, which had to do wonders for their confidence as they headed for the locker room.

I suspected it was going to be a struggle for the Colts, even though they were only down by seven, to pull themselves together and play something close to their maximum. You're either ready to play or not, and attitudes can't be controlled by merely telling yourself at that late juncture, halfway through the sixty minutes, that "now I'm ready to go win." It doesn't work that way.

From a "game plan" perspective, the Jets designed their offense to run away from linebacker Mike Curtis, who was highly respected. Their intention was to avoid him as much as possible. They went, instead, to the other side, where end Ordell Braase was trying to hide an injury and Namath believed that two other veterans, Don Shinnick and Lenny Lyles, were ready to be exploited.

The most controversial play occurred as the first half was about to end. The Colts were at the Jets' 41 yard line, second and nine. Morrall handed off to Matte, who ran to the right, stopped, and tossed back to Morrall. It was the old "flea-flicker," a dusted-off play that had its origin with Bob Zuppke, a coaching legend at Illinois. Morrall had to stretch somewhat for the return of the ball but made the catch and looked downfield for his target. He was trying to locate Jimmy Orr, who was so wide open he couldn't be found (by Morrall or the Jets). Orr was signaling with his hand, perhaps 15 yards behind the nearest defender. Still, Morrall couldn't find him. Why?

He still doesn't know. One theory advanced is that a marching band, wearing blue uniforms, was assembling behind that corner of the end zone in preparation for the half-time show. Perhaps the Colts-blue jersey Orr was wearing blended in with those of the bandsmen. Morrall didn't have time to sort them out or send up a flare. He quickly turned to another option, looking almost directly down the center of the field and firing the pass for Jerry Hill. But the Jets, out of position in their coverage, quickly recovered, and Jim Hudson got there in time not only to get in the way but to intercept.

The Colts had an earlier chance to score when they recovered a George Sauer fumble at the Jets' 12. Tom Mitchell came open in the end zone and could have made the catch but Al Atkinson, a linebacker, barely tipped the ball and took it off its trajectory. Instead of going into Mitchell's hands it was deflected, bounced off his shoulder pads and into the hands of Randy Beverly for an interception. After the game and even years later, Mitchell refused to offer any kind of an excuse. "They pay off on the final score," he said. "There's no reason to dissect the game and try to wonder what happened. They beat us. That's it. They won, we lost. Over and done with."

The Jets were ahead and for the Colts there was a slight feeling of desperation. Things didn't improve in the second half. Jim Turner added two field goals in the third period and another in the fourth to extend the count to 16–0. Shula had been debating with himself whether to lift Morrall and put in Unitas, who was eager to play. But Morrall had taken the Colts this far, to a record of 16 and 1, and Shula wanted to give him every chance to get the offense moving. There was still time to turn it around. But the Colts only had four offensive plays the entire third period while the Jets, with time-killing drives, dominated the clock and the ball.

Finally, in the fourth period, with 13:26 remaining, Unitas got a belated call. He helped advance the Colts to the Jets' 25 and on second down a pass intended for Orr in the end zone was picked off by Beverly, a clean interception. The next time the Colts' offense went to work, Unitas took the team in a well-orchestrated march of 80 yards, with a smart mix of plays, and Hill went over from the one, behind Bob Vogel and Glenn Ressler, for what was Baltimore's only touchdown. It appeared, yet only for an instant, that Unitas might again do the "impossible" and bring the Colts back, as had happened so many times in the past. But on this day of deep disappointment it wasn't to be. The Jets were using up the clock and playing keep-away. Unitas, asked why he didn't get in the game earlier, said, "I would have if Shula's big ego hadn't gotten in the way," which was another way of saying the coach wanted to win with Morrall to show he didn't need Unitas.

The Jets' locker room, with Namath's father present, was close to pandemonium. As for the Colts, they were in a state of bewilderment, shocked by what had happened. They couldn't wait to be somewhere else—just anywhere. The Rosenbloom postgame party went on as scheduled, but it was more a wake than anything else.

The drinkers on the team lost themselves Sunday night and into Monday morning. Alex Hawkins sat at a bar analyzing the Jets' roster, listed in a program, and wondered how few of them were capable of making the Colts. He was right. But the Jets had won, 16–7, and it was history. Michaels was so crestfallen he cried—that's how much victory meant to him—and wondered what his brother, Walt, an assistant coach for the Jets, was doing. Lou, though, had promised, win or lose, a sizable donation to his church in Swoyersville, Pennsylvania, and followed through to make it good, even though it was coming from the loser's share.

From another standpoint, yet of no consolation to the Colts, was that the result established the Super Bowl as an American sporting staple. A team ranked as a 16½-point underdog had, by winning, given a certain authenticity to an event that all the hype in the world couldn't have provided. For Ewbank, it was total vindication, not that he needed any. And he now had the distinction of coaching in two of the most notable games in NFL history and winning both of them. Ewbank didn't chortle but he could have. Beating Rosenbloom and the Colts in something as prestigious as the Super Bowl had to carry profound satisfaction. The overly confident Colts, in a manner of speaking, figured they could win by merely showing up—but it didn't happen that way. It never does.

The Colts promised they'd get back to the Super Bowl to rectify the embarrassment and they did, only two years later. In 1969 they played with injuries that were bothersome to three of their receivers, John Mackey, Mitchell, and Orr. By the next year, Szymanski, Braase, and Bob Boyd, with outstanding careers behind them, took retirement. Rosenbloom was unhappy over the way things were going. The Colts could do no better than 8 and 6, a season-long hangover from the Super Bowl loss. Maybe it was time for another change.

Rosenbloom said Shula had given him a legacy—the first National Football League owner to lose to the American Football League. It was true but still a cheap shot. This, too, would change, because the NFL and AFL were to complete another important phase of their amalgamation agreement. Pittsburgh, Cleveland, and Baltimore were handsomely compensated for making the switch ($3 million apiece for agreeing to join the American Conference) which set up a Colts and Dallas Cowboys meeting in Super Bowl V. They were going back to the scene of the earlier disaster, Miami's Orange Bowl, and this time there would be a different ending and a change of leadership.

Shula wouldn't be around and neither would Hulmes. Both left when they could see and feel that things were going to be decidedly different. In early January, the appointment of Don Klosterman as general manager was announced. Hulmes even officiated at his own replacement party. Only he could have done it, this man of quiet decency and graciousness. Hulmes later moved on to the New Orleans

Saints as executive administrator. And, within a matter of weeks, Shula was gone, too. In a way, he beat Rosenbloom to the punch.

The exit process began when Shula got a phone call from Bill Braucher, a former college teammate, who was a sportswriter for the *Miami Herald*. Braucher was doing a favor for Joe Robbie, owner of the Miami Dolphins, who was upset when he learned that Paul "Bear" Bryant was not going to leave the University of Alabama to assume the coaching position Robbie was offering. Braucher volunteered to call his friend of long standing, Shula, and sound him out on his interest and availability. Shula listened to Braucher and wasn't about to close the door on opportunity. He immediately went to see Steve Rosenbloom, the club president, Carroll's son, and asked if he could talk to Robbie in Miami. Permission was granted. Carroll was away on a trip to the Orient, and Steve had total authority to run the club in his absence.

When Rosenbloom arrived in Hawaii on February 18, Shula telephoned to tell him of his decision. At first there was little reaction within the Colts hierarchy. The feeling I had was they were generally pleased to see Shula leave without having to fire him. Shula also was a club vice president and when Steve was asked about that role, he simply joked, "that's because we needed someone to sign the checks." Shula burned. Reaction in the media was that Robbie had scored a coup and the Colts had taken a major hit with the loss of Shula. As Rosenbloom gathered the public reaction to Shula leaving, he began to scream that Robbie had tampered with his coach while he was out of the country. Shula said he had been given approval by his son, Steve, who was the officer in charge of the ship while his father was away. Still Rosenbloom wouldn't let up. He put pressure on Rozelle and the commissioner caved in when he shouldn't have.

Instead of taking a strong stance and letting the Shula move remain as is, Rozelle endeavored to keep peace in the NFL family by awarding the Colts something they weren't entitled to have, a first-round draft choice, who turned out to be Don McCauley, a strong, reliable halfback from the University of North Carolina. At this point in his ownership, Rosenbloom looked on coaches as not much more than a necessary evil. He waited forty-four days before making an appointment, almost as if he was sending Shula a message that he was so unimportant to the Colts there wasn't any real need to hurry the naming of a replacement.

The new coach was a popular choice, the familiar Don McCafferty, who had been the backfield coach and offensive coordinator under Shula and had originally been hired by Ewbank. He was the antithesis of Shula. An entirely different personality with a style of his own. The players called him "The Easy Rider." While Shula was intense, demanding, and given to shouting, McCafferty was low key and patient. The players reacted in a positive way. Here it was, a new decade, the 1970s, and for the Colts it was going to be different. As a result of the merger, a new set of teams would play in the reorganized NFL and they had an incoming general manager in Klosterman and a rookie head coach in McCafferty.

Yet in spite of all these changes, the Colts reached the pinnacle—another trip to the Super Bowl. It was as if all the bad luck of the previous ten years had been exorcised. Instead of calls and measurements going against them, they went in their favor. In the opening game there was a positive omen of what was to come. Playing in San Diego, rookie kicker Jim O'Brien clicked on three field goals, the last one coming with fifty-six seconds left to give the Colts a 16–14 win over the Chargers. One of his kicks, similar to what Gossett had done to the Colts in 1967, hit the post and caromed inside. They won games, not by blowouts, but by the narrowest of margins—one, two, three, and four points. It wasn't pretty but it was good, a case of the breaks finally evening up for a team that had been dogged by what seemed an unending avalanche of bad luck for much too long.

It was a season that accumulated eleven wins, two losses, and a tie in the regular season and victories over the Cincinnati Bengals and Oakland Raiders in the playoffs. On to the Super Bowl.

This time the Colts established a businesslike atmosphere in their preparations. The players' wives and children were not around during the week. Families arrived the day before the game and were registered in another hotel. The team was headquartered in Miami Lakes, a short walk from where Shula was living since joining the Dolphins as coach, general manager, and part owner. At night, some of the players, along with equipment manager Fred Schubach, visited Shula's house. They didn't want it known for fear Rosenbloom would take a dim view of their friendly relationship with his ex-coach. They drank a few beers and relaxed.

As for the game against the Cowboys, it became either the sloppiest or the most exciting of all Super Bowls, depending on the point of view. There were eleven turnovers between the teams. Unitas was intercepted twice and fumbled; Morrall was intercepted once and also fumbled but recovered it before the Cowboys could. Overall, the Colts gave up the ball on fumbles four times. Unitas was taken down in the second period with a vicious tackle, tore a rib cartilage, and had to give way to Morrall, a thirty-six-year-old backup replacing a thirty-seven-year-old starter.

Unitas rarely showed he was hurt or gave into pain but it appeared he was under duress. As George Andrie powered into Unitas, or almost through him, he was in the act of throwing, and the ball was short-fielded by Mel Renfro for an interception. The Cowboys put impressive midsized drives together, but each ended with field goals by Mike Clark and a margin of 6–0. Then came one of the most astonishing "accidents" in Super Bowl history. Unitas, before the injury dealt by Andrie, attempted a pass to Eddie Hinton, who was running a medium deep pattern against the Cowboys.

After enduring so many arm injuries, Unitas's touch on short passes wasn't the same. He could throw long with accuracy but when it came to lobs and taking something off the ball, there appeared to be a problem that originated with an accumulation of so many blows to his hand, elbow, and shoulder. The pass to Hinton was high but he tipped it as he attempted to pull it down. Then Dallas defensive back Ray Renfro reached for the interception, barely touched it, and the ball traveled on—right into the arms of John Mackey at the Cowboys' 45. If Renfro had not contacted the ball, the pass would have been an illegal reception, the play called back. Mackey, with the football, stormed untouched the rest of the way to the goal line. It was a freakish 75-yard touchdown, but the points looked good on the scoreboard regardless of how they got there. In keeping with the day, O'Brien's conversion try was blocked, and the score was 6–6.

Two possessions later, after Unitas was pounded by Lee Roy Jordan and fumbled, the Cowboys rode for a touchdown, as Craig Morton flipped to Duane Thomas from seven yards out. It was 13–6 at the half and, at the end of three periods, it remained the same. Thomas had a chance to directly influence the outcome when he fumbled at the Colts' one-yard line at the start of the third quarter. It came after he was stopped and then made a second effort to get to the goal line. The ball came loose. A scramble. And Billy Ray Smith kept screaming, "It's our ball . . . it's our ball." Meanwhile, the Cowboys insisted they had it. Dave Manders, the Cowboys' center, contended, then and now, during the game and after, that he was the one who had the ball and his team deserved to maintain control instead of giving it up when they were so close to the goal line.

The Cowboys, including coach Tom Landry, claimed Smith pulled a perfect con job on the officials. As for Smith, he won't say what happened. Not for the record anyhow. The recovery went to Jim Duncan, Colts halfback, who had put the Dallas drive in motion after fumbling the second-half kickoff. Again, it was that kind of a game, replete with mistakes and players coming back to redeem themselves. The Colts, most assuredly, had gotten off the hook because if Thomas had reached the end zone it would have put Dallas ahead, 20–6. "And there was no

⇑ Approachable and amiable, John Unitas stops to sign an autograph as he heads for the locker room at Memorial Stadium before a game with the Detroit Lions.

⇑ Trying to stop John Mackey when he had the football was akin to attempting to stand in the way of an eighteen-wheel tractor-trailer running wide open. He was also a devastating blocker. (Courtesy Pro Football Hall of Fame)

⇐ Mike Curtis, who played with all-out zeal and determination, qualifies as one of the best linebackers in the thirty-five years of the Colts' franchise.

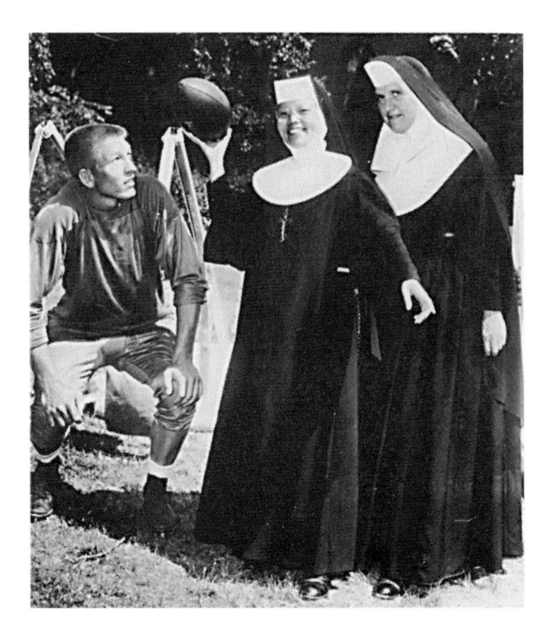

⇑ Rookie John Unitas, then with the Pittsburgh Steelers, watches as Sister Mary Theresa Hung of Shishi, China, and Sister Mary Mercedes of Philadelphia visit training camp while attending a 1955 seminar at St. Bonaventure College in Olean, New York.

⇓ John Unitas, with graceful style, delivers a pass against the Detroit Lions. Notice the pitcher-like rhythm of the follow-through. Jim Parker (No. 77) and Alan "The Horse" Ameche (No. 35) block out the Lions.

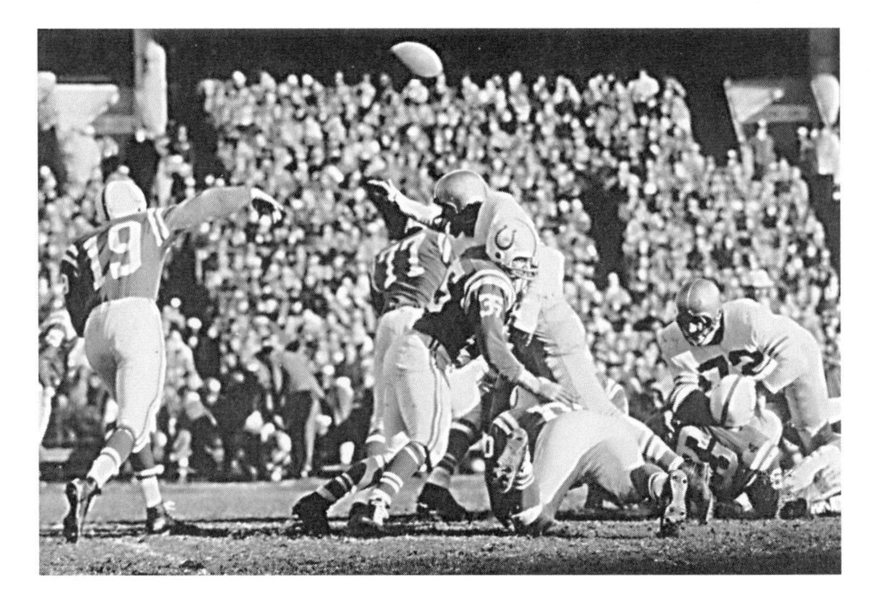

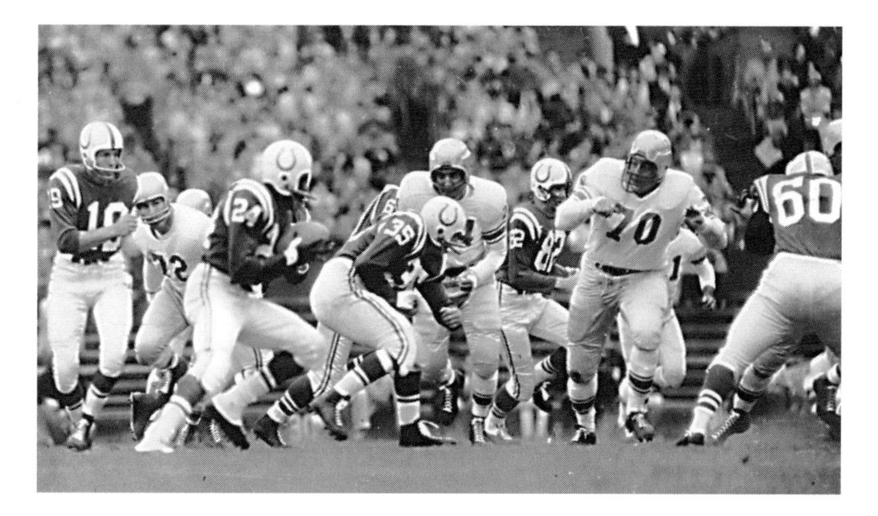

⥣ Ready to accelerate: Lenny Moore (No. 24) takes a handoff from John Unitas (No. 19) and, with blocking assistance from Alan "The Horse" Ameche (No. 35) and George Preas (No. 60), is about to find running room against the Detroit Lions.

⥥ John Unitas, prepared to set up and throw behind Tony Lorick (No. 33), Bob Vogel (No. 72), and Jim Parker (No. 77) in a game against Green Bay.

⇑ Classroom teacher/coach Don Shula, with assistants Don McCafferty and John Sandusky in the background, reviews fundamentals during training camp. Bob Vogel *(left)* and Fred Miller are two of the students/players.

⇓ Hall of Fame honors would subsequently come to Lenny Moore, who participates here in retiring his jersey number in pregame ceremonies in 1968. Moore once scored touchdowns in eighteen consecutive games—an NFL record.

⇐ Fullback Jerry Hill, at the window seat, and punter Tom Gilburg play cards while en route to Detroit in 1963.

⇐ Jim Parker, the only Colt to be enshrined in the college and pro football halls of fame. He played both guard and tackle and is considered among the foremost offensive linemen of all time. (Courtesy Pro Football Hall of Fame)

⇑ As John Mackey (No. 88) gets in position to help clear the way, the nimble, slick Jimmy Orr (No. 28) dances for yardage against the Detroit Lions. Orr combined sure hands and clever moves to become one of the Colts' most capable receivers.

⇓ Here's the most famous touchdown in Baltimore football history. Alan "The Horse" Ameche drives toward the goal line in the Colts' 23–17 win over the New York Giants. Lenny Moore *(left)* gets an effective block on Emlen Tunnell after John Unitas (No. 19) hands off to Ameche. Jim Patton (No. 20) tries to fill the gap in vain. (Courtesy Pro Football Hall of Fame)

⇑ Part of the crowd of 30,000 fans overwhelming the Colts on their return to the Baltimore airport after winning the 1958 sudden-death game over the New York Giants.

⇓ Preparing to catch the ball deep in New York Giants' territory, Jim Mutscheller looks over his shoulder just yards away from the goal line in the third quarter of the Colts' sudden-death game. Raymond Berry (No. 82) ran a shallow pass route on the play. Giants pictured are Sam Huff (No. 70), Karl Karilivacz (No. 21), and Jim Patton (No. 20).

⥣ The actual ball used in the historic sudden-death game of 1958. (Courtesy Pro Football Hall of Fame)

⥣ A Colts' decal from bygone days.

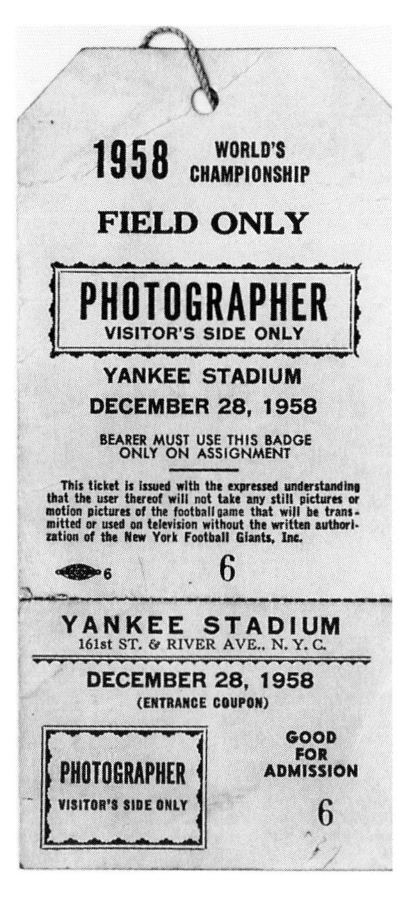


⇐ A rarity: An unused photographer's badge for the 1958 title game in New York's Yankee Stadium.

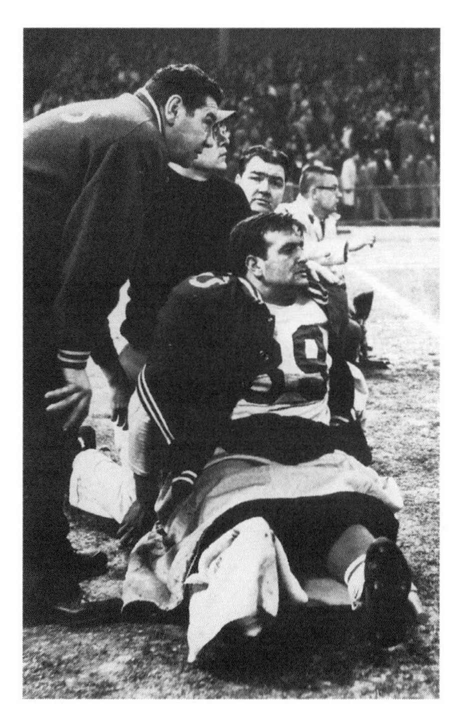

⇐ With only minutes to play in the epic Colts-Giants struggle in 1958, Gino Marchetti broke his ankle. He refused to leave the sidelines while the clock wound down. Here he is attended by Vince DePaula, trainer Bill Neill, and Bill Naylor. (Courtesy Pro Football Hall of Fame)

⇓ Assistant trainer Dimitri Spasoff *(left)* raises his fist in a menacing gesture against the Giants' Sam Huff (No. 70) in the title game. Huff and coach Weeb Ewbank exchanged heated words in this sideline confrontation. In the background are equipment manager Fred Schubach *(left)* and Bob Shaw, assistant coach.

⥣ Lydell Mitchell, a strong and reliable runner and a sure-handed receiver, gave the Colts six exceptional years.

⥣ Quarterback Bert Jones had it all—a powerful passing arm, strong running ability, and the durability to take a hit.

⥣ Gary Cuozzo set a team record of five touchdown passes against the Minnesota Vikings on a day in 1965 when John Unitas was sidelined by an injury. Later in the same season Cuozzo suffered a separated shoulder.

⥣ He later wore No. 41 on his jersey, but Tom Matte is recognizable at any age—even before he was running with a football. Matte grew up to be a Colts first-round draft selection from Ohio State.

⇐ With Don McCauley (No. 23) preparing to offer protection, the Colts' Bert Jones, endowed with extraordinary physical skills, is about to deliver the ball downfield.

⇓ Three close friends with ties to the Colts: Buddy Young *(left)*, Billy Vessels *(right)*, and a certain sportswriter gather at a Chesapeake Restaurant reception.

⇑ An infamous kick in a 1965 Green Bay Packers-Colts game, clearly high and wide of the goal post. After thirty-one years, kicker Don Chandler finally admitted that from his perspective it was the wrong call by the official.

⇐ An innovative wristband, offering a ready list of plays, was worn by Tom Matte in the 1965 playoff with Green Bay. Pictured is the display at the Pro Football Hall of Fame. Matte was used as an emergency quarterback after injuries to John Unitas and Gary Cuozzo. (Courtesy Pro Football Hall of Fame)

⇐ Part of the fun of a Colts game was watching the fans. At every home game *(left to right)* Dominick DeAmico, Bill Gattus, Buddie Janowicz, and Gene "Reds" Hubbe would circle the field carrying signs and provide an amusing sideshow.

⇓ Colts followers hold up a sign proclaiming championships in 1958, 1959, and 1964. The latter claim was somewhat premature; the Cleveland Browns shut out the Colts, 27–0.

⇑ Team owner Bob Irsay, who liked to flash the thumbs-up sign, stands between Sgt. Paul Reese and PFC Emanuel Terna at Memorial Stadium. The marines were involved in the annual "Toys for Tots" program that benefits kids at Christmas.

⇓ John Unitas, Lenny Lyles, and Dick Szymanski gather at a Colts reunion. Unitas and Lyles were teammates at the University of Louisville and as Baltimore Colts.

⇑ It's time for a picnic and some of the standout Colts gather for an informal reunion. *Left to right:* Lloyd Colteryahn, Doug Eggers, Joe Campanella, Gino Marchetti, Jim Mutscheller, Elmer Wingate, Don Shula, and Bill Pellington. All played for the Colts during the 1950s.

⇓ With this ring, Gino Marchetti is wed to the Pro Football Hall of Fame in 1972. Making the presentation is the late Dick Gallagher, former director of the Hall of Fame and onetime Cleveland Browns assistant coach.

⇑ Coach Weeb Ewbank and Raymond Berry at a Pro Football Hall of Fame installation ceremony at Canton, Ohio, in 1973. (Courtesy Pro Football Hall of Fame)

⇓ Ready for the snap: Center George Radosevich is over the ball and quarterback George Shaw is ready for the exchange. The deep backs are *(left to right)* Claude "Buddy" Young, Alan "The Horse" Ameche, and Billy Vessels. The presence of Ameche and Vessels in 1956 represented the only time in Baltimore football history that two former Heisman Trophy winners were teammates.

way if we go up two touchdowns they were going to get two touchdowns off us," said Bob Lilly, the Cowboys' outstanding tackle.

During the entire third period, the Cowboys never attempted a pass. Morton had arm trouble late in the season and Landry was trying to minimize the passing game. In the final period, he had no choice. Morton put the ball in the air ten times, completed four for only 27 yards, and three of his passes were intercepted. The first was by Rick Volk, who picked off Morton's hurried toss after Roy Hilton put on a strong rush at the Cowboys' 33 and returned it to the three. In two plays, Tom Nowatzke crashed the line for a touchdown and O'Brien's kick for the point tied the score at 13–13.

Morrall was to call the Volk interception the "play of the game" because it gave the team a lift or the breakthrough it needed. "We knew then that Dallas was going to have to pass again and that's what we were waiting for," added Volk. With 1:52 to play, the Cowboys fielded a punt at the Colts' 48 and were in position to either win or force overtime. On second down, Morton was sacked by Fred Miller but a Cowboy was called for holding. The penalty was stepped off from the point of the foul, which took it all the way back to the Cowboys' 27, where it was now second and 35 yards for a first down.

The next year, the rules were altered so that the penalty would be calculated from the line of scrimmage and not from where the foul occurred. Again, the Colts were the beneficiaries of a break. Their luck had changed. Morton was under a strong rush again and attempted to reach Dan Reeves near the sidelines. The pass was high. Reeves jumped, the ball bouncing off his hands and into the arms of Mike Curtis, the Colt linebacker who the Cowboys, based on their scouting reports and personal observations, held in the highest regard. He was respected as a contact type player, a punishing tackler who was always around the ball.

After the interception, Curtis returned to the Dallas 28 yard line, which had been the Cowboys' line of scrimmage when Morton tried to throw to Reeves. Two running plays by Norm Bulaich and the clock was down to nine seconds. Jim O'Brien said he had been watching from the sidelines and hoping the entire time that it wouldn't come down to this—where it all depended on him. But it couldn't be avoided.

O'Brien tried to pick up blades of grass to scatter in the air to determine which way the wind was blowing. "I reminded him it was artificial turf and that grass wasn't growing there," Morrall recalls. "I just told him to forget the wind and meet the ball square." Morrall took the snap from center Tom Goode and set it down at the 32 yard line. O'Brien kicked and the Super Bowl crowned a new champion. Baltimore had won, 16–13.

Unlike a previous Super Bowl, the loss to the Jets, the best team had prevailed. It was a momentous victory for McCafferty, the new head coach; Rosenbloom, the owner; and all the Colts.

In the stands, Shula watched with interest, trying to put out of his mind what happened to his team and to himself only two years and five days before on that same field. He would have liked to have been on the sidelines, riding to a victory, but the experience of winning a Super Bowl would come later for him—in a new city, Miami, and with a different team, the Dolphins. The next morning, Shula gave me a ride to the airport, along the same expressway that later, when he gained more victories, including Super Bowls, and increased his fame, would be named after him.

As to how the Colts, jubilant after so many near-misses to get there, viewed their new football achievement, it remained for tackle Bob Vogel to put it in perspective. When the luck aspect of the 1970 regular season was brought up, he said, "So what? I've had luck decide against us so many times I'm sick of it. I quit being proud years ago when we lost games we should have won. The way I look at it is we're going to get the Super Bowl ring because we won the games that counted this year. We deserve it."

Another tackle, Lilly, of the Cowboys, after the O'Brien kick decided the issue, pulled off his helmet and gave it a mighty heave. If it wasn't an Olympic record it sure qualified as a Super Bowl distance mark for how far a Riddell headgear could be thrown. The Colts knew exactly how he felt; they had been there and could empathize with his frustration. Landry, not given to idle chatter, realized the game had been replete with miscues but offered a substantial reason why it happened—the way the teams were banging away at each other. Andrie's tackle of Unitas, when he put him out of the game, for instance, was clean but devastating.

"I haven't been around many games where the players hit harder," Landry commented. "Sometimes people watch a game and see turnovers and they talk about how sloppy the play was. The mistakes in that game weren't invented, at least not by the people who made them. Most were forced."

The victory earned a $15,000 check for each of the players and a lug-nut sized ring, with a horseshoe design, that provided them a more permanent reminder of Baltimore's first and only Super Bowl success. It had been a long and arduous adventure.

CHAPTER 13

# TALE OF TWO CITIES

Astonishing things continued to occur in Baltimore's eventful football life . . . and not just on the field. What was in the throes of developing was the unprecedented trade of the Colts for the Rams, one franchise handed over for another. East and west. Baltimore for Los Angeles. Almost an even exchange, except for a few million extra dollars thrown in to make it more appealing.

Carroll Rosenbloom orchestrated the move, indicative of how big business swaps companies, inventories, and even office managers, salesmen, secretaries, and file clerks. At face value, Los Angeles and the Rams represented more of everything, a larger fan base, prestige, money to be made, show biz celebrities, and sunshine. The Rams' owner Dan Reeves was a part of the family that founded and owned the Reeves grocery chain in New York. He had been afflicted with Parkinson's Disease and supposedly told Rosenbloom that when "something happened" to him that he, Carroll, should have the team. That's what Rosenbloom said Reeves told him while walking across the field before a Rams-Colts game in Los Angeles. I don't believe it, nor do others. Those of us who knew Reeves, such as Tex Schramm, Bert Rose, and Rozelle, found he was always upbeat, figuring he would somehow survive the illness. This was a man who always had a positive outlook; he was also honest and forthright.

Rosenbloom had become disenchanted in Baltimore. He had earlier pressured his co-owners, Livie, the Hilgenberg estate, Mullan, and Krieger to sell out. Carroll told them he wanted the team for his two sons, Steve and Danny. Finally, Krieger and Mullan, in late 1961 or early 1962, said they didn't want to stand in the way of such a beautiful idea and reluctantly agreed to let Carroll have their shares of ownership. They were getting little attention. Their names were rarely mentioned; it was Rosenbloom's show. At one point, Rosenbloom had Chuck Thompson, who was doing play-by-play of the games, refer to the team as "Carroll's Colts." That brought a negative reaction all over Baltimore and was especially offensive to Krieger.

Within a matter of days after Krieger capitulated and sold to Rosenbloom, the league signed a massive television deal with CBS—the first one that called for enormous income for all the teams. Krieger believed Rosenbloom had advance information of the pending contract and, as an attorney and businessman, knew this to be a violation of the legal relationship between a majority owner and his minority partners. But instead of bringing suit, Krieger called Kellett and told him that he had changed his mind and wasn't going to sell. "I reminded Don," said Krieger, "that when I agreed to let Carroll have my percentage of ownership that he had told me I could 'come back in' any time I wanted. So I was electing to exercise that option. I wanted to 'come back in.' Kellett told me he would talk to Carroll. He called back and said, 'Carroll doesn't ever remember making any such promise.'" Krieger had a case but didn't pursue it, realizing again what he already knew—that Rosenbloom's word was suspect. In the years that ensued, Krieger, usually extremely charitable, never kept it a secret that Rosenbloom had maneuvered him out of the ownership picture and continued to express a low personal regard for the man.

Rosenbloom ultimately realized the new stadium he wanted in Baltimore wasn't going to be forthcoming. There was no hue and cry on the part of the fans for another place to play; it is the owners who demand better facilities, paid for, of course, by the public. Rosenbloom had stopped speaking to Jerry Hoffberger, the National Brewing Co. president who bought the Orioles, and attempted to feud with him over petty issues. Hoffberger continued to run his brewery interests and ignored the Rosenbloom insults. In short, Carroll didn't believe he was getting the full attention, or adulation, he deserved. That's when he threatened to take the Colts to Tampa. A survey of other NFL owners indicated this wouldn't happen, and Rozelle was on record with Congress that all present franchises would remain in their current locations. He made this part of his testimony when he asked for permission to merge the NFL with the AFL.

In 1970, the Colts beat Shula's Dolphins with little trouble in their first meeting, causing a gloating Rosenbloom to tell the sportswriters, "I thought they would be better coached." That was ridiculous. The young Dolphins, as anyone could see, were not ready to win, but it didn't take Shula long to make it happen. The next year he more than returned the fire, beating the Colts in a season-ending game, a 21–0 shutout—the first time Baltimore hadn't scored a point since December 13, 1965, or 95 games before. Two of the Colts' most productive runners, Norm Bulaich and Tom Matte, were injured and didn't play. In the fourth period, with the heat on, Bubba Smith left the field because, he said, he was having trouble breathing in the saunalike temperatures of the Orange Bowl. The Colts got a quality performance from Unitas, even though they didn't score, or the margin would probably have escalated.

A Dick Anderson return with an interception for 62 yards, with vicious blocking wiping out all pursuers, was a backbreaker for the Colts. The Dolphins were on their way to the Super Bowl. Meanwhile, Upton Bell, who had been the club's personnel director, left to become general manager of the New England Patriots and helped put that franchise on the road to respectability. Rosenbloom was eager to unload Bell, even though it was Upton's father, the late commissioner, who had "gift wrapped" him for the Baltimore franchise in 1953. Bell's other son, Bert, Jr., the business manager, resigned in the mid-1960s when he said the league no longer represented what his father had intended, but there was another reason, which he refused to discuss publicly, but says I am free to reveal after his death.

Rosenbloom said he wouldn't stand in the way of Upton advancing himself and, indeed, worked to promote the possibility with Billy Sullivan, the Patriots' owner. So it wouldn't appear too obvious that Rosenbloom was trying to push Bell to the Patriots, he told him to go to San Diego and to call Sullivan from there, so as to indicate the Chargers were interested in him, even if they weren't. When it came to weaving a fictitious game plan, Carroll led the league.

George Young filled the position vacated by Bell. He had been an assistant in the scouting department and in 1970 was offensive line coach when the team won the Super Bowl. He had played at Calvert Hall in Baltimore and went to Bucknell where he was a Little All-America tackle and then was drafted by the Dallas Texans of the NFL. Young first impressed Shula with his knowledge of the game after grading films for the Colts on a part-time basis while he was still coaching football at Baltimore City College.

Rosenbloom, who frequently worked in devious ways, played to the speculation that Tampa might be trying to woo the Colts by saying the team would be leaving Western Maryland College, after twenty-one years, to train at the University of South Florida. Tampa, simultaneously, agreed to host three exhibitions. This pleased both Rosenbloom and Baltimore, too, because Colts' fans didn't want to patronize games in the heat of summer when they would much prefer to be enjoying the breezes of Ocean City, Deep Creek Lake, or some getaway on the Chesapeake Bay.

A man known as the "Trophy King" of Baltimore, one Larry Beck, put out bumper stickers that read: "Don't TAMPA With Our Colts." But, as it developed, Rosenbloom never got to see the Colts in Tampa. The opportunity to make the switch to Los Angeles was getting closer all the time. Bottom line—he knew a good business deal when he saw one.

The Rams were one of the most profitable teams in the NFL and had potential to do even better. Melvin Durslag, one of the best and most reliable sportswriters in the business, reported in 1971, after the death of Ram's owner Dan Reeves, that Rosenbloom was Los Angeles-bound.

There was immediate criticism of the story in Baltimore and Los Angeles but not from me. I knew Durslag too well; he didn't invent such things to create a passing headline. He was a highly intelligent, probing, well-informed columnist with all the right contacts. Rosenbloom also was miffed that Baltimore wouldn't accept exhibition games tied into the season ticket package. He had earlier made up his mind that he was going to force them on the public, whether it was wanted or not. I took a firm stand on behalf of the fans. Why not? Isn't that what newspapers are for, to attempt some defense for a public that's being violated?

The minds of some owners, similar to politicians, work in selfish ways. They strain to think of new methods to be used to extract money from the customers. Rosenbloom had gotten the Colts for virtually a "song" and had increased his wealth because of the enormous support Baltimore provided him. It also enabled him to gain a notoriety he otherwise wouldn't have had, a chance to be identified as the owner of an NFL team rather than merely a man who owned a manufacturing business. At this juncture, it seemed he was trying to take advantage of the same fans who had been good to him. The three exhibitions he staged in Baltimore in 1971 got the silent treatment. Over ten years before, the Colts had experimented with exhibitions at home and the idea fizzled. In 1960, coming off two world championships, the Colts drew a "crowd" of 6,218 for an exhibition in Memorial Stadium with the Redskins. This was a rivalry? And the next year, only 10,208 showed up to watch the Colts and Vikings. In 1971 the Colts booked not one but three exhibitions instead of holding to the usual plan of playing preseason games in nonleague cities. It was simply a case of trying to trick the fans into believing they were going to get a legitimate product when, of course, an exhibition bears little resemblance to a regular game, even though the cost of admission is the same.

Admittedly, with the AFL-NFL merger and expansion on the drawing board, they were running out of places to go. The three-game exhibition caper followed their only Super Bowl victory. But even the incumbent champion Colts weren't able to draw in their own hometown for anything remotely resembling an exhibition. The average season ticket buyer figured he was paying to see them play home games when the regular season started and didn't want to bother with meaningless preseason skirmishes.

The meager turnouts signified Baltimore couldn't be pushed, by Rosenbloom or anyone else, to accept the near-zero appeal of exhibitions. Against the Chiefs, the attendance was 16,771; against the Bears, 17,593; and the Cowboys (a replay of the Super Bowl of two years before), 22,191. Far from a success. Rosenbloom was unhappy. He had overestimated his magic. Men of power aren't used to being told that what they are attempting to do is ethically wrong. I was the source of most of his criticism and, although some reporters were in agreement, they weren't about to say that exhibitions were unpopular.

Some writers and columnists either didn't care about taking a position or else wanted to stay on good terms with Rosenbloom. Still others had been accepting his gifts and, to use a political reference, were "in his pocket," one way or the other. One reporter's wife had earlier "borrowed" $1,000 from the team and never gave it back. Stock market deals were offered and Rosenbloom guaranteed a select few sportswriters they would not lose any money if the offerings went bad since he would cover their investments. It was a no-lose proposition. The regular reporters covering the team, Cameron Snyder of *The Sun*, Walter Taylor and Larry Harris of the *Evening Sun*, and N. P. "Swami" Clark of the *News American* didn't know the extent of the favors Rosenbloom was offering. His charm and personality could be overwhelming.

With these "pay as we go" methods Rosenbloom could do virtually anything he wanted and be assured of a favorable press. He figured every man had a price. At one point in the disagreement over the exhibitions, Mark Collins, the publisher at the *News American*, called me to his office and said a lawyer who had years before helped resolve the complex estate affairs between the children of William Randolph Hearst and Marion Davies, an actress friend, had gone to the newspaper's New York headquarters to ask that I be ordered to back off the issue.

Collins wasn't telling me to go "easy," but wanted me to know that Rosenbloom was working all angles to get his way. During the turmoil, a "peace" overture was made. It was one of those agreements to "let bygones be bygones." But the cooling-off period didn't last long. When I believed things were wrong, I said so. The Colts, about this time, had a pretraining camp outing at the Woodholme Country Club: lunch, golf, and dinner. I played with Rosenbloom, an excellent amateur golfer; Klosterman; and Sig Hyman, who owned Pension Planners, Inc., a Baltimore firm that administered the league's retirement fund. At the gathering, there also was a raffle for a $100 savings bond. Close to two hundred guests were present and, of all things, my ticket was the lucky one pulled. I didn't know until later that the drawing was rigged for me to win. An employee of the Colts told me. I had mentioned to Eddie Rosenbloom, a nephew of Carroll's, who was team business manager, that I didn't want the savings bond but to make sure it went to Mary Dobkin, a woman who lived in a poor section of Baltimore and sponsored baseball, football, and softball teams for children. Unfortunately, something went awry. Mary never got the $100 bond. The Colts kept it.

As Rosenbloom's fury increased, and when I supported Shula's right to leave without the Dolphins having to give up a draft choice, he decided I should no longer have the same opportunity as other reporters to travel on the team charter for road trips. Traveling with the team was a tremendous convenience for reporters from the Sunpapers and *News American* and also the Baltimore radio and TV stations. It's the way a team should be covered, enabling the reporters and the public to learn from a close-up perspective the stories that are developing. Club officials and players also were instructed not to talk to me but they did, especially Dick Szymanski, Harry Hulmes, and Ernie Accorsi.

Szymanski went out of his way to offer assistance and didn't care if Rosenbloom knew about it or not. Others were always looking over their shoulders to see if Rosenbloom was around when we talked. I made my own travel and hotel arrangements and never missed a game. Rosenbloom had now moved in another direction. He wanted any and all negatives about Baltimore to be emphasized; he put down Baltimore and the condition of Memorial Stadium in every way he could, telling a Sunpapers columnist that the visiting locker room was rodent-infested and that one of the minority owners of the Bills, Pat McGroder, had complained. This was disturbing to McGroder and, years later, when he had me in Buffalo to talk before the Quarterback Club, said, "That was a downright lie and I was deeply embarrassed." Rosenbloom, by innuendo and outright criticism, was painting Baltimore as an unfit place for a football team, even if he had to plant a story about rats running around the dressing room. He had endeavored to pull out of Memorial Stadium if he could find a location in Baltimore County or Howard County. Property not far from the Baltimore Beltway, near Falls Road and the eastern sector of Green Spring Valley, was viewed as a possible site for a stadium.

Zoning for turning spacious farms into commercial use would have been virtually impossible. The neighbors were ready to marshal an all-out fight to resist any intrusion on this magnificent natural setting. Dale Anderson, a strong, outspoken leader, the chief executive of Baltimore County, wanted nothing to do with any such plan. He made Mayor William Donald Schaefer happy when he said, "The Colts belong to Baltimore. They are important to the city. We don't want them because they are Baltimore's property and always have been. I love to go to Memorial Stadium to watch them play."

If other political chiefs about the country held to such basic beliefs, similar to those voiced by Anderson, the National Football League wouldn't have cities trying to steal teams from each other.

The rebuffed Rosenbloom, eager to improve his status and at the same time teach Baltimore a "lesson," had the bright lights of Hollywood drawing his interest. The Rams were going to be sold after the death of Reeves. The life-style of Los Angeles and ownership of the Rams appealed to him. But how could he circumvent the tax angle on such an enormous transaction? At one point it appeared Hugh Culverhouse had the Rams to himself and the agreement was close to being signed. But Rosenbloom put on a full-court press and the Culverhouse effort was sidetracked. Culverhouse threatened legal action but was appeased by the league and Rosenbloom with a promise he would get ownership of an expansion team to be awarded Tampa Bay. Finally, the arrangements were worked out in a rather convoluted way. Culverhouse pulled away; Rosenbloom pushed toward Los Angeles, and a third party became involved.

A man named Bob Irsay (or Bob Isray, as some early reports had his name spelled) would buy the Rams and then trade them to Rosenbloom for the Colts. But where did this Irsay or Isray come from? Who was he? He had been born in Chicago, attended the University of Illinois, where he didn't play on the football varsity, despite what he said; served in the Marines but was discharged during World War II—a time when America had its back to the wall in the fight for survival and needed all the manpower it could either recruit or draft. The Marines say he enlisted October 23, 1942 and was separated April 3, 1943, not as a lieutenant, which he alleged, but as a sergeant. He never served overseas but claimed he did. Sometimes, when he coughed, he'd say "that's from the malaria I picked up on New Guinea."

Irsay, as it turned out, was a "discovery" of Joe Thomas, who had quit the Miami Dolphins as personnel director because the owner, Joe Robbie, wouldn't make him general manager. Thomas had a prominent hand in scouting and signing players. That was his forte. But he wanted desperately to be a general manager. Robbie told him he could stay on with the Dolphins as the head of personnel with a new three-year contract that guaranteed salary raises every season. But Thomas, impetuous, decided to leave. He walked out but left behind such young prospects for Shula to coach as Bob Griese, Larry Csonka, and Jim Kiick. He also made a trade for Paul Warfield.

For six months, Thomas continued to live in Miami without a job and watched the newspapers for developments within the NFL. He was eager to get back in action and was interested to read that Rosenbloom was trying to get the Rams. Thomas had coached in both Baltimore and Los Angeles and was on good terms with Commissioner Rozelle, who had a role in seeing that he was hired as a personnel director for the Minnesota Vikings when that franchise was founded in 1961. With the Rams' ownership future still not defined, Thomas called Rozelle to inquire about the possibility of putting a group together to make an offer for the Colts or Rams. Rozelle, fully aware of what was going on behind the scenes, told Thomas that he should surely make the effort.

One of Thomas's doctors, a man who had performed his open heart surgery, told Thomas that his brother, attorney George Elias, might be able to put him in touch with some substantial investors. This led Thomas to W. H. "Bud" Keland, who had been a minor partner in the Dolphins, and to Irsay as potential owners of the team that Thomas wanted them to buy. The proviso was that since Thomas was organizing the effort, he would be placed in charge as general manager. A different kind of a finder's fee—the promise to be the GM. That was one way for Joe to guarantee fulfillment of his longtime ambition. It was expected that Keland would be the major player. But, at the eleventh hour, Keland backed away. This left Irsay, who had gone to great heights in the sheet metal and air conditioning business, as the man Thomas turned to when it came time to guarantee the money. As Irsay said later, "I ate the whole thing," a reference to a rather coarse description that was being used at the time in a national television commercial. It was so gross people liked it.

The football franchise trade announcement said that Irsay bought the Rams from the Reeves' estate for $19 million and then swapped them to Rosenbloom for the Colts. What would have happened if Irsay said he wanted to keep the Rams? An interesting concept but that wasn't the way the deal was arranged. Rosenbloom gave other financial inducements to Irsay. At various times, the sale price Irsay paid for the Rams was downgraded to $16 million. This may have been the case, especially if he picked up another $3 million from Rosenbloom in the exchange, including what was in the Colts' operating fund. Thomas and Rosenbloom met frequently during the time the Rams were on the market. They were in accord. Now to work out the details of this unprecedented manipulation.

The Reeves family wanted to dispose of the football assets as quickly as possible and turn their attentions to other things. The sale and trade, when it was in the making, was so sensitive that even general manager Klosterman, a gregarious individual, had little to add . . . certainly not on this subject. He wanted it to happen, too, because it would take him back to Los Angeles, which was his home and where he had quarterbacked Loyola University to football success and had excelled to the point of being a third-round draft choice of the Cleveland Browns in 1952. Klosterman knew what was going on but wasn't about to tip his hand because Rosenbloom impressed upon him, with the strongest of instructions, that they could not afford any trickle of a leak as the proceedings neared completion.

By making the move a "trade" and not a "sale," Rosenbloom didn't have to pay capital gains. It was hailed as a masterstroke of financial cunning. Carroll and son Steve, a straight-shooter and popular figure with the team, were off to Los Angeles and Irsay was bound for Baltimore.

The press conference in Baltimore to introduce Irsay and Thomas was held at the Chesapeake Restaurant. I didn't buy into Irsay's rambling mutterings and felt, without even knowing him, that he wasn't equipped to own a team. The column in the next day's *News American* was far from a ringing glorification of the new owner in town. Irsay didn't talk the language of a man who had been around sports and understood them. In short, he was a likely misfit in a game he knew little about, even if he was buying the Colts. But, then again, others had been similarly inept, and I had been wrong before. Certainly Irsay deserved the chance to see if he could succeed. Bob said how pleased he was to be in Baltimore and suggested the name of the city be changed to "Unitasville." He fumbled and stumbled but, of course, wasn't accustomed to speaking before a group, or so it seemed.

Irsay claimed he had played football at Illinois, on the "scrub" team was the way he put it. But "scrub" was a reference that went out with dime novels, a term that was around in the 1920s but rarely, if ever, used by coaches or football people. When the introductory meeting ended, Irsay came over and said, "Halas told me in Chicago I should have twenty minutes with you so you can tell me something about Baltimore."

I said, "Sure. When do you want to do it?"

"How about tomorrow morning? Call me at ten o'clock at the Village of Cross Keys." I then asked if he had been coached by Bob Zuppke or Ray Eliot at Illinois. It was as if he had never heard either name, two of the legendary figures in Illinois football history.

The next morning, per the request, I called Irsay at the hotel, figuring he wanted to see me for breakfast or lunch or even a quick visit to fill him in on the flavor of Baltimore and the history of the franchise. After telling him who I was and reminding him that he asked me to call, he had nothing else to talk about. No mention of a meeting or anything pertinent to his first day as owner of the Colts. I was sorry I called and went out to mow the front lawn. Days later, while I was playing golf at Hillendale Country Club with Frank Cuccia, a prominent businessman, I was handed a note to call Halas in Chicago. I made the call from the locker room. Halas said Irsay wanted to do a good job and was hoping I'd be as helpful to him as possible. I thought so much of Halas that anything he requested, I'd try to do. That's the way the sportswriting game used to be played.

Meanwhile, Thomas darted off to Tampa, where Rosenbloom had earlier arranged for the team to train. This was what Thomas wanted . . . to at last fulfill his dream of becoming a general manager. The Colts were relaxed. The Florida camp was new, but it never takes a team long to get acclimated. While there, Joe, however, had little to say. When players complained that he hadn't introduced himself to the team he said that wasn't important. "I know your number" is what he answered, which meant that when it came time to arrange a cut-list, or put them in a trade, he wouldn't be at a loss to remember their jersey numbers and who they were.

At that stage, Thomas was regarded as some kind of a mystery man to the coaches and players—a name and a face. Little else was known because Joe wasn't much for small talk. But he was watching. Although promising to be patient and insisting he wasn't interested in making changes, he did exactly the opposite. Before leaving Tampa, he told the press the team wouldn't be back there to train, which was disappointing to the natives and the Chamber of Commerce. But that was Thomas, blunt and hardly ingratiating. When the season started the Colts got off at a slow pace, losing four of five games, and they didn't look good. Thomas reacted—bang. He fired head coach Don McCafferty and told John Sandusky, the offensive line coach, to take the club the rest of the way.

Sandusky got the Colts to playing well and did a creditable job under difficult circumstances. After they had a win in Cincinnati, I was about to write a column stating that Sandusky deserved to be retained. To reinforce the idea, I wanted a statement from Thomas. "Don't write that unless you want to look bad," he said. He obviously had plans to jettison Sandusky, and that's exactly what happened.

Thomas, meanwhile, began sending players to all kinds of places, taking what he could get in draft choices, and showing a cold exterior in his personal dealings. He said the Colts had gotten old, which was true. Yet he wasn't about to proceed in a slow, orderly fashion to remedy a situation that wasn't as bad as he said it was. Instead, he dismantled the team with the devastation of a cyclone—no quiet, patient rebuilding with an infusion of rookies, mingling them with holdover veterans.

As Baltimore found out, this was not going to be Thomas's way of doing business. He'd make an evaluation and, just like that, a player was gone. He traded for Marty Domres and late in the season called Unitas in the locker room. Joe said he was notifying him in advance that he was going to tell the coach to use Domres. This meant Unitas wouldn't be around much longer either. John was disgusted about the way he was being treated and with reason.

At the last game of the season, against the Buffalo Bills, a plane flew overhead with a trailing message: "Unitas We Stand." The crowd applauded then, but a real roar erupted when Unitas entered the game to replace an injured Domres. In typical Unitas style, he put the ball in the air and it was a touchdown. Just like that. The pass wasn't particularly well thrown and it was intended for Eddie Hinton, who was surrounded by a crowd of Bills' defenders, but it clicked. Hinton went up for the ball, made the catch, and somehow eluded the clutches of all those Bills defenders who had him covered. At the end of the season, Thomas fired the entire coaching staff. This was only two years after they had won the Super Bowl. It also became apparent that Unitas had no future in Baltimore with Thomas calling the shots. I tried to talk Thomas out of sending Unitas to another team but, alas, it was to no avail.

I was wrong in even making the attempt and it seemed totally ludicrous that anyone should be presenting a case for Unitas. Joe always resisted advice. Still, at the end of a working day, I arranged to meet Thomas and Accorsi, then the publicity director but later to be general manager, at the 3900 Restaurant on North Charles Street, for a conversation, not an interview. I was glad Accorsi was there to hear the full context of the discussion. I looked at Thomas and told him: "America doesn't have many heroes left. You can't put Unitas on waivers." I thought that to be a rather forceful way to start but Joe brushed it aside by replying, "Why not, he was there before wasn't he?" I next mentioned he also should consider all that Unitas had contributed to football, his rags-to-riches success story, and much-revered and deserved reputation. "I don't look at it that way," he answered. "Look what football has done for Unitas. The game is always more important than the player."

Once the season shut down, Unitas was gone—sold to the San Diego Chargers for $150,000. The only good thing from Unitas's standpoint is that he held out for a contract paying him $250,000 per season for two years in San Diego. In Baltimore, under the Rosenbloom regime, he had been making $125,000 in salary and had been promised the chance to remain with the organization in an unspecified capacity when his playing career was over. But Unitas didn't want to be around Thomas or Irsay and thus worked out a buyout at a meeting in the office of

Commissioner Rozelle, who John insisted sided with management and not the player.

Thomas, moving in all trading directions, not only sold off Unitas but made deals to get rid of Tom Matte, John Mackey, Bill Curry, Billy Newsome, Norm Bulaich, Danny Sullivan, Fred Miller, Tom Nowatzke, Charley Stukes, Jerry Logan, and Jim O'Brien, among others. Maybe he felt if Rosenbloom could swap the whole franchise then he could certainly trade the players. But it was all so impersonal. Timing was unimportant to Thomas, and he wasn't as smart as he thought he was. In a sound professional move he waited until July 16, the day camp opened at Towson State University, to watch Bubba Smith move on his injured knee, didn't like what he saw and quickly sent Bubba to the Oakland Raiders for Raymond Chester.

Some of his moves and the draft choices he obtained worked out to be pluses. No question of that. But you don't initiate as many changes in personnel as Thomas did without alienating friends of the players and destroying morale. For Joe, it was like playing the stock market or a slot machine. He had his misses but he also hit the jackpot. Baltimore, or few NFL cities for that matter, had ever seen the likes of Thomas and his demolition derby. Was this a madman on the loose in a football office or a true genius at work? He was neither; rather, he had an overwhelming belief in his ability to know more about players than anyone else, at least in his own mind, and he wasn't reluctant to say so. Maybe he was driven by the fact that he had gotten so little credit for building with draft choices and engineering trades for two teams that had made previous visits to the Super Bowl, the Vikings and the Dolphins. No question, he had serviced them well with quality personnel.

He had, in truth, done much of the work but the acclaim went to the coaches, Bud Grant with the Vikings and Shula with the Dolphins. Both Thomas and Rosenbloom believed that coaches were not important, so when he hired Howard Schnellenberger to replace Sandusky, Joe said: "It's like a cabinetmaker working with wood. Give him a piece of maple and he'll make a good piece of furniture. But let him have cottonwood to work with and it won't look like much and it won't last. Players make coaches." What he might have realized is that there are also bad cabinetmakers who take good wood and turn out bad products. Coaches are important even if they aren't any better than the personnel at their disposal.

The most productive move Thomas made was getting quarterback Bert Jones in 1973. He dealt away tackle Billy Newsome and a fourth-round pick for the first draft choice of the Saints, plus keeping the Colts' own first-round choice and also drafting Joe Ehrmann, a strong, active defensive tackle. Jones had all the capabilities to go far, bringing with him as much natural ability as any athlete could be expected to have.

As for the new coach, Schnellenberger, he was a studious pipe-smoking type. He had been the offensive coordinator of the Dolphins and Thomas knew him when he was there. With a collection of new faces, not much could be expected. Schnellenberger was 4 and 10 and Domres was his quarterback. He intended to bring Jones along in a patient, orderly way, and Thomas must have approved. Joe had traded for Domres in one of his first major moves and he wasn't going to knock his own merchandise.

Midway in the season, Thomas was upset because the coaches were slow to recognize Lydell Mitchell. The year before, under McCafferty, the rookie runner had been given only brief appearances and, at one point, there was a chance that Mitchell was a free agent and eligible for signing by another team. Thomas wanted him to be played to see what he could do. But the coaches continued to use Don Nottingham, a hard worker who never stopped trying. That wasn't what Thomas was after. He preferred Mitchell to be in the game and he got his way. Without consulting anyone, certainly not the coaches, he traded Nottingham to the Dolphins in the middle of the season and said, sarcastically, "I'd like to see them use Nottingham now."

At one point, during all the off-season dealing, I had an artist superimpose a broom in Thomas's hands and ran a picture in the paper of Joe cleaning out the place. The Associated Press wanted to circulate the photo on its national wire but decided against it when it was explained it was merely intended as a joke.

The 1974 season was only three games old when another bomb exploded. In Philadelphia, with the Colts being routed, Irsay told Schnellenberger to "play Jones." The Schnellenberger reply was about what you might expect.

When the game ended, Irsay thundered into the locker room and notified all the Colts that Schnellenberger had been fired and Thomas was the new coach. They were astonished. With that, Thomas, nervous and perspiring, jumped up on a table and tried to get the attention of the team as he made announcements to the players. It was reminiscent of a scene from a bad movie. The players didn't know what was going to happen next. Some team members said Joe looked frightened when Irsay broke the news. The last thing he wanted to do was coach again. He didn't mind second-guessing coaches as a general manager, but he wasn't prepared to be placed on the firing line, which is where Irsay put him.

It meant the Colts' season was just about over, even though only three games had been played. Irsay had managed to ruin any chance the Colts had of being even halfway successful. Thomas stayed as "coach" the rest of the season, in over his head with a team in disarray. Another bad record, 2 wins, 12 losses. Time to hire a professional coach. Thomas suggested Hank Stram, formerly of the New Orleans Saints and Kansas City Chiefs, but Irsay didn't want him. And there was the same reaction when Thomas brought up the possibility of hiring Paul Wiggins. Maybe Bob didn't like the sound of their names because he certainly wasn't aware of their football credentials. Next Thomas brought up the possibility of Ted Marchibroda, who had spent fourteen years as an assistant with the Redskins and Rams. Irsay said yes and the Colts had another new coach.

They had already gone through McCafferty, Sandusky, Schnellenberger, and Thomas. Marchibroda was next. It was believed the strong-willed Thomas would overpower Marchibroda. At the press conference there was no doubt who was going to be in charge. Thomas made that point positively clear, even if Marchibroda said later he didn't know all the decisions on playing personnel weren't his to make. There was no way to misunderstand what was said. Maybe Marchibroda, carried away with the excitement of the moment, didn't hear the question or the answer Thomas gave when he was asked about the chain of command. The rookie coach, who had waited so long for his chance to operate his own show, jumped right into the preparation for his first season. He had Domres and Jones together for a spring indoctrination. They liked him and what he was saying. Meanwhile, in Pittsburgh, the owner of the Steelers, Art Rooney, whose team had made Marchibroda its first draft pick in 1953, said, "If they can't play for Ted they can't play for anybody." He was, indeed, a player's coach. And Rooney was never more right.

The Colts opened with an upset of the Bears, 35–7, and then had to meet three playoff clubs from the previous season. All the games were close. In fact, the Colts led in all of them before losing to the Raiders, 31–20; to the Rams, 24–13; and the Bills, 38–31. Then there was another tough defeat, to the Patriots, 21–10. From that point, the Colts took off, winning nine in a row and closing the year with a 10–4 record. Against the Bills, in the rematch, they were down 28–7 before exploding for five straight touchdowns, including an 89-yard touchdown pass, catch and run to Roger Carr, one of the fastest receivers in team history.

They also had beaten the Dolphins twice, including a sudden-death victory in the rain and fog of Memorial Stadium. Punter Larry Seiple had them backed up at the 4 yard line, but for the next seventeen plays the Colts moved the ball in short takes. They got to the Dolphins' 14 yard line. Finally, Toni Linhart was called on for a field goal from 31 yards away and it was all over. The Colts won, 10–7. Shula gave them immense credit. "It hurts us to lose that way," he said, "but the Colts earned it." It was then on to Pittsburgh for a playoff with the Steelers, where Jones got hurt, had to leave, and Domres took over. Eventually, Jones came back but the Colts still lost, 28–10. The Steelers went on to the Super Bowl and won it for the second straight time.

Thomas and Marchibroda were the talk of football. A team that had been 2 and 12 the year before went 10 and 4. A remarkable turnaround. The NFL had never known such a transformation. The talented new players drafted by Thomas, such as Jones, Ehrmann, Carr, Mike Barnes, John Dutton, Fred Cook, David Taylor, Ray Oldham, Ken Huff, Marshall Johnson, and Roosevelt Leaks, had made telling contributions. The defensive front of Cook, Dutton, Ehrmann, and Barnes was putting heavy pressure on the passers, running various types of stunts that confused opposing blockers. They were all over the passer so I called them the "Sack Pack," a name that quickly caught favor due to its simplicity. Marchibroda was voted "coach of the year," Thomas "executive of the year"—the highest awards in their respective positions—but all was not well. Thomas seemed to resent the accolades coming to Marchibroda, as if he wasn't getting enough credit himself—a case of envy eating away at a man and doing him no good.

The coach was honored at a Baltimore testimonial put on by the Polish American community and Robert Alfie Kramer, a Colts' fan, wrote the "Marchibroda Magic March Polka," with lyrics and music by David Bannach. Marchibroda was enjoying the fruits of victory. Thomas should have been, too, but he was obviously unhappy.

The next season found the Colts getting off to a fast exhibition start and, just as quickly, flattening out to lose their last four games. The final exhibition was against the Lions in the Pontiac Silverdome and they were beaten, 24–9, and looked sorry in the process. Then the lid blew off. Irsay and his contingent of hangers-on reached the locker room almost simultaneously with the players. After such a poor game, team morale was low. And one of their own, Ehrmann, had everyone worried. He had hyperventilated and was being carried out by ambulance attendants for a trip to an emergency room and an overnight hospital stay.

Irsay was screaming about how badly the team had played and even told Oldham to go stand in the corner, much the way a child used to be punished for misbehaving in school. He didn't know who Oldham was, except that he was one of the players. Richard Kucner, a reporter for the *News American*, was standing outside the locker room door and could hear shouting inside. At first he thought it was a fight. Not that at all, just Irsay performing with gusto, threatening to fire the coaches and bring in a new staff. The players hollered, "No, don't do that." All this turmoil after losing something as innocuous as an exhibition. When Jones was later confronted and asked to talk about what happened, he said, "We've been through a traumatic experience and would appreciate it if you reporters didn't ask us questions about what went on."

On the two buses to the airport, Kucner took one; I boarded the other. No point in having two of us in the same place. Kucner said it was a rather pathetic scene when Jimmy Irsay, then only fifteen, got up in the front of the bus and, in tears, apologized for his father's actions. He said, "My dad means well. It's just that sometimes it doesn't come out right." In the Detroit airport, waiting to be called to the gate for departure, I sat with Marchibroda and Dr. Edmund McDonnell, the team physician. Marchibroda had never spent a coaching night like that one. He realized he couldn't continue with such ongoing, explosive distractions and interruptions caused by the owner. Thomas also was making his life miserable.

So, with little to lose, he asked for a meeting with Irsay to review the situation. Irsay, Marchibroda, and Thomas met at the Milwaukee Yacht Club, where Irsay had his sixty-foot boat, the *Mighty I*, docked. Irsay reaffirmed that Thomas was in charge but he hoped Ted would stay on as coach. Marchibroda insisted he couldn't coach that way. He decided to quit. Irsay and Thomas attempted to change his mind but he was insistent. What he heard wasn't to his liking.

The announcement soon came that Marchibroda had resigned, which put Irsay and Thomas in the position of being the heels, as they say in wrestling. Next, the players began to sound off. They supported Marchibroda all the way. Jones was fond of saying, "I was a pumpkin when I showed up and Ted made me into a jack-o-lantern." He added, "We back him 100 percent." Mayor William Donald Schaefer, alarmed over what he was reading, got involved. He came to a team meeting and told Thomas he was ready to do whatever he wanted to restore order.

Schaefer pointed a finger directly at Jones and said, "I don't like you telling people not to come to the games." Although under the gun, Thomas wasn't backing down either. "He walked out so let him keep walking," he said about Marchibroda.

Unknown to anyone, I called Rozelle in New York and explained the situation. He obviously didn't want to get involved in the internal problems of a team. It wasn't the regular role of a commissioner. But I told him it was in the best interests of the league and certainly of Baltimore that it be resolved. He realized it was important and worked quietly in his usually effective manner and achieved a solution—the return of Marchibroda for the opening game of the season against the New England Patriots in Foxboro.

Jones was superb in that game, as if he was on a mission. Mitchell, too, had an outstanding performance running and catching. When it was over, linebacker Jim Cheyunski said, "We felt like somebody had pulled a weight off our chest when we won. The pressure was really on us to win." From that point, the Colts went on to another banner year. Marchibroda's position had been strengthened as he continued to win games, eleven this time, one more than the year before, and another playoff opportunity. Mitchell had gained 1,200 yards, Carr averaged an impressive 25.9 yards a reception, the best ever by a Colt, and Jones just missed winning the passing championship, barely losing to the Raiders' Ken Stabler. Jones, though, was voted "player of the year" in the NFL.

But nothing changed in their playoff effort against the Steelers. They were blown away, 40–14, no contest, as the Steelers gained 526 yards to only 170 for the Colts. The game wasn't even two minutes old and Pittsburgh was on the board. Terry Bradshaw, who liked to bomb, reached a wide-open Frank Lewis on a 79-yard touchdown play. Marchibroda knew his team gave a bad performance. "What disturbs me the most is that we didn't give ourselves a chance to win," he said. "We were never in it. I thought the team was ready to play, but we couldn't get into our game plan. We never did stop them and right from the start we were having to play catch-up. We never got to find out if our game plan would work." Frustrating? No doubt. Linebacker Stan White, representing a player's point of view, remarked, "Last year, everybody on the team made tentative plans concerning what they'd do if we lost the final playoff game. But this time, we not only thought we could win, we expected it. Nobody was prepared for what happened."

Most of the crowd of 60,020 became so disillusioned with the Colts' collapse they went home early. It was fortunate. When the disappointing rout was over, a single-engine airplane, operated by a thrill-seeking pilot, one Donald Kroner, tried to land at the 50 yard line. Two reporters actually witnessed the subsequent crash and I happened to be one of them. In the press box David Ailes, sports editor of the Greensburg, Pennsylvania, *Tribune-Review*, asked if I'd show him the way to the locker room. I said yes but explained I usually waited until the end of the game and made it a practice not to leave when the final two-minute warning was given, which was the routine of the majority of the reporters. I told him I didn't use the elevator but had my own escape route, if he didn't mind taking it, and invited him to follow.

We made it from the press box to the second deck ramp and down to the lower level, then walked through the empty stands. At the first row of seats, I put a leg over the rail, and was on the field. It was easy then to cut across the end zone, enter the dugout, and follow the tunnel to the locker room. This time, as we descended the steps, an airplane, with running lights on, was coming in over the open area of the stadium. It was a strange sight. Preposterous. The plane was lower than the rooftops on 36th Street in the Ednor Gardens section of the city. Naturally, it caught our attention. Then it was at a level no higher than the scoreboard. It somehow avoided a light tower. My first thought was the pilot's gas supply was short so he had to make an attempt at an emergency landing.

The plane appeared to be preparing to touch down at the 50 yard line. It was maybe ten feet off the ground. Suddenly, it accelerated and attempted a 30- to 40-degree climb. As it gained altitude, it was on a course directly over our heads. We both looked up to see the underside of the plane. It turned left, towards the east, and tried to follow the horseshoe curvature of the top deck. Then, it lost power, as if too much stress had been applied to the engine. The plane dropped, pancaked right there, in the upper deck of the end zone, looking the part of a wounded bird. A policeman ran over to help. There was no fire and pilot Donald Kroner suffered only minor injuries. During the previous week a plane had flown over the stadium, relatively low, while the team was practicing and an old Colts' commemorative necktie, blue with silver markings, had floated down on the field. I had it and the police wanted it for evidence. What unfolded was a bizarre story. Kroner had rented one plane, flown across the Chesapeake Bay to the Eastern Shore and back to a Harford County airport. Then he got out of the original plane and took another one without proper authorization, according to airport officials. He said he was attracted to it because it was blue and white, Colts' colors. This was the one that crashed and had to be crane-lifted out of the seats the next day. Police charged him with reckless flying, flying over the stadium, and destruction of property.

Bill Pellington, a highly competent Colts linebacker of the past, remembered he had ejected a man from his Iron Horse restaurant in Lutherville for bothering other guests. Subsequently, a plane flew over his place at a low height and "bombed" the roof with rolls of toilet paper. He believed it to be the same pilot who had flown into the stadium. In sobering retrospect, had the Colts been involved in a game that was more closely contested with Pittsburgh and the score not a runaway, it's reasonable to fear a number of fans would have still been sitting in the section, waiting for the crowd to disperse before heading for the exits. No telling what the casualty count might have been. As it was, no one was hurt except the daredevil pilot.

CHAPTER 14

# TOUGH TIMES

It can be said without the slightest hesitation that the Colts years during the Bob Irsay regime were the most difficult. Turbulence was the order of every day, or so it seemed. It wasn't that he planned it. The reporters found they were covering Irsay more than the team, which was unfortunate, but the spectacles he created left them little choice.

Attention was directed toward Bob and his behavior rather than the players and their deeds on the field. There was no telling what he might do or say. Bo Jackson was a freshman at Auburn, still a bright new name on the sports pages, when Irsay declared, out of the blue, that the Colts would make him their number one pick in the upcoming draft. That was contrary to what the NFL would ordinarily permit. Jackson, when asked for reaction, didn't have any idea who Irsay was or what he was talking about. Newspapers and wire services were too often going around in circles trying to determine the validity of Irsay's statements or describing his latest caper. His face was usually flushed and it was no secret he liked to drink.

The firing of Thomas by Irsay came after the season and it was unexpected. Joe had been at a luncheon honoring Bert Jones and George Kunz. When he got to his Hunt Valley office, two lawyers were waiting to tell him his services were no longer needed. Marchibroda, at that point, could have had his hand raised in victory for winning the power struggle but the coach didn't perceive it to be anything of the kind. For him, it meant the chance to breathe and get out from under Thomas's dictatorial ways.

Joe, though, claimed he never had any difficulty with Irsay but that the "little altar boy," referring to Marchibroda, had caused the problems. Thomas also said Jones had become too important and had so much influence with Irsay that he was running the team. I doubted that because Irsay wouldn't listen to anyone, be it Bert Jones or John Paul Jones. One of the lowlights of the year was Irsay's explosion in the dressing room after the Lions game, when he created such a wild scene. That was more upsetting to Marchibroda than anything Thomas had been doing to him. I also believed, right or wrong, that Marchibroda originally wanted to complain to Irsay about his conduct in the locker room but didn't make that the primary topic of contention when they huddled in Milwaukee for their summit meeting.

Maybe it was something about going head-to-head with the club owner that made him direct his fire toward Thomas instead. There is no doubt Thomas could be a problem to work for, unreasonable and unyielding but certainly not volatile. My own read on the situation, which became such a crucial point in the history of the Colts, might not be entirely accurate. It's based on instinct. But that one occasion, the meeting in Milwaukee, when Marchibroda chastised Thomas in front of Irsay, served only to create a wider split between them. It seemed the most pressing problem for Marchibroda would have been dealing with Irsay and trying to get him to stay under control when he visited the locker room rather than airing complaints about the general manager's heavy-handed ways. But it made for an untenable situation.

Thomas insisted he spelled out to Marchibroda, when he was hired, that final personnel decisions would be his and were not going to be left up to the coach. Marchibroda didn't remember any such stipulation. Certainly, McCafferty, Sandusky, Schnellenberger, and others in the NFL realized this all too well. Thomas's strong, hands-on influence was such that we reporters believed coaches—and most of them are desperate when they are out of a job—would be reluctant to come to Baltimore. But Thomas reacted by saying, "My telephone won't stop ringing. I'd have to go out in the woods to hide to keep them from finding me. That's a laugh . . . that they wouldn't want to coach the Colts because Joe Thomas is here."

Anyhow, there was more than a slight difference of opinion between Marchibroda and the man who hired him. At season's end, the coach, by winning another Eastern Division title, was in a more commanding position. So Thomas, not Marchibroda, was the one who went out the door. The Irsays, Bob and wife, Harriet, admired Dick Szymanski, the scout in charge of pro personnel. Szymanski was elevated to the general manager's position after the Thomas firing and his first move was to bring back Ernie Accorsi from the NFL office, where he was assistant to the president of the National Conference.

The discharged Thomas, no doubt, brought on his own problems. Although invested with authority to run the club and make decisions, he forget one basic fact—Irsay owned the team. Thomas often talked down to him, almost condescending, and you can't expect an owner to be happy with that kind of treatment. It was almost as if Joe was telling him that if he "wasn't a good boy he wouldn't be able to come to the game on Sunday." Even so, early in that same season, Irsay talked to Thomas about signing a new contract but again Joe overplayed his hand, saying he wanted more money. Not only did he not get a raise, but less than three months later he was out of a job.

The 1977 season, free of Thomas as general manager, was another divisional winner for Marchibroda and the Colts. This time, instead of being eliminated by the Steelers, they met the Oakland Raiders on Christmas Eve in Baltimore. The game was an epic, certainly one of the best ever witnessed in Memorial Stadium. It wasn't over until 2:17 of the second overtime period, or after 77 minutes and 17 seconds of intense football had been played.

In the first quarter of overtime, Jones had Raymond Chester wide open but overthrew him. When the game was finally over, Chester said he knew it would have been a sure touchdown but then said, "Don't say anything about the Boy Wonder," meaning Jones. Some players were annoyed when Marchibroda made a statement earlier that Jones represented the "franchise." Even though there was respect for Bert's immense natural ability, they didn't believe the coach should have gone quite that far in assessing the quarterback. It made the rest of them appear to be nothing more than a collection of nonentity walk-ons and that certainly wasn't true.

Ken Stabler had a brilliant afternoon for Oakland. Three times he connected with tight end Dave Casper for touchdowns. One reception was truly spectacular, over his head, running away from the ball, and it qualified as a memorable catch, almost make-believe. The game ended with the Raiders closing out the Colts, 37–31, in a game that had been tied or saw the lead change eight times. It was a bitter loss, causing residual pain. The Colts, you see, were never going to get this close again.

In the off-season there was another regrettable Irsay story, this one told by Hal Deutsch, then the general manager of the Colts' radio outlet, WCBM. Deutsch emphasized to Irsay that his station was prepared to do all it could to promote the team and help sell tickets for the next season. WCBM was ready to make an all-out push, a twelve-month involvement with the club. A date was finally selected to meet for lunch to discuss details and Deutsch took an early morning flight to Chicago. He was to meet Irsay at one of his favorite restaurants. Irsay showed up, had a couple of belts, and before they could even get into the matter of business, the team owner got up and said, "I'll be back." Deutsch waited. An hour went by. Then another fifteen minutes. Finally, Deutsch went to the manager to ask if he knew Bob Irsay. The man said he most certainly did. In fact, he had watched him drive off the parking lot well over an hour before. So Deutsch was shocked that Irsay walked out on him. He had to take the afternoon plane for home. And where was Irsay? No one seemed to know.

He was always unpredictable. In the Orange Bowl, after a Colts' loss to the Dolphins, he suddenly showed up in the radio booth where announcers Tom Davis and Dave Humphrey were doing the postgame show. The next thing they knew, their uninvited visitor was in the middle of the wrapup, complaining about the work of Pat Heagerty, one of the game officials. This was certainly conduct not becoming the owner of a major league franchise.

If you coach long enough in the NFL, as Marchibroda has found out, you're going to have seasons where problems arise that never had to be dealt with before. To open the season against the Dallas Cowboys, incumbent world champions, the Colts found themselves without either of their first two quarterbacks. Bert Jones and Bill Troup had been injured so they went with relatively untested Mike Kirkland. Jones had suffered a serious shoulder separation when he went down hard on the artificial turf of the Pontiac Silverdome. His shoulder took the full burden of the hit, with nearly a ton of Lions piled on top of him. With Jones and Troup unavailable, the Cowboys trampled the Colts, piling up 583 yards and, in the process, walloping them 38–0. Stan White and Norm Thompson had to leave early because of knee damage and were lost for a month. The next week, it was more of the same, only worse, blown out by the Dolphins, 42–0, in Baltimore. It was the worst start in Colts history, giving up 80 points in two games and shooting nothing but blanks.

Marchibroda somehow pulled them together for an outstanding effort against the New England Patriots in a Monday night nationally televised game, played in the rain. Going into the last period, the Patriots led 13–7. Then the scoreboard lights began to flash. The two teams, taking on the tempo of a track meet, quickly ran up 41 points. Joe Washington had a show-stopping performance. He took a pitch-out from Troup, stopped suddenly, fooled the Patriots, and passed to Roger Carr for a 54-yard touchdown to ignite the Colts' rally. Next, Washington was on the receiving end from Troup—another touchdown. Once more Troup passed, this time to Carr from 67 yards. But inside two minutes, just when it appeared the Colts had it won, the Patriots tied the game.

Overtime was in the offing. But Washington, a dynamo of speed and action, wasn't through. The next time he touched the ball, he breezed with a kickoff for 90 yards, giving the Colts a pulsating 34–27 win. The

Colts won only four more games the rest of the way, which was not surprising. Having quarterbacks wiped out with injuries and the secondary torn apart with the loss of key players spelled trouble. It became Marchibroda's first losing season as a head coach.

The next year, 1979, was a repeat, another 5 and 11 showing. Irsay and Szymanski agreed, with the season over, that a coaching change was needed. But it might well have been, as matters evolved, that they pulled the trigger much too quickly. "Do you want me to tell him?" asked Irsay of Szymanski, who thanked him but said he felt it was his responsibility to break the news. Accorsi accompanied Szymanski to the stadium to deliver a message they didn't enjoy giving, and the Marchibroda years were over (but only for the first time) in Baltimore.

He left with the third best Colts' coaching record, 41 and 33, behind Ewbank and Shula, and in his résumé was the well-documented achievement of being the first man in NFL history to take a team from last place to a divisional title in his rookie year. That was too quickly forgotten. He had made a contribution, and if injuries hadn't deprived him of six starters in 1978, there's no telling what might have been achieved. If Marchibroda came in for criticism it was, as other coaches in similar situations have heard, that he was too conservative. Coaches who play it wide open and go for broke might be entertaining to watch but, as a fundamental fact, few of them get to enjoy long careers in the business. Marchibroda rarely gambled but preferred to utilize his personnel in a way that the team, more times than not, was always going to be "in the game." Fault him for his philosophy, if you wish, but he could coach, handle players, and had a burning desire to win.

The Colts that year had opened with five straight losses, including two successive three-point defeats, which proved their competitiveness. In losing 13–10 to the Browns in Cleveland, kicker Toni Linhart, who had been a reliable point-maker, had a day he would like to forget. He missed three field goals from short to medium range. When it was over, Irsay stood in front of an obviously upset Linhart and made a different kind of a promise. He told Linhart he was going to give him a $10,000 bonus for trying hard. It was delivered in a tone of compassion, not in any way sarcastic. I was standing there as Irsay talked to Toni, who was born in Donawitz, Austria, where he made his country's all-star soccer team seven times and earned a degree in architecture from Austria Tech.

At that point, the kicker wasn't entirely sure of American football ways but he knew it was out of the norm in any sport to be rewarded for failure. He just listened. Then Irsay turned to guard Robert Pratt and asked him how he played. Pratt, with his jersey off but still wearing shoulder pads, was taken aback. He looked up from the four-cornered stool in front of his locker and forced a smile. "We're going to give you a $25 raise," Irsay added. When defensive end Fred Cook heard of the Linhart bonus, he held his stomach, rolled around on a bench in a heap of laughter and said, "It's the wildest thing I ever heard about. Are you telling me the absolute truth? I've heard it all now. You have to say our owner is different. This is so unbelievable it can't be real." Three weeks later, Linhart was released. No, he never got the $10,000 bonus Irsay had promised—not even as a going-away present.

For Marchibroda it was another season of being without his regular quarterback, Jones, for most of the way. Jones had reinjured his shoulder twice within two months, bringing in veteran Greg Landry, who had played eleven years with the Lions and was acquired for two future draft choices. In one year, Landry put the ball in the air more times than Unitas had in any season of the seventeen he played in Baltimore. Of course, there were two more games on the schedule, which gave him the opportunity to have higher totals in attempts and completions. Landry had a "live" arm and was respected for his ability and maturity but he didn't have Jones's mobility.

Looking at the owner from a positive standpoint, Irsay built a $5-million training and office complex for the organization in Owings Mills. It was such a momentous occasion that Commissioner Rozelle and State Comptroller Louis Goldstein showed up for the dedication. Goldstein charmed the audience with his down-home humor and Rozelle enjoyed him so much he got up to say, "After listening to Mr. Goldstein, I know where we're going to get next year's half-time show for the Super Bowl. We'll just put him on and let him talk."

With Marchibroda gone, the Baltimore coaching log would add another new name, that of Mike McCormack, who had once been included on the roster the Colts inherited from the Dallas Texans. He had been traded to Cleveland in the ten-for-five trade in 1953. He spent nine outstanding seasons with the Browns, where Paul Brown called him the smartest offensive lineman he ever had and, subsequently, he went on to Hall of Fame enshrinement.

Like Marchibroda, McCormack had amassed an impressive coaching background, having worked under Vince Lombardi, George Allen, and Brown as an assistant. Coaching tutors don't get much better than that. He also spent three seasons as head coach of the Eagles and enjoyed a good reputation, even though his teams had only a 16–25–1 record. The Colts also were having trouble at the draft table, utilizing first-round choices for players who never fulfilled the high hopes held for them, as witness Ken Novak in 1976, Randy Burke in 1977, Reese McCall in 1978.

Thomas had been fired before the draft in 1977 so only Novak was his choice. He couldn't be blamed for the others. In 1979, as number 1, they took Barry Krause, an aggressive linebacker, and in 1980 Curtis Dickey and Derrick Hackett as double first-round picks. Krause and Dickey were productive but never attained the heights predicted.

It's interesting, by way of a draft flashback, to note what happened in 1975, when Thomas was calling all the signals. Schubach, in charge of college personnel, doing the leg-work and much of the preparation, had visited Jackson State University and came upon a running back named Walter Payton. The coach there, Bob Hill, had once been in the Colts camp; in fact I had signed him to a contract, and he wanted to see Payton join the Colts, his old team. "Look, Fred," Hill told him, "this fellow can play. I know he can. And let me do this for you. I have my own personal film I put together on his runs in college that I'm not letting any other scouts see. Take it back to Baltimore so you can review it over and over again. I hope you get the chance to draft him."

Schubach, who had been around football since he was a small child, having worked for his father with the Eagles, didn't need to see the film because what he saw in Payton during practices left little doubt he was an NFL player. What he would need to do is let Thomas see Payton on film and then await his reaction. "You're right," Thomas told Schubach after checking out Payton. "I agree he's a great looking prospect. But what we need right now, more than a running back, is to get some help for the offensive line." So the Colts, thinking they needed to improve their blocking, took Ken Huff, a 6-foot-4, 250-pound guard from North Carolina.

To bring this about, Thomas bluffed the Falcons into believing he was going for quarterback Steve Bartkowski of California and then would probably use him in a major deal with another team that was drafting near the bottom. The Falcons became interested and took the bait. Thomas then dealt the Colts' first pick in the draft to the Falcons, who took Bartkowski. In turn, the Falcons gave the Colts their first choice, who was to be the third player taken, plus a proven veteran offensive tackle, George Kunz. So what Thomas wanted to do he achieved, dropping down two notches and coming away with two first-string offensive linemen in Huff and Kunz. No doubt, Thomas could wheel and deal. He knew how to maneuver, but in the case of Payton, missed an elite performer who would have been Baltimore's selection if left up to Schubach. He had input, of course, but Joe made the final call. It's easy to describe how good the Colts thought Payton was going to be, but Thomas clearly outsmarted himself, negating some of his earlier success with personnel.

The Bears were to name Payton as their first choice and watched with satisfaction as he distinguished himself for the next thirteen years while on his way to becoming the league's leading rusher of all time. His Hall of Fame entrance was automatic. Baltimore can only ponder, with much regret, what Payton would have meant to the Colts. Certainly, Jones, Mitchell, and Payton together would have made for a combination that knew how to move the ball and been difficult to stop. After Payton was drafted, Schubach told a Bears' scout, "You've just gotten yourself a tremendous running back." Words that were all too true.

McCormack had a 7 and 9 start, commendable enough, and was in position to win the division in a game at Cincinnati if his team could have won. The Colts were ahead of the Bengals, 33–31, with 1:45 remaining, but couldn't stop them. Starting at the Colts' 31, Jack Thompson, another highly regarded quarterback who never fulfilled his potential, took his team from the Colts' 20 to the Bengals' 31 in six plays. Then Thompson attempted to pass to Pat McInally on the 6 but the ball fell short. Corner back Larry Braziel, who had earlier intercepted to set up a Colts' touchdown, was called for pass interference. This made it perfectly easy for a 21-yard chip shot by Jim Breech, who kicked the ball through the posts for the victory. Dickey came in with a productive first season, joining Alan Ameche and Norm Bulaich as the only rookies to ever lead the Colts in rushing yardage.

McCormack's second time around as a head coach—first Philadelphia and then Baltimore—turned into a major disaster. The Colts opened and closed his second season with wins over the same team, the Patriots, yet in between lost fourteen straight games, a club record. In Philadelphia, which seemed to bring out the worst in Irsay, the Colts got hammered 38–13 by the Eagles. That also was the afternoon when he invaded the scout's booth in the second half and commandeered the headphones. He proceeded to alternate Landry and Jones every other play. No coach would try that. It was a bizarre and upsetting picture that unfolded in Veterans Stadium. There was McCormack, humiliated by a clown of an owner, standing on the sidelines with the quarterbacks passing each other en route to the huddle, running on and off, like two ships sailing in opposite directions. And from high above, where some of the coaches are stationed to call in plays, Irsay was sending in his version of whether the team should try a run or a pass. Jones said he defied the suggestions and was doing just the opposite of what Irsay wanted. The day after the season ended, McCormack was gone. In his place came Frank Kush, who had spent the previous year coaching the Hamilton Tiger Cats of the Canadian Football League after being out of football for two years following his troubled demise at Arizona State. He was one of the nation's most successful college coaches with a record of 176 wins, 54 losses, and 1 tie. Kush was a fanatic on physical conditioning and drove his teams hard.

Kush had been signed by Szymanski who went along with the general thinking in football, and other sports, too, that you follow a coach with a soft hand (McCormack) by one who cracks a mean whip (Kush). The new coach tolerated no loafing, excuses, or malcontents, yet treated the players as men, not children. His two-fisted reputation from Arizona State preceded him but the Kush from college and the Kush of the pros were vastly different. "I hear all these things about how tough I am," he once said. "I only wish that were true. I really would like to be as hard-nosed and as rough a guy as they say I am. But I know myself. I'm not that tough."

With Kush arriving and McCormack leaving, the Colts had a major problem in trying to resolve a dispute with Jones, who thought he had a contract agreement with the Colts for four more years. But then he didn't, not in writing anyhow. Irsay said he made no such verbal commitment. But Jones claimed Irsay reneged. It led to Jones filing a protest with the players' association and Irsay saying, "I'll kick his ass right out. Kush doesn't like him either, doesn't like his attitude."

On the eve of the draft, after nine years as a Colt, the gifted Jones was gone, sent to the Rams for their first- and second-round choices, who turned out to be Ohio State quarterback Art Schlichter and Florida State punter Rohn Stark. The Colts were interested in the best offer any other team could make. (Irsay kept talking about Schlichter as Dave Schuster; he had a penchant for getting names wrong.) So Jones, the young phenomenon with extraordinary talent, the kind made for Hall of Fame recognition, was gone to the Rams. Before he could complete the season in Los Angeles, his career, at age thirty-one, was over. Jones suffered a neck injury against the Falcons and aggravated the problem the next week when he tried to face the Chiefs. Doctors, after operating, advised him not to play again. "They didn't tell me I shouldn't play," he said. "They told me I couldn't play." Instead of enjoying what should have been the most productive phase of his career, since quarterbacks generally have longevity, he was all through. The neck injury was far more serious than originally believed. He had no alternative but to give up and get on with his life, joining the family lumber business in Ruston, Louisiana.

Before Kush could coach a single game for the Colts, the man who hired him, Szymanski, was an ex-general manager. He was dumped by Irsay and no reason was given. Szymanski merely walked the plank at Irsay's pleasure. He said he lost count of the number of times Irsay had fired him, even laughing about it, but Szymanski kept coming to the office and Irsay would make no mention that he intended for him to be an ex-employee. It would be business as usual. Thomas, when he was with the Colts, always said he learned early never to discuss anything of a serious nature with Irsay after 10 A.M. because he usually began drinking at this hour. But now Szymanski was gone from the circuslike atmosphere. Baltimore was a revolving door, or so it seemed.

Hired to replace him as general manager was Ernie Accorsi, who started with the Colts in 1970, their one and only Super Bowl winning year, as public relations director. Then he went with the NFL office and returned as assistant general manager under Szymanski in 1977. He had written sports for the *Charlotte News*, *The* [Baltimore] *Evening Sun* and *The Philadelphia Inquirer* besides working at St. Joseph's College in Philadelphia as sports publicity director and then assistant sports information director at Penn State. Enthusiastic, well-liked, and articulate, he was to become the third Colts' general manager with a Philadelphia background, the others being Kellett and Hulmes.

Kush didn't have much opportunity to help the Colts in his rookie season because the National Football League Players Association called a strike. The players went out after two games, both losses for the Colts, and stayed away fifty-seven days, forcing the schedule, when they returned, to be reduced to nine games instead of sixteen. Of course, the players' association scored all the winning points in its new collective bargaining agreement, and the owners took another hard hit.

Kush, in analyzing his personnel, waived or traded away two-thirds of the squad. He was, as the coaches before him, headed for a rebuilding effort in Baltimore. What he saw in the films that he had inherited from McCormack he didn't like. It was his nature to make quick judgments and never look back. Players complained but Kush didn't figure he had to explain.

The Colts of 1982, Kush's first creation, had not been able to win a game in the strike-shortened schedule. This was the first time the Colts had drawn a complete blank. For the last home game, played as a "make-up" on January 2, the crowd that watched them lose, 34–7, to the Dolphins was a mere 19,073. The strike action had thrown the entire sport for a loss, but only temporarily. In the playoffs, which was really a contrived postseason tournament, there were more teams included, sixteen, than those excluded. The NFL seeded the clubs for the first time, eight from each conference, and began an elimination series.

The Dolphins became a Super Bowl finalist but lost to the Washington Redskins, 27–17, in the Rose Bowl, as John Riggins dominated the day, gaining 166 yards, or only 10 fewer yards than the entire Dolphins offense was able to generate.

A leading question in Baltimore had to do with Kush. Was he in over his head when he couldn't recruit? He had learned in a hurry that Baltimore wasn't Arizona State, where the talent pipeline produced an almost nonstop flow of prospects. There weren't many blue-chip youngsters Kush went after when he was coaching in college that he didn't get. With the pros it was a different game. The strike year had been a bad experience for all concerned. The Colts, undeniably, were the worst club in football, which was covering a lot of territory since there were now twenty-eight franchises in the NFL. From a numbers standpoint, they had thirty-one new additions to the roster of forty-nine (a 63 percent turnover), and there was no way they could be expected to win when saddled with so much inexperience. If you were looking for encouragement, it was found in the fact the Colts were the youngest team in the league, having an average age of 24.87 years. They could only get better.

In the 1983 draft, Baltimore, for only the third time in the NFL, was going to have the chance to select the first player from college football. In 1955 it had taken quarterback George Shaw of Oregon and in 1967 end/tackle Bubba Smith of Michigan. The choice in 1983 was John Elway, quarterback of Stanford. But there were immediate complications. Elway and his father, a coach, had earlier rejected Kush's overtures for him to attend Arizona State.

They didn't like what they were hearing about the football program and there was a personality clash, certainly from the standpoint of the Elways. Now the gifted young athlete was in similar straits as he prepared to turn from college football to the professionals. He had played a season of minor league baseball for a New York Yankees' farm club at Oneonta of the New York-Penn League and showed some promise. But football was what he wanted for a career.

He could start at the top and didn't have to struggle his way through the minors, which would have been his lot in baseball. This was similar to the situation that had confronted Shaw in 1955 when he, too, was the Colts' first-round pick and baseball was a possibility. Elway was adamant in not wanting to come to Baltimore. Nothing against the city. And he most emphatically didn't want to get involved in controversy with Kush. The agent for Elway, one Marvin Demoff, merely said his client didn't want to play in the East. Occasionally, players use this type of an excuse as a ruse in contract negotiations.

Usually, after the opening salvo, a player will soften his position. He will come around to management's way of thinking. There will be a meeting of the minds. Not with Elway, though, who was being "quarterbacked" by his agent, who played it perfectly. Within just six days, Elway heard the news that made him happy, thanks to Irsay's intervention at the trading table. Irsay, without Kush or Accorsi knowing about it, had met with the Denver Broncos and worked a deal. Elway would be turned over to the Broncos for their first player in the draft, offensive tackle Chris Hinton, plus quarterback Mark Hermann, and their first-round pick of the next year, who turned out to be Maryland guard Ron Solt.

And, oh yes, there was another inducement in the deal for Irsay. This was no doubt the first time anything of such a crass monetary nature had been agreed to in the NFL, which most assuredly does not live by bread alone. The Broncos were going to give Irsay the chance for the Colts to play two future exhibitions in Denver, where crowds reached close to 75,000, and the visiting team took home a hefty paycheck. The opportunity to take a lot of money out of Denver was especially appealing to Irsay.

As the unpredictable elements of the schedule were decided, the Broncos were to play the Colts in Baltimore's home opener. Many in the crowd of 52,316 were there to harass Elway, considering he had passed up coming to Baltimore and the fans took the rejection personally. But what Elway didn't want to do was play for Kush as his coach and Irsay as the owner. In my memory there was never a player in any sport, for the home or visiting team, who was subjected to as much ridicule from the stands as Elway caught in Baltimore. When he came to the line of scrimmage to set the offense a torrent of boos engulfed the stadium, and it was constant. Almost nonstop.

Here was a rookie quarterback, with enough to worry about in running an offense, let alone being bothered by a hostile crowd, who held up remarkably well under adverse circumstances. During the game and in the locker room later he never uttered a complaint. He took it all in stride, the inherent mark of a professional. If there were such a thing, Elway would hold the unofficial Baltimore record for creating negative noise, the boo factor award.

That afternoon he played most of the game and looked impressive for a kid quarterback being exposed to a tough defense and a crowd that zeroed-in on him and wouldn't let up. The Broncos, however, didn't score until the fourth quarter when veteran quarterback Steve Deberg came in to throw a touchdown pass to Steve Watson and then connect with Watson again to set up the winning touchdown at 17–10.

In the rematch, later in the season, Elway had shown remarkable improvement. He bombed the Colts with three touchdown passes, completing 23 of 44 for 385 yards, and scrambled for 23 yards on three carries. He lived up to the profile of a first-round draft choice. It turned out to be a close finish, 21–19, as Raul Allegre tried a record NFL field goal from 64 yards away and the ball fell short by 6 feet as the clock ran out on a Baltimore bid for victory.

Before the game, Irsay was in a spirited mood as he visited with Baltimore reporters. He only knew two of their names, even though he had been seeing most of them for all the time he owned the Colts. He was, on this occasion, wearing, of all things, a cap that identified him as a member of the John Elway Fan Club. Bob couldn't be accused of not having a sense of humor. There was no question he was drawing considerable attention to himself and, in the adjoining owner's box, was more than enamored of a woman friend as they hugged and kissed—necking, as in high school.

Once, after a controversial reception by Watson, he left his seat, walked up the steps, and entered the press box, where I was seated with Jim West of WBAL and Bernie Miklasz of *The News American*. Irsay leaned over and asked, as if I were some kind of an omnipotent authority, instead of a sportswriter, "Was he in or out?" I remember telling him, "Too close to call," and with that he seemed satisfied. Quickly, he made an about-face and retraced his steps to the owner's box. Overall, the Colts won seven games, which meant they were much better than in Kush's first year. They finished at 7 and 9, not a threat to the Super Bowl in the near future, but encouraging.

The last game of the season, in Baltimore, on December 18, 1983, was a farewell to the Colts. The party was over, only the guests weren't told. They played and beat the Houston Oilers, 20–10, before an assemblage of only 20,418. The conduct of some fans in the modest-sized gathering was embarrassing. Through much of the second half, building to a crescendo, there was a unified voice from the stands screaming "Irsay sucks . . . Irsay sucks." Most of the bitterness came about because Irsay had been in a standoff dispute with Curtis Dickey, who was asking for a substantial raise, and Irsay didn't want to give it to him. The public had taken sides and was in general support of Dickey. When the game ended, I packed up and left the press box, with the thought that no owner, not even Irsay, would be comfortable with the kind of insults he heard directed towards him. But I certainly didn't think it would be a thirteen-year wait, accompanied by frustration and disappointment, before another NFL game would be played there.

It was obvious that Mayor William Donald Schaefer realized Irsay presented problems and made every effort to understand him, showing good humor and consideration in every way possible. He would rebuke reporters for being "too rough on him." But deep within himself he knew that if he as the mayor joined in the denunciation, it would jeopardize the Colts remaining in Baltimore.

Certainly, the Baltimore media—the *News American*, Sunpapers, *AFRO-American*, and the radio-television stations—were not going to give Irsay the same type of kid-glove protection he was getting from Schaefer, who no doubt envisioned Irsay as a walking, talking "time bomb."

Most of what Bob said and did made the papers and the broadcast outlets. So Schaefer went the other way, defending the actions of Irsay and never offering a word of rebuke. He was attempting to demonstrate to Irsay in person and by all of his public comments that he wanted to be his friend. Even if Schaefer thought the stories making headlines were correct—and they were—he tried to "humor" the man. They got along. Irsay, when talking about Schaefer, frequently called him the "little mayor." It sounded almost, from the way Irsay said it, as if Schaefer was the size of a jockey. No one else ever thought he was the "little mayor" or called him such except Bob.

While controversy never seemed far away, a story came over the wire services quoting Irsay's mother as saying she hadn't seen him in thirty-five years and that her son was the devil. Bernie Miklasz, who worked with me at the *News American* before going to the *St. Louis Post-Dispatch*, reached Irsay's brother by telephone for an interview and found out how much personal animosity existed between them. Before the conversation was completed, Bernie introduced me to Irsay's brother via phone. What I heard was likewise astonishing. "Bob is a no good son-of-a-bitch," his brother said. "He claims to be a Roman Catholic. We were both bar mitzvahed at the same temple near Chicago." Next he brought up the subject of Lionel trains. "Do you remember them as a kid?" he asked. "Absolutely," I replied. "Well, he stole my train and sold it for $5 claiming it was his."

Irsay often said whatever came in his mind, be it fancy or fact. He once reported in Chicago that he had been shot at in a parking garage and that he had asked the FBI to investigate. When I called the FBI to inquire, they knew nothing about the incident and had no such record. My belief was that it might have been the sound of a car motor backfiring and Bob interpreted the noise as a gunshot.

What Schaefer was trying to do was keep Irsay happy until he could get something in place by way of a long-term contract for the Colts to continue in Baltimore. In 1981, the team had signed a two-year rental contract for Memorial Stadium but Irsay never accepted another one. He kept insisting that when "Bennett [meaning Edward Bennett Williams, the Orioles' owner] signs one then I will, too." Most of the time Irsay referred to him as "Bennett," rarely using Ed, as he was usually called. This was during the time period when Williams was saying the Orioles needed a new stadium and he played the cause to the maximum, which gave Irsay reason to do the same, only he was far less eloquent and not as clever.

Irsay had difficulty remembering names, which is why he generally called everyone "Tiger." It would have been funny, except it was sad. At a Baltimore banquet, attended by the Colts, he referred to Bubba Smith as "Bo Bo." But Bubba didn't seem to mind. It was what the players had come to expect. After an exhibition game in Atlanta, his second season of ownership, I was using a wall telephone in the press box. I had phoned the newspaper office to make sure all the copy had cleared. Along came Irsay, who was having trouble with his equilibrium. When he saw me, it was as if he felt compelled to say something. "The gamblers got Marty," he said. I assumed he meant Marty Domres, the quarterback. Such an assertion was totally irresponsible and without any semblance of truth. Domres was a tremendous competitor who gave the game a full and honest commitment.

That same night, Irsay made a trip to the locker room, either before or after he left the press box, and confronted Marty. He told him he was throwing passes to players in the wrong-colored jerseys. "It's something I'll never forget," says Domres. "He was wearing a madras sport coat and yellow pants and also had a load on. He was slurring his words. I had left the game after giving the team the lead. Bert Jones, who was a rookie, came in and Atlanta got ahead. Then I went back in to try to win it.

"I thought Bob was kidding around when he first came in the dressing room. Then he wanted to know why I threw the ball to the other team. I told him that if he knew anything about the game he wouldn't ask a question like that. He had that entourage with him and I was getting heated. I had just played a game I thought we should have won and my two interceptions came from a ball that bounced off Don Nottingham's shoulder pads and another one that was similarly tainted when I tried to pass to Cotton Speyrer. Finally, Mike Curtis and Joe Thomas rushed over to quiet the situation."

Domres was disgusted. The players knew he had played well but there was Irsay showing the worst side of himself. Schnellenberger, the coach, was disturbed over what had happened. It was so unnecessary. After the team bus left the stadium for the airport and had gone about two blocks, Domres hollered to the driver to stop. Then he got off. He had a change of mind and decided he would spend the night in Atlanta and come back to training camp the next day at his own expense. Domres was visibly upset over the confrontation with Irsay and the things the owner said.

What Irsay said about "the gamblers having Marty" was the worst thing that can ever be said about an athlete. And it was totally inaccurate, a drunken lie. The next afternoon, a Sunday, I reached Jim Kensil, who was Rozelle's assistant, at his Long Island home and told him of the erroneous and reckless accusation of the previous night. I mentioned that the league had a role in this since he was a club owner, and if Irsay was going to become any kind of a respected member of their fraternity then he needed to act in a responsible manner. Talking about a player being involved with a gambler, when no such thing had occurred, was reason for banishing an owner from the league or at least suspending him. Naturally, Kensil was concerned and said he would see that Irsay was talked to and told not to invent such charges.

After Irsay bought the Colts, it was learned that he also had been a part-owner of the Montreal Expos baseball team but the association had lasted for only for a brief time. It was understood that he was invited to leave, which Kensil didn't know. In fact, the league didn't even realize he once had a baseball connection. I always felt the NFL entered into a once-over-lightly examination of Irsay without finding out as much background as it should have. This was true of some other owners, too, and it was a serious error considering the type of men buying their way into the league.

The *News American*, endeavoring to get an early look at Irsay, had sent reporter Bob Blatchley to Chicago to interview him. Irsay took Bob on a tour of his old neighborhood, "Bucktown," and talked about how it was to grow up there. He pointed to a bar and said that was where he and his friends once congregated. Irsay decided to go inside and buy Blatchley a drink to quench his thirst. After entering, they saw it had become a package store. Irsay ordered a bottle of whiskey and asked for a couple of paper cups. In a minute or so, he was outside pouring a drink for Blatchley on a street corner. "If anyone would have come along they would have sworn we were a couple of guys so down on our luck we were sharing a bottle of booze on the sidewalk," Blatchley recalled.

As for taking the team away from Baltimore, the first report surfaced in 1976, eight years before, when he said he had "an attractive offer" from Phoenix. Then it was Indianapolis in 1977 and Los Angeles as a possibility two years later. Jacksonville entertained him at a pep rally, complete with fireworks and cheerleaders, in the summer of 1979. At a meeting with Jacksonville officials, he reportedly said three different times, "It's not a matter of if I'm leaving but where I'm going." This was the kind of negative talk Baltimore kept hearing and it was bothersome. It separated the team from the fans. It also made it difficult for Governor Harry Hughes and Mayor Schaefer to make an accurate assessment of the situation. But they made every attempt to appease the man. After all, he had the football.

CHAPTER 15

# ACHING HEARTS

There was no way to forecast what turn Irsay might take with the Colts or if he would remain in Baltimore. It was doubtful if even he knew, considering his penchant for saying so many things and then reversing himself. General feeling was, after all the turmoil, he wouldn't leave and that what was going on was mere subterfuge, a condition not uncommon to sports franchise owners. But how were the governor and mayor to know, considering the type of bombastic and unpredictable personality they were dealing with? All Schaefer would say is "he's an interesting man." It was likewise assumed that Irsay, once again, had been scouting and flirting with other cities to increase the element of fear while helping to arrange a better deal with the man he called the "little mayor." Ten weeks before, Governor Hughes disclosed he was ready to spend $22 million on major stadium improvements. That was after Irsay said he was misquoted about leaving Baltimore and would stay if he could be assured of enough good seats—whatever that meant—being put into place. But January of 1984 was an unsettling month for getting a clear projection on the Colts' future.

First it was revealed that Irsay had reopened talks with Phoenix. Then he turned up at a press conference at BWI Airport, flying in from Las Vegas, and not appearing to be in the best of condition. With Schaefer and reporters present, he said his trip to Baltimore had covered 6,000 miles. Gordon Beard, of the Associated Press, quickly asked, "Where did you come from, China?" At one instance he took a roll of money out of his pocket and let Bill Glauber of *The* [Morning] *Sun* count it. When Glauber handed it back, Irsay playfully asked for the rest of it, as if some of the bills had vanished. This was Irsay's attempt to laugh and have fun. He wanted so much to be liked and didn't know how. Then he started his rambling discourse about the future of the Colts and reminded the group that "I'm a good Catholic boy." He insisted, "I haven't any intention of moving the goddamn team."

The impromptu meeting with the media at the airport was covered by television and it was the first time a majority of fans had ever seen him in action. This was all going on two nights before Super Bowl XVIII was played in Tampa. Had the Irsay tape been replayed in opposition to the Super Bowl in Baltimore, there's little doubt which one would have drawn the top rating. Accorsi, the team general manager, was at the airport for Irsay's fly-in press conference. "Soon thereafter, I decided to quit," he said. "I had enough. But had I been making a prediction at that moment, I would have said the team was headed to Phoenix, not Indianapolis." That was because Kush was pushing in that direction and he had a friend, a real estate developer named Anthony Nicoli, interested in either buying the team from Irsay or else helping him to move it there. Accorsi was deeply concerned.

On February 7, Accorsi resigned from the Colts, appropriately wearing a blue and white necktie, and seemed relieved. He was the only employee in a major position, either general manager or coach, who wasn't fired in the twelve years Irsay owned the team; he quit on his own terms. Ernie probably beat him to the punch, which may have made Irsay unhappy when he got around to thinking about it. Two years later, with the Colts about to play the Browns in Indianapolis, the employees were told not to talk to Accorsi on orders from Irsay.

After Accorsi was gone and the Colts were rudderless, so far as front office leadership was concerned, the NFL office had no one it could consult for a view of what was going on in Baltimore. Don Weiss and Jim Heffernan, two of Rozelle's assistants, called to find out if I knew what was going to happen. A month went by and there was no replacement for Accorsi. I called Rozelle and said I was hoping Jim Finks, who had left the Bears, might be enticed to come to Baltimore. Rozelle said the idea had merit and enthusiastically encouraged me to pursue it. I called Finks at his home and outlined the situation, asking him if he would be interested. "John, thanks for thinking of me," he said. "The answer is no. Bob Irsay is an accident waiting to happen." How prophetic.

Indianapolis, when it began to pursue the Colts, had completed what it called the Hoosier Dome and Convention Center at a cost of $82 million and supposedly was on the waiting list for an NFL expansion team. When it learned Irsay was interested in seeing what it had to offer, Indianapolis pushed with even more gusto. Michael Chernoff, the team attorney for Irsay, was busy dealing with Indianapolis and negotiated the contract that put the team there.

Indianapolis promised a $15-million loan at 8 percent interest, a guaranteed number of ticket sales, use of the Hoosier Dome, and a new practice facility. Phoenix interests reacted by offering virtually the same kind of a deal. It didn't have a domed stadium in place but made promises to build one.

Rozelle and the National Football League owners, at a meeting in Chicago, said they didn't intend to attempt to block any move Irsay contemplated because of what was going on in the case of Al Davis, who was endeavoring to transfer the Oakland Raiders to Los Angeles to replace the Rams, who had fled to Anaheim. As minutes of a previous NFL meeting showed, Irsay had voted against allowing such a move. Now he was doing the same thing. At the March 19 NFL owners meeting in Hawaii, he was a no-show.

Six days later Irsay met with Schaefer and Frank DeFrancis, who was Maryland's secretary of economic development. They had earlier offered him a $15-million loan at 8 percent, and agreed to take care of his $2.2-million debt on the Colts' training complex. This time they improved on the "financials," describing how a group of businessmen would put up $450,000 a year to make up the difference between the prime interest rate of 11 percent and the 8 percent he was being offered. On March 26, the Maryland Legislature had two bills relative to the Colts. One had to do with the state buying the team for $40 million from Irsay and then selling it to investors in Maryland. The other proposal was for the state to condemn the Colts and begin eminent domain proceedings.

Senator Thomas Bromwell, who sponsored eminent domain, said, "We are sitting on the bills. We don't want to tip the scales. It is a very sensitive position we are in. The way Mr. Irsay is, I don't want to be the guy who makes him jump off the deep end." The call to implement would, no doubt, reflect what Schaefer and Hughes believed was in the best interest of keeping the Colts in Baltimore.

Meanwhile, Hughes, Schaefer, DeFrancis, and Baltimore County Executive Don Hutchinson were aware that Irsay had tempting invitations in his pocket from other places, including Phoenix and Indianapolis, and they were trying to sweeten the deal to keep him in Baltimore. Irsay and DeFrancis talked on March 27 and the owner had a new list of demands. He now wanted a guaranteed home attendance of 43,000 per game and $6.6 million to purchase the complex, up from $4.4 million. Before the day was out, the State Senate voted by 38–4 to grant Baltimore authority to seize ownership of the team, but the measure had not yet gone to the House of Delegates.

On the morning of March 28, DeFrancis and Schaefer tried to contact Irsay by phone but weren't able to reach him. Irsay later said, repeatedly, that "Schaefer stabbed me in the back with eminent domain."

Whether that finally put Irsay on the road to Indianapolis isn't known, but there are those who believe it played a part. Maybe he would have remained in Baltimore. No one will ever know. But the eminent domain threat surely triggered his final decision—to get out of Baltimore as fast as he could, before the bill was enacted. Schaefer said Irsay broke his word in not telling him a move was imminent after promising him that he would be in touch. The "eminent domain" aspect caused Irsay to react. It forced his hand, one way or the other. There was no reason to wait and wonder what his next move would be. That's when he flashed word to his son, Jimmy, to prepare to get out of Baltimore.

Kush, who earlier had been hoping if Irsay moved it would be to Phoenix, near where he lived, was doing yard work outside his house in Tempe, Arizona, when he got a call from Irsay and was told to return to Baltimore. He was informed the team was moving but Irsay wouldn't say where. By ten o'clock that night the movers were packing cartons of equipment, office records, films, and furniture. A fleet of Mayflower Vans, all shined and glistening, were on the property, ready to collect the cargo, and head west on route 70 for the Colts' new home. Lights were on in the complex and, from a distance, it looked like a prison under siege. Adding to the downcast mood for Baltimore was the weather. A light rain and sleet storm had arrived. A few fans were outside the complex fence watching from afar, including Hurst "Loudy" Loudenslager, the team's premier follower. The NFL didn't know what was going on. Irsay hadn't bothered to check with Rozelle. He was only intent on getting his show on the road to Indianapolis. Meanwhile, the fifteen Mayflower vans were rolling towards Indiana in the predawn darkness.

Most of the Colts' employees left at the end of the working day on March 28 and had no idea what had been planned for the evening. Assistant coach Hal Hunter had been told earlier in the day what was in the works but was pledged to secrecy. Meanwhile, Kush was on a plane bound for Baltimore, per Irsay's instructions. Hunter informed the other members of the coaching staff at 5 P.M. what was going to happen. Meanwhile, Walter Gutowski, the public relations director, and Pete Ward, administrative assistant, were playing racquetball inside the facility. After Gutowski showered, dressed, and left the building, he noticed more cars than usual on the parking lot. He thought it to be strange. This time of the year the coaching staff didn't put in long hours. During the season, yes, but not in March. Then he noticed that lights were on in the offices where the coaches worked but the blinds were pulled down. "I just had an unusual feeling that something wasn't right," he recalls. "For some reason, I went back in the building, went to my desk and put some personal belongings in a box. You know, pictures, a clock radio, and other things that belonged to me. Then I drove home and got the word of the move a couple hours later. I always believed Ernie Accorsi left because he had an inkling something like that was going to happen and didn't want any part of it."

When Schaefer turned on his radio in the morning he heard the grim details of the deed. "That's a final humiliation," he said with a weary voice and a troubled mind. "It degrades a great city." Hughes added, "I'm not only disappointed, but I'm slightly angry. It's as if we were not being treated in good faith. We felt we met every reasonable demand he made. But the demands kept changing."

The day after the defection, Hughes signed the eminent domain papers, and the city wired a $40-million offer to Irsay. Hall of Fame member Art Donovan, who talked frequently with Irsay over the years and recognized him for what he was, said, "I always thought he must have gotten hit with a hand grenade when he was in the Marines. Now I think it was a 155mm cannon shell. This whole thing is a mess and if it wasn't so damn sad it would be funny. Imagine a great town like Baltimore being done in this way." Gil Griggs, known as "General Griggs," who had presided over a "Save the Colts for Baltimore" movement while amassing a group of public-spirited vigilantes, added, "Look, this is no different than what happened in some European countries where there have been bad kings but the people live through them to regain their glory. We can do the same."

On March 30, Baltimore made the eminent domain suit official, but it was too late. Nine months later, U.S. District Court Judge Walter Black, Jr., in Baltimore, ruled the team had already moved when the city acted. But the tears wouldn't go away. The Colts were gone.

CHAPTER 16

# AFTER THE CRIME

Baltimore, which had found the Colts to be a way of life, was in mourning over its loss. The team name had been linked to the city since 1947, all the way back to Truman's time, when a horse raced around the field after every score. And the band played and the cheerleaders cheered. And Unitas connected to Berry. And Donovan and Marchetti buried the passer. And Moore ran with the speed of sound and the grace of an adagio dancer.

There were years, all so long ago, when the Colts had trouble paying their bills, before the age of television, but they survived because of the passion of the fans. With only one interruption, in the seasons of 1951 and 1952, they stayed intact. From a humble beginning, taking over the bankrupt Miami Seahawks, they climbed to a level of respectability, won championships, and made an enormous amount of money for the owners, who weren't satisfied and wanted more. It was indeed a one-way love affair. The fans gave. The owners, Rosenbloom and Irsay, took.

After Accorsi was hired by the Cleveland Browns, months after he quit the Colts, he was talking to Art Rooney, owner of the Steelers, during a recess at a league meeting. Rooney asked if it was true that Accorsi had worked for both Rosenbloom and Irsay. He answered in the affirmative. Rooney, rarely a critic, pulled on his cigar and said, "Boy, you really did come up the hard way." It couldn't be said anymore perceptively than that.

To get Irsay to come to Indianapolis, that city's Capital Improvement Board gave him a twenty-year lease which provided two five-year options to renew. The Colts also got a guaranteed revenue of $7 million a year for the first twelve seasons from ticket sales, broadcast rights (preseason TV and regular season radio), and a training facility to cost $4 million. Additionally, the team received a $12.5-million loan for ten years at 8 percent. The team would pay $250,000 in rent, plus $25,000 per playoff game. Not a bad deal, but nothing to compare to what the

Browns received eleven years later to come to Baltimore to fill the void caused by the Colts' departure. No wonder John Moag of the Maryland Stadium Authority said the Colts were calling in 1995 but he didn't bother to call them back. Did they have ideas about coming home again?

In the summer of 1984 I visited the Indianapolis training camp, in Anderson, Indiana, and my trip just happened to coincide with an Irsay press conference. Kush seemed content to be an Indianapolis Colt and was especially interested in what the sportswriters were telling him about Bobby Knight, the Indiana basketball coach, and some of the tactics he used—Kush making it sound as if he only wished he had the same chance. Irsay flew in by helicopter and answered questions. When I asked about why he rejected Baltimore, he brought up the eminent domain aspect and said, "Schaefer stabbed me in the back." I flew to Indianapolis for the Colts' opener with the New York Jets. As I prepared to enter the dome, the team bus drove up. The coaches and players recognized me but only quarterback Mike Pagel made a courtesy call. It seemed as if they didn't want to be seen talking to anyone from Baltimore. Pro athletes are like that.

Later, Raul Allegre, a man of remarkable intelligence and sensitivity, said when he went out on the field for early practice, "my thoughts, I couldn't help it, were with the people of Baltimore who had their team taken away." I had a seat in the first row of the press box inside the dome and I was enjoying pregame practice. The punters were airing out the ball, the passers were warming up their arms, and the individual talents were on display for inspection and appreciation. Suddenly, behind me, came the sound of heavy feet pounding the steps. I looked over my left shoulder to see that it was Irsay himself. I thought maybe he was coming to gloat over the new "house" his team was playing in, compared to Memorial Stadium. He appeared to put out his hand and I got up to say hello. With that he pulled me in close to him and said, "How does it feel to be a shit-heel?" I pushed him away and replied, "How does it feel to be devoid of common decency?" With that, he hurried back up the steps. A front office member, the highly competent and respected Bob Eller, who witnessed the entire episode, said he was embarrassed for himself and apologized for the team. That wasn't necessary. Two other sportswriters around me, Michael Wilbon of *The Washington Post* and Fred Klein of *The Wall Street Journal*, were surprised by the interruption but didn't hear what Irsay had said. I called Jim Toedtman, managing editor of the *News American*, and asked him if he wanted a story about the confrontation. "Yes," he said, "by all means." Regarding Irsay's language, he said, "in this situation it should be used to convey for the reader exactly what had transpired." After Irsay bounded back up the steps, he saw Scott Garceau of WMAR-TV and told him, "Steadman just attacked me." Garceau laughed. He knew better than to believe Bob.

Some Baltimore followers of the Colts said it was a tough price to pay, losing the team, but to be rid of Irsay made it a fair trade-off. That wasn't necessarily true because young son Jimmy, the heir apparent, seemed to be a fair-minded individual and certainly represented hope for the future. The Indianapolis newspapers gave Irsay a warm welcome; it appeared the editors had talked it over and decided to go "soft" on him. That's the way the stories read. In Baltimore, for the next eleven years, the city endured the conjecture of possible team moves from New Orleans, St. Louis, Los Angeles, New England, Oakland, or, as it turned out, the remote chance of getting an expansion franchise. Hopes would build and then there would be the inevitable letdown.

Baltimore had never participated in the robbery of a sports franchise. In football, it had picked up two bankrupt teams, the Miami Seahawks and the Dallas Texans, and rescued them from failure in other cities. And in baseball, the Browns had come from St. Louis to Baltimore when it was determined they couldn't draw enough to pay their bills. And, of course, St. Louis still had the Cardinals. Schaefer said he didn't want to do to some other city what Indianapolis had done to Baltimore.

But under a different governor, that's precisely what happened. Glendening and Moag trampled on Cleveland. To attract Art Modell and his Browns the city provided him with a new $200-million stadium and a rent-free ride for thirty years. The team went through all the cacophony of trying to select a nickname and finally decided on the Ravens. A Sunpapers poll showed Ravens with an overwhelming tally and the other two finalists, Americans and Marauders as distant also-rans. My personal selection would have been Baltimore Bees, providing a short word for headline writers and an easy alliteration.

The Ravens had a new logo created and selected colors of black, purple, and gold. There was an association with Edgar Allan Poe, the author, who died in Baltimore, but the team didn't want too close a tie with Poe because he had been an opium user—not a good role model, so to speak. Poe was related to the famous Poe brothers of Princeton, who were among the pioneers of college football.

Baltimore prepared for another football adventure. It would be played before new generations of followers who deserve the chance to have a team of their own. The Baltimore Colts' past, like with all history, would be preserved from the years 1947 through 1983. The Ravens were off on their own, setting out to create a reputation and a record. But, always, there would be this fondness for a team that meant so much to Baltimore. The Colts remain irreplaceable.

# EPILOGUE

Coming back from Indianapolis, after the first game I saw the Colts play there, the opener of 1984, I pushed a small piece of luggage under the seat. The plastic, imprinted bag tag, issued by United Airlines to all reporters traveling with NFL teams, read "John Steadman, Baltimore Colts."

I sat there and looked at it. Then, without my even touching or moving toward it, the identification tag and the leather strap holding it fell off. It just happened. So surreal. The Baltimore Colts were gone, and some higher power was telling me they'd never be back.

Hold dear the memory.

# INDEX